ETHICAL SYSTEMS AND LEGAL IDEALS

ETHICAL SYSTEMS AND LEGAL IDEALS

AN ESSAY ON THE FOUNDATIONS OF LEGAL CRITICISM

By
FELIX S. COHEN, PH.D.
Member of the New York Bar

GREENWOOD PRESS, PUBLISHERS
WESTPORT, CONNECTICUT

Library of Congress Cataloging in Publication Data

Cohen, Felix S 1907-1953.
Ethical systems and legal ideals.

Reprint of the ed..published by Falcon Press, New York.
Includes index.
1. Law--Philosophy. 2. Ethics. 3. Legal ethics.
I. Title.
Law 174'.3 75-40440
ISBN 0-8371-8643-9

Originally published in 1933 by Falcon Press, New York

Reprinted in 1976 by Greenwood Press,
a division of Williamhouse-Regency Inc.

Library of Congress Catalog Card Number 75-40440

ISBN 0-8371-8643-9

Printed in the United States of America

TO

L. M. K.

TABLE OF CONTENTS

PREFACE

In an age marked by the phenomenal growth of science, the shifting winds of theory and the sporadic emergence of hitherto unformulated problems make men acutely aware of the extent of human ignorance. But along with this awareness arises a demand for universally recognized norms of human conduct, a demand which science nourishes by putting into the hands of the individual new capacities for making his neighbors miserable. Moralist and jurist are therefore called upon to produce authoritative truth in the midst of the shifting sands of scientific doctrine.

Thus arises the barren divorce between normative theories of law and mortality and the natural and social sciences. Moralists, fearing to venture where scientists rear their fortresses and tear down their fellows', retreat to a realm where the missiles of science seldom land, the realm of man's inner thought and feeling. Against those who, under the banners of psychology, would follow even into this holy land, they barricade themselves with the metaphysical doctrine of the freedom of the will.

Shut off from the doubts and the achievements of positive science, our moralists may deal without fear of contradiction (except from themselves) with human conscience and human volition. But they have abandoned the sovereignty which Greek and medieval moralists once exercised over the really important realms of human conduct, the realms of art, thought, industry, the distribution of economic and political power, friendship, and war. Our moralists speak only of petty things, of lying, stealing, and murdering in their retail forms, of barren desires, of ugly manners. It would not be unfair to say that no avowed ethical philosopher in the last hundred years has made a single fundamental criticism of the established institutions of modern society.

Jurists, no less than moralists, have succumbed to agoraphobia. Morality no longer gives its orders in the realm of law's activities. The law owns allegiance only to itself. Ingrown legal philosophy takes law as the standard for evaluating law. Aesthetic harmonies within the legal system supply the touchstones of criticism which a universal moral science once provided. Such non-legal norms as are given a half-hearted verbal obeisance only reveal the narrowness of the responsibilities which the jurist will recognize: Let law restrict itself to the meager essentials of social life, security, liberty, a modicum of fairness in men's dealings. There is no authority beyond its own hallowed past to which the law will look when society throws to it the task of revising an industrial system, or solving new problems in domestic relations.

Beyond the circle where jurists nervously thresh thrice-threshed straw is the fearful land of scientific doubts. And the authority of law must remain pure.

There are many signs today that this traditional picture of morality and law is disintegrating. But the conception of morality freed from science and of law freed from morality retains enough vitality in contemporary thought to endow philosophical criticism with responsibilities and consequences other than those of funeral oratory. If I am presumptuous in venturing to hope that the simple and obvious truths elaborated in the following pages offer any permanent contribution to the critique of social ideals, I can offer in excuse only the too generous encouragement of my revered teachers (within and without academic walls), Ralph Barton Perry, Roscoe Pound, Henry M. Sheffer, Felix Frankfurter, Herman Oliphant, Karl N. Llewellyn and Morris R. Cohen. Thanks are due my friends Ernest Nagel, Ambrose Doskow, and Maurice Goldbloom, who have been kind enough to read and criticize this essay.

Acknowledgment is made to the editors of the *International Journal of Ethics* and the *Yale Law Journal* for permission to reprint portions of the first and third chapters of the essay.

Ethical Systems and Legal Ideals

CHAPTER ONE

THE ETHICAL BASIS OF LEGAL CRITICISM

1. THE PROBLEMS OF LEGAL CRITICISM

AT THE heart of man's ancient quest for justice is the search for some measure of good and bad in the most powerful and flexible instrument of social control, the law. This problem of the ethical appraisal of law is no pseudo-question invented by philosophers. It is inescapably presented by the most fundamental of man's social institutions, and no philosopher of the first rank has been able to overlook it. Indeed, historically, most of the distinctive problems of metaphysics and epistemology have arisen in the attempt to clarify discussion of social ideals. The nature of ideas or essences, the relation of reason to life and to the cosmos, the status of "natural laws," the meaning of possibility and necessity, the validity of knowledge, the reality of the individual will and mind, the relation of universal laws to particular facts—each of these cardinal problems of philosophy has roots deep in legal-ethical controversy. Without the vision of these connections, philosophy tends to become simply the noblest of games and social reform the most pathetic of humanity's aspirations.

Shifting terminologies cannot obscure the continuity with which the Western world has faced the problem of the ethical valuation of law. Whether treated by Greek philosophers analyzing the nature of "justice," by Roman and medieval jurists under the rubric of "natural law and equity," by scholars of modern Europe speaking in the language of "natural rights," or by social scientists of our own day who are concerned with "social interests," the problem has remained essentially the same. Fundamental to all adequate thought on politics and society lies the question of what law ought to do, the search for valid standards of legal criticism.

The problem is, in the first place, an ethical one, since legal criticism is a passing of judgments of good and bad, right and wrong, upon human acts and works. This has led to a tendency apparent in most modern "scientific" studies of law to disclaim responsibility for its solution, to pass the buck to the ethical philosopher. But in the second place, the problem involves a calculation of the nature, effects, and potentialities of legal machinery which only the jurist or social scientist as such can attempt, and this has led most ethical philosophers to ignore crucial legal problems, throwing responsibility back to the jurist. This game of battledore and shuttlecock, or, to put the analogy in modern terms, volley ball, is carried on through most of the social sciences today. The historian, the economist, the political scientist, the sociologist, all argue that science is non-moral, and that their task is done when they have portrayed the facts. Ethical philosophers, on the other hand, are seldom anxious to descend from the ethereal realm of abstract duties and intrinsic goods to the mud of social statistics. Indeed, a Platonic reluctance to recognize that there is any essence or idea of mud has persisted through the most diverse currents of philosophical thought. But it is of mud that human edifices are built, and no dainty philosophy can pass adequate judgment upon the buildings of men, their weakness and their strength. Only when freed from the last vestiges of professional snobbery can philosophy offer to an unphilosophical world tributes worthy of her dignity.

Shunned alike by scientists and philosophers, most social-ethical questions are left today in a No Man's Land where only those with strong practical and emotional interests will make a stand. This arbitrary and inadequate division of intellectual labor would be pitiable enough if the limitations it imposes upon social thought were regularly recognized. But the moral philosopher who disdains the data sheets of social science as irrelevant to questions of value continues to assume human desires and human abilities which those data refute; and the social scientist (not least of all the jurist) continues to assume ethical norms which have not withstood the test of philosophical analysis.

An ethics, like a metaphysics, is no more certain and no less dangerous because it is unconsciously held. There are few judges, psychoanalysts, or economists today who do not begin a consideration of their typical problems with some formula designed to cause all moral ideals to disappear and to produce an issue purified for the procedure of positive empirical science. But the ideals have generally retired to hats from which later wonders will magically arise. A historical school of law disclaims concern with ethics[1] and repeatedly invokes a *Zeitgeist* or a *Volksgeist* to decide what the law ought to be.[2] An analytical school of jurisprudence again dismisses questions of morality,[3] and again decides what the law ought to be by reference to a so-called logical ideal, which is not an ideal of logic at all, but an aesthetic ideal of symmetrical analogical development.[4] Those who derive the law from the will of the sovereign usually introduce without further justification the premise that it is good to obey that will.[5] And those who define law in terms of actually prevailing social de-

1 See Savigny, "Ueber den Zweck dieser Zeitschrift" (1815) 1 *Zeitschrift für geschicht. Rechtswissenschaft* pp. 4-5; Maine, *Early History of Institutions* (7th ed. 1914) p. 370 and Lectures 12 and 13 *passim.*

2 See J. C. Carter, *The Proposed Codification of our Common Law* (A Paper Prepared at the Request of the Committee of the Bar Association of the City of New York, Appointed to Oppose the Measure) (1884) pp. 86 *et seq.* This pamphlet is largely based upon Savigny's essay, *The Vocation of Our Age for Legislation and Jurisprudence* (1814, trans. by Hayward 1831), which was written under somewhat similar circumstances in answer to the demand for codification of German law (See Thibaut, *Ueber die Nothwendigkeit eines allgemeinen bürgerlichen Rechts für Deutschland,* reprinted in Thibaut, *Civilistische Abhandlungen* [1814] p. 404).

It was characteristic that Maine's famous generalization "the movement of the progressive societies has hitherto been a movement *from Status to Contract*" (*Ancient Law* [1861] ch. 5), was proposed and generally received as an indication of the *desirability* of free contract.

3 See Amos, *Science of Jurisprudence* (1872) p. 18; Pollock, *Essays in Jurisprudence and Ethics* (1882) ch. 1 (The Nature of Jurisprudence), pp. 18-32.

4 A good example of this ethical use of analysis is found in the development of the *prima facie* theory of torts (See Pollock, *Law of Torts,* 1st ed. [1887] ch. 1), which purports to be merely an analysis of what has always been the law but actually gives the old doctrine of conspiracy a new impetus (see Note [1930] 30 *Columbia Law Rev.* 510), and threatens to extend the vagaries of that doctrine over individual conduct.

5 "Legislatures and courts formulate or seek to formulate the will of all of us as to the conduct of each of us in our relations with each other and with all. That will ought to be wholly effective. That it fails of effect in any degree is a misfortune." Pound, "Enforcement of Law" (1908) 20 *Green Bag* 401.

mands or interests make frequent use of the undisclosed principle that these demands *ought* to be satisfied.[6]

The objection, then, is not that jurists have renounced ethical judgment but that they have renounced ethical science. Ethical science involves an analysis of ethical judgments, a clarification of ethical premises. Among the current legal crypto-idealisms there can be no edifying controversy, since there is no recognition of the moral issues to which their differences reduce. One looks in vain in legal treatises and law-review articles for legal criticism conscious of its moral presuppositions. The vocabularies of logic and aesthetics are freely drawn upon in the attempt to avoid the disagreeable assertion that something or other is intrinsically better than something else. Particular decisions or legal rules are "anomalous" or "illogical," "incorrect" or "impractical," "reactionary" or "liberal," and unarguable ethical innuendo takes the place of critical analysis.[7] Little wonder then that on a more abstract plane

[6] "In the actual practice of courts and jurists, after stating claims or demands in general terms as social interests, attempt is made, more or less consciously, to secure as much as possible of the whole scheme of social interests with the least sacrifice. This is the pragmatist ethical principle stated by William James. How far it is a sound ethical criterion we need not inquire. . . . The task of the jurist is to make us conscious of the method that actually obtains and to give it more precision. He should aim at all times, and in all the compromises and adjustments and reconcilings involved in the legal order, to give effect to as much of the whole body of social interests as possible." Pound, "Jurisprudence" in *History and Prospects of the Social Sciences* (1925) p. 472. See also Pound, *Introduction to the Philosophy of Law* (1922) pp. 95-99.

[7] One might expect to find in the American Law Institute's attempted "Restatements" of various branches of the common law some attempt to work out the meaning of controversial rules of law in terms of social consequences and some indication of the moral standards which make the rule laid down in Mississippi (say) preferable to the rule laid down in Ohio. Instead, one meets the pious fiction, implicit in the very title of the enterprise, that the common law is a system within which in-

of thought the classification of ideas has taken the place of legal philosophy,[8] while Hegelian pictures of inevitable trends are offered as substitutes for the delineation of the desirable.[9]

But the relevance of ethics to the philosophy of law would be clear even if it were not unconsciously assumed by those who appear to deny or to ignore the connection.

---

tellectual inspection reveals a definite answer for every legal question. Decisions are hailed as "correct" or "incorrect" rather than "good" or "bad," and truth is obtained either in accordance with the mathematical precepts of the Valentinian Law of Citations (426 A.D.), or by projecting evolutionary "tendencies" found in the past decisions of courts, or by reacting aesthetically to the harmony or discord between a questioned rule and the rest of the legal "system." *Cf.* the strictures of Professor Kantorowicz upon the German Civil Code, in *Rechtswissenschaft und Soziologie* (1911) p. 8.

8 All who appreciate Dean Pound's unparalleled equipment in legal philosophy must hope that such taxonomic studies as *Law and Morals* (1924); "The Scope and Purpose of Sociological Jurisprudence" (1911) 24 *Harvard Law Rev.* 591, (1911-12) 25 *Harvard Law Rev.* 140, 489; "The End of Law as Developed in Legal Rules and Doctrines" (1914) 27 *Harvard Law Rev.* 195; "The End of Law as Developed in Juristic Thought" (1914) 27 *Harvard Law Rev.* 605, (1917) 30 *Harvard Law Rev.* 201, are preludes to some affirmative statement of valid legal standards or ideals.

9 Courts frequently rely not on actual decisions but on tendencies in series of past decisions. The fact that two earlier cases have each stretched a rule a little further than existing precedents in each case warranted is taken to indicate the desirability of stretching the rule still further in a third case. The assumption seems to be that all change is for the better and is infinitely capable of extension. The philosophical generalization of this type of argument is, of course, evolutionism. Dean Pound has frequently followed Hegel, Marx, and Spencer in putting forward evolutionary schemes of legal history in answer to strictly ethical questions. See *Introduction to the Philosophy of Law* (1922) pp. 95-99; "Justice According to Law" (1913) 13 *Columbia Law Rev.* 696, (1914) 14 *Columbia Law Rev.* 1,103, esp. at 117-121; "The Theory of Judicial Decision" (1923) 36 *Harvard Law Rev.* 641, 802, 940, esp. at 954-958. But this identification of the inevitable and the desirable under the banner of Progress is, as Huxley, Sidgwick, G. E. Moore, and M. R. Cohen have demonstrated, intellectually indefensible, however gratifying emotionally it may be to feel that cheering for the winning side is the substance of morality.

For ethics is the study of the meaning and application of judgments of *good*, *bad*, *right*, *wrong*, etc., and every final valuation of law involves an ethical judgment. When we say, for instance, that a given law is bad, that one judicial decision is better than another, that the American constitution ought to be revised, or that laws ought to be obeyed, we are passing judgments whose truth or falsity cannot be established without a consideration of ethics. That portion of jurisprudence which is not concerned merely with the positive nature of law or with its technical relation to assumed ends is, accordingly, a part of the domain of ethics.

There is no way of avoiding this ultimate responsibility of law to ethics. Every final determination of the general end of law, the standard of legal criticism, (whether this be labeled "justice," "natural law," "the protection of natural rights," or "the organization of social interests"), must reduce to the general form, "The law ought to bring about as much good as it can."

Our problem is to give content to this formal principle by defining the nature of the good and indicating the extent of the law's actual powers over that realm. In attacking this problem our first concern will be to formulate precisely the relation between ethics and legal criticism. Having established the dependence of critical thought in law upon the ethical concept of the good life, we shall turn in our second chapter to an examination of certain more specific legal ideals in the light of this general conception, paying particular attention to the significance of the good life and rival ideals for positive legal science. To fill in the abstract conception of the good life with the content which a scientific ethics can support will be the purpose of the third chapter. Finally an attempt will be made to sketch the lines of positive scientific inquiry which legal criticism must undertake in the application of its ethical ideal.

2. HISTORY, PHILOLOGY, AND ETHICS

A few words as to the method of our inquiry may not be amiss. The problem which the foregoing considerations delineate is not a problem of history, and in its solution the historical method is peculiarly inappropriate. We face the question of what law ought to do, and no statement that law has done something or that somebody thought the law ought to do something else can answer this question.

The answers which past thinkers have given to our problem are either true or false. If any of them is true, our present task is unnecessary. If all are false, our present attempt cannot be founded upon them. Philosophical literature too frequently reminds one of a dog show, where only entrants with a sufficiently long pedigree may have their merits tested. There is something equally objectionable in the practice of fighting one's predecessors, alive and dead, to prove the virtue of the lady for whom one fights. To both of these ills the habit of classifying philosophies as a foundation or substitute for philosophizing is naturally heir.

The pathways beaten by intellectual pioneers are valuable guides in most fields of human thought. To follow them until they lead to insurmountable difficulty or intolerable misdirection is our only alternative to an exhausting battle against the primeval waste. When, however, a field has become so intricately laced with divergent paths as has the field we now face, it may be better to take compass in hand and seek our goal without thought of past adventurers, lest we find in the end that we have charted our journey instead of traveling it. We shall be comforted if we find, perhaps, that on most of our route we follow the tracks of illustrious pioneers. We shall attempt to confine the expression of such jubilation to footnotes that may easily be skipped.

It is clear, in the second place, that our problem is not a philological one.

To trace the ways in which words like *law* and *morality* and *justice* have been used is not our task. We have to trace relations between ideas, between entities, and clarity of thought is to be sought even at the cost of some arbitrariness in our definition of terms. Humpty Dumpty gave voice to a methodological postulate of all advanced scientific thought in his much-quoted utterance, "When I use a word it means just what I choose it to mean—neither more nor less. The question is which is to be master—that's all." The only limitation upon our mastery of words lies in the requirement that we make our use of them clear. A verbal definition is neither true nor false—it is convenient or misleading. And unless we are careful to distinguish questions of philology from questions of ethics, we shall become involved in the absurd sort of argument to which G. E. Moore has called attention in his discussion of verbal definitions of *good*. If one person means by the word *good* "conducive to pleasure" and another means by the same term "desired," their controversies as to what constitutes goodness or as to what things are good must be quite without ethical significance. "The position is like this. One man says a triangle is a circle; another replies 'A triangle is a straight line, and I will prove to you that I am right: *for*' (this is the only argument) 'a straight line is not a circle.' 'That is quite true,' the other may reply; 'but nevertheless a triangle is a circle, and you have said nothing whatever to prove the contrary . . . which is wrong there can be no earthly means of proving, since you define a triangle as a straight line and I define it as a circle.' "[10]

Such meaningless arguments are by no means uncommon, and they are the source of much confusion in philosophy as in other fields of thought. One frequently finds heated discussions as to whether certain things are real, or beautiful, or good, or practical, when the parties to the controversy mean quite different things by the same words. Jurists are wont to argue whether the rules of war, for instance, are law or not. But we usually find in this dispute that the upholder of the negative uses the term *law* to mean simply the rules utilized by the courts of a sovereign state in settling disputes, while his adversary attaches a much wider meaning to the term *law*. The two opponents are both right in what they affirm and both wrong in believing that they are contradicting each other.

Arguments of this sort we must avoid at all costs. Nothing could be more destructive of clear thinking than to imagine that words like *good* and *justice* have always meant the same thing to those who have uttered them, or to hope that by a critical comparison of different people's ideas of what comes under these ambiguous terms we shall be led to discover a definite content. A dispute between an

[10] G. E. Moore, *Principia Ethica* (1903) p. 11.

Englishman and a German as to what things we can describe by the word *Gift* would be no more absurd than many disputes as to what constitutes goodness or justice. An understanding of what we mean by the words *good* or *just* does not prejudge the question of what things are good or just, or even the question of how the content of these concepts is to be analyzed. It is rather the first condition of the intelligibility and significance of these questions. Not every collection of words followed by a question mark asks a question.[11] Our final responsibility in the process of defining such terms as *good* and *just* is not that we be faithful in perpetuating the ambiguities of common speech, but that we provide an efficient vocabulary for the adequate and intelligible treatment of our problems.

3. THE NATURE OF LAW AND THE SCOPE OF ETHICS

We cannot by definition eliminate ambiguity from our speech. The terms of a definition always carry their own aura of indeterminateness. But there are some traditional ambiguities in the slippery words *law* and *ethics* that we can definitely eliminate.

By the term *law* we shall mean a body of rules according to which the courts, that is the judicial organs of a political body, decide cases. This definition is in essence that adopted by Gray,[12] who has so thoroughly demolished the superficial objections commonly brought against this definition[13] that it would be a work of supererogation to

[11] For an attempted analysis of the conditions of interrogatory significance, see F. S. Cohen, "What is a Question?" (1929) 39 *Monist* 350.
[12] *Nature and Sources of the Law* (1909) § 191.
[13] *Ibid.*, ch. 4.

review them. There is, however, an unfortunate vagueness in the phrase used by Gray, "rules which the courts . . . lay down," that is avoided by the definition given above. It is not clear whether Gray meant to equate law with rules *enunciated* by courts, but if he did, Mr. Frank's criticism[14] that such rules are often merely verbal and always subject to interpretation, so that on Gray's analysis they must be considered themselves *sources of law*, like statutes, rather than *law*, is irrefutable. Judges make law only in the way that electrons make physics, amoebae make biology, and Trobriand Islanders make anthropology. What is law, as that term is most commonly used by lawyers, is the way or pattern in which judges decide cases, and this way or pattern may be as remote from the mind of the judge as is the Gestalt psychology from Köhler's anthropoid subjects.[15] As a matter of fact a lawyer looking for "the law" on a point will generally pay more attention to a wholly unofficial schematization of decided cases found in a legal treatise than to a judicial opinion which purports to "lay down" the law. Where this is not the case it is because of the scholarship of the particular judge rather than his authority.

There is thus ample reason to believe that the definition of *law* given above is faithful to the usage of lawyers and litigants, as well as of those who merely observe the processes of law administration.[16] But whether or not that be

14 *Law and the Modern Mind* (1930) pp. 121-132.

15 See Bingham, "What is the Law?" (1912) 11 *Mich. Law Rev.* 1, 16; "Legal Philosophy and the Law" (1914) 9 *Ill. Law Rev.* 98, 107-108; C. J. Keyser, "On the Study of Legal Science" (1929) 38 *Yale Law Jour.* 413.

16 In a recent article Professor Dickinson has attacked the realistic or positive definition of law on the ground that it does not fit the problem

so, the institutional complex defined by these terms is an important one and it is the one we mean to write about. Usefulness rather than truth, we have said, is the only standard by which a verbal definition can be judged. This definition is useful because it denotes an important concept and because this denotation is as clear as the subject permits. There are, to be sure, twilight zones about this definition. What is a *court*? How is a *judicial organ* distinguished from an administrative organ? What is a *political body*? When do the interests of litigants become so nominal that we can no longer say that a *case* (as distinguished,

---

of the judge himself, who does not want to know what he is about to do. ("Legal Rules: Their Function in the Process of Decision" (1931) 79 *U. of Pa. Law Rev.* 833, 843-844). But this is to assume that a judge's duty is to *find* the law rather than to *mould* it, an assumption which no realist makes. In a similar vein Dickinson argues that if we should call judicial responsiveness to unworthy motives law, it would become "difficult . . . to find any proper standard for criticizing the behavior of the judge." (*Ibid.* 838). Again by assuming without question the traditional premises which realists have been attacking, Dickinson arrives at an absurdity which he ascribes to his opponents. Unless one assumes that law is above ethical criticism, there is no difficulty in criticising a judge for making or perpetuating bad law. The confusion becomes evident when Dickinson asserts that "a legal rule, even though derived by generalization from what has been done, is not a rule of 'isness' because it either may or may not be applied in the next case, *i.e.*, the case for which the rule is sought, depending on the volition of the judge." (*Ibid.* 860, n. 51) Obviously, if a legal rule is a formulation of judicial behavior, it must explain the next case as well as the last case. The existence of legal rules is not disturbed by judicial volition, since rules are simply descriptions of the way judicial volition works. And a description of judicial volition is a rule of *isness.* Dickinson has confused normative and descriptive science by failing to recognize that a description of purposive behavior is not itself purposive. He has said nothing which reveals the impossibility or undesirability of a descriptive science of judicial conduct. He has offered no reason for believing that *law* as the realists understand the term is not a more precise concept (his own criterion of definition) than the amorphous Something which is neither a description of what courts actually do nor a formulation of what they ought to do (*Ibid.* 861-862) but a jumble of the two notions whose only merit is faithfulness to the fundamental confusions in modern juristic thought.

say, from a request for a declaratory judgment or for an "executive" veto or approval of legislation) is before the court. Legal phenomena shade off imperceptibly into non-legal phenomena. We may say that the enforced rules of the Federal Trade Commission are more legal than those of a trade union, that the latter are more legal than those of a game. A definition of law which faithfully reflects these twilight zones and gradations is probably more useful than the more exact and artificial definition we should get by incorporating definite answers to the questions suggested above.

The important thing about the definition here adopted is that it reveals the concept of law as something purely positive or natural, involving no connotations of approval or disapproval. We are thus able to avoid the confusions following inevitably upon commendatory definitions of law. Blackstone could define law as "a rule of civil conduct prescribed by the supreme power in a state, commanding what is right and prohibiting what is wrong."[17] Upon such a definition the question of whether law is good cannot be significant, and ethical questions are either evaded by denying the appellation *law* to certain enactments and courses of judicial decision, or settled by the complacent and pre-

[17] Blackstone, *Commentaries* p. 44. That "right" and "wrong" in this definition are ethical rather than strictly legal terms is made clear in Blackstone's own exegesis upon his definition, at pp. 54-55.

Much confusion in the reading, and, it may be suspected, in the writing, of continental legal philosophy arises from the fact that *Recht*, *droit*, *diritto*, etc. denote at the same time the positive concept of law and the normative notion of right, justice, or ideal law.

That a similar confusion did not perish in Anglo-Saxon juristic thought with the death of Blackstone is revealed in such a passage as the following: "Thus all things made legal are at the same time made legally ethical because it is law, and law must be deemed ethical, or the system itself must perish." Brumbaugh, *Legal Reasoning and Briefing* (1917) p. 7.

posterous assumption that whatever sovereigns have commanded is good. Law is law, whether it be good or bad, and only on the admission of this platitude can a meaningful discussion of the goodness and badness of law rest.

Much of what must be said concerning the relation of ethics to law applies to a wider concept than strict law, that is, to the whole social complex which includes legislation and law enforcement, as well as pure judicial action. We shall refer to this complex as the *legal order*, and to its constituent parts (*i.e.* particular laws, methods of trial, acts of police, judicial decisions, etc.) as *legal elements*. It is clear that these two notions are positive derivatives of our first concept, and that they give rise to significant ethical problems.

By *ethics* we shall mean the science of the significance and application of judgments of *good, bad, right, wrong, better, worse, best, worst, ought,* and their derivatives, in so far as these terms are applied categorically. By this qualification we exclude only such use of these terms as is exemplified when we say that medicine is good *for* colds, without implying any judgment as to the value of colds or of the curing of colds. We do not thereby exclude the judgment that medicine is good *because* it cures colds. That is to say, ethics deals with instrumental as well as intrinsic values, but it does not deal with physical causality as such.[18] Finally, we mean by *judgment* a logical rather than a psychological or linguistic entity, and ethics is therefore

[18] It is ancient wisdom that efficiency or usefulness presupposes intrinsic values or final ends. Only a failure to recognize clearly that "social engineering" and "efficiency" may be directed to mutually destructive ends can explain such a sentence as, "What we seek is a picture which will best enable us to understand what we are doing and to do it most effectively." Pound, "The Theory of Judicial Decision" (1923) 36 *Harvard Law Rev.* 954.

not restricted to a study of propositions which have been actually believed. The truth of any proposition of the form *A is good* (or *bad*, *better*, etc.) is relevant to the science of ethics.[19]

Moral science or philosophy we define as that branch of ethics which is concerned with voluntary human activity.

4. LAW AND THE GOOD LIFE

On the basis of the foregoing definitions the indispensability of ethics in legal criticism is immediately obvious. Ethics involves all final applications of the terms *good*, *bad*, etc. We may decide whether law is good for strengthening social bonds or bad for the peace of mind of criminals, without any appeal to ethics, but when we come to the question of whether the strengthening of social bonds or the peace of mind of criminals is good, and whether law which has the described effects is good, we are in the realm of ethics. Thus every valuation of law, every formulation of the ideal object or end of law, must be either categorical and ethical, or conditional, in terms of some ulterior aim which can itself be valued ethically. In either case, there is no way of escaping the final responsibility of law to ethics, and, since the field of law lies within the

[19] We follow G. E. Moore in this use of the word *ethics* to cover all problems of goodness and its related concepts, whether or not concerned with human conduct. This usage is too well substantiated, historically, to require apology. "Axiology" or "theory of values" may be more accurate appellations for our subject from a philological point of view, since they avoid the suggestion of a particular reference to human conduct. But both names are much too clumsy for consistent usage, and the latter at least carries its own aura of ambiguity, being extended in application to "values" other than goodness (*e.g.* truth and beauty) while frequently restricted, from the viewpoint of method, to a particular naturalistic philosophy.

field of human conduct, to morality.[20] It is the task of legal philosophy to demonstrate the precise scope and character of those ethical judgments which form the base or the content of valuations of law.

Although the valuation of law is ethical, it does not exhaust the realm of ethics, for ethical judgments can certainly be passed upon other things than law, and even upon things which law can in no wise affect. To delimit the realm of ethics which is relevant to law is merely to outline the realm of ethically justiciable facts which law can comprehend or affect. And that is a task involving positive science. But we may here presume upon its conclusions to the extent of affirming that the law can affect only human activities and such other happenings as depend upon them. It follows from this that law has instrumental value[21] in so far as it promotes good human activity, or more briefly, the good life.[22] The good life involves both intrinsic and instrumental values, so that possible non-human goods (*e.g.* the well-being of domestic animals) which law can attain indirectly by affecting human conduct are not excluded from our valuations, appearing as results which endow human life with instrumental value. And on the other hand, since law is the work of human beings, any intrinsic values which may appear in the legal order will be accounted for in an evaluation of the lives of those

[20] *Cf.* Laird, *Study in Moral Theory* (1926) pp. 26-29; Demogue, *Analysis of Fundamental Notions* (1911, trans. by Scott and Chamberlain 1916), in *Modern French Legal Philosophy*, Modern Legal Philosophy Series, vol. 7, §§ 206-221; Pound: "Jurisprudence," in *History and Prospects of the Social Sciences* (1925) p. 472.

[21] *Cf.* pp. 52 *et seq.*, *infra.*

[22] In speaking of *the good life* we do not mean to imply that different sorts of living may not be equally valuable. *The good life* is simply a concept common, though applying in various degrees, to all lives worth living.

directly implicated in this order. Accordingly, the valuation of law is part of that branch of ethics which we have called moral science, and every legal element can receive a final evaluation in terms of the good life.

Strangely enough, only two writers on law and politics have distinctly affirmed that the value of law depends simply upon its success in promoting the good life. But since both of these writers have been philosophers and logicians, their loneliness in the ranks of political scientists, on this point, does not detract from the enticing strength of their basic position.[23] This position, to the elaboration of which the rest of this essay is devoted, has been attacked on two grounds. In the first place, it is claimed, we do not know what the effects of law will be. And in the second place, we do not know what the good life is.

Both of these objections are true in a certain sense, but in that sense they do not contradict our conclusion. It is certainly true that we cannot calculate all the effects of law or of anything else. And it is equally obvious that our knowledge of ethics and of human nature is not great enough to permit us to describe completely and in detail what constitutes the good life for each person or even for man in the abstract. But if there is any such thing as human knowledge, we certainly have enough of it upon both these subjects to formulate definite problems and to reject unsatisfactory solutions. And, as a great French jurist, M. Pierre Tourtoulon, has said, "There is no need to throw

23 Aristotle, *Nichomachean Ethics,* Book I, ch. 2; *Politics,* Book 7, ch. 1; Russell, *Political Ideals* (1917) p. 4. We do not mean to suggest that all other philosophers have denied this proposition. Plato, Mill, Bentham, and many other leaders of political-ethical thought have accepted this basis of valuation, but without thinking it necessary explicitly to formulate it.

to the dogs everything that is not fit for the altars of the gods." A recognition of the inadequacy of our knowledge in these fields can bring a sweet scepticism into our political beliefs, but it cannot deny them. To quote again from Tourtoulon, "The greatest jurist has only very vague ideas concerning the services that the laws which he expounds and explains render to society. . . . The first step toward wisdom is the knowledge that we are ignorant of nearly all the functions of our laws, or of the evil or the good which they may bring us."[24] And one more quotation: "A little scepticism will render him [the judge] more scrupulous, more indulgent to every one and consequently more just."[25]

The inadequacy of human knowledge, we may fairly assume, does not destroy the usefulness of our fundamental principle of legal criticism. In fact, a judgment of ethical values the truth of which is recognized to be partially dependent upon the accuracy of human scientific knowledge seems to be far more useful than the sort of judgment which assumes that, however uncertain the physical results of an act may be, we can know clearly in advance whether they will be good or bad.[26]

Suppose, however, that this assumption as to the useful-

[24] Tourtoulon, *Philosophy in the Development of Law* (1919, trans. by Read 1922), Modern Legal Philosophy Series, vol. 13, p. 24.

[25] *Ibid.* p. 487.

[26] *Cf.* Bentham, "The Influence of Time and Place in Matters of Legislation" ch. 3, 1 *Works* (ed. by Bowring, 1843) 183: "In all such matters, the cautious statesman will avoid the tone of peremptoriness and decision: his conclusions will always, in the first instance, be hypothetical. If such and such events are the likeliest to take place: But are they? This is a matter which ought to be stated as accompanied with the degree of uncertainty that belongs to it. Beware of those who by the vehemence of their assertions, by the confidence of their predictions, make up for the weakness of their reasons."

ness of ethical vision in law is erroneous, and that our human appraisals of law in terms of the good life are wholly unreliable and useless. Still it does not follow that the theory which reveals legal values as dependent upon such causal efficacy is false. Great confusion has been caused in ethics by the belief that knowing and publishing the truth is always good, and that it is therefore unnecessary to distinguish between the goodness or usefulness of an ethical theory and its truth. The proposition that the value of law depends upon the law's efficacy in promoting the good life remains true though it be wholly useless in legal criticism. We believe, however, that this proposition is far from useless, for although it offers no material measure of legal values, it provides a logical base upon which all significant discussion of the subject can rest. In this field of the valuation of law, as in most other domains of thought, confusion is a more potent source of evil than is error. A formal principle of this sort cannot insure against error, but it can bring light to the foundations of our thinking. It can bring our traditional legal controversies into the fertilizing context of ethical science. It can free legal criticism from blind deduction from obsolete moral postulates. It can illumine "social engineering" by inducing a critical attitude towards the social interests that the law is asked to protect.[27] It can bring legal scholarship into a

[27] The current notion that the function of the jurist is simply to secure adequate enforcement for the expressed demands of society (see L. K. Frank, "Institutional Analysis of the Law" (1924) 24 *Columbia Law Rev.* 480, 497-498 for an interesting reductio ad absurdum of this view) derives from a dangerous metaphor. Society is not vocal. The expressed demands of society are the demands of vocally organized groups, and a discreet deference to the power of such groups should not lead us to confuse their demands with "social welfare." *Cf.* Judge Hough's criticism of this confusion in his review of Dean Pound's *Spirit of the Common Law*, in (1922)

more intimate contact with practical legal problems by reminding jurists that logical, historical, and sociological analyses of law are merely necessary introductions to the argument: This decision or statute is desirable because in some way it promotes the good life.

It is, however, only with the *truth* of this fundamental doctrine that we are immediately concerned. To deny it, one would have to deny either that the law ought to do as much good as it can or that the law can exist only in and through human activity. The real danger is not that our conclusion from these premises is false, but that it is too inclusive or too vague to have real significance. This is a difficulty for which the rest of this essay may be regarded as an attempted remedy. And yet, as we have suggested, even the bare principle that law is to be measured in terms of the good life has significant and important logical consequences.

5. CRYPTO-IDEALISM

No less significant and important, then, must be the consequences of a denial of this basic principle. For although it is, indeed, a truism, it is not a commonplace. The ignoring or tacit repudiation of this principle is extremely general in juristic literature, although few legal writers have made their disavowal explicit. To M. Leon Duguit we may profitably appeal for a statement of the typical

---

22 *Columbia Law Rev.* 385: "The present lecturer can and does sum up the judicial duty of decision by saying that the jurists of to-day (and judges are presumably jurists) are content to seek the jural postulates of the civilization of the time,—a phrase extremely easy of translation into keeping one's ear to the ground to hear the tramp of insistent crowds."

position that the field of law is independent of ethics and morality. To show the inadequacy of his doctrine is to point to the fallacy upon which a vast amount of legal philosophizing is squarely based.

Law, according to Duguit, has for its sole purpose social solidarity. Solidarity, he insists, is a fact, not a rule of conduct. "It is not an imperative."[28] Duguit shows inductively that law makes for social solidarity and that such solidarity is a feature of all societies. But, as with so many other jurists, this inductive generalization suffers a gradual metamorphosis[29] and is finally used as the sole basis for such commands or ethical judgments as the following: "Respect every act of individual will determined by an end of social solidarity";[30] "Every individual ought to abstain from any act that would be determined by an end contrary to social solidarity";[31] "It is a crime to preach the struggle of classes."[32] Since it is impossible to derive the goodness of an act from its frequency or uni-

28 Duguit, *Theory of Objective Law Anterior to the State* (1901, trans. by Scott and Chamberlain 1916), in *Modern French Legal Philosophy*, Modern Legal Philosophy Series, vol. 7, p. 259.

29 Professor Husik, in a review of Tourtoulon's *Philosophy in the Development of Law* (71 *U. of Pa. Law Rev.* (1923) 416, 418-419) thus summarizes the procedure: ". . . one starts with the proposition, 'Men live in society,' which is perfectly true, and ends up with the statement, 'The aim of the life of the individual is to contribute to the development of the social body,' which is far from being a scientific statement and may easily be denied. Moreover if the last proposition is intended as imposing an obligation, it can never be logically derived from the statement of a fact. Most if not all of the books dealing with natural law by advocates of that doctrine, such as Thomas Aquinas, Grotius, Lorimer, are guilty of this fallacy."

30 Duguit, *op. cit.* p. 290.

31 *Ibid.* p. 292.

32 Duguit, *Changes of Principle in the Field of Liberty, Contract, Liability, and Property* (1912, trans. by Register 1918), in *The Progress of Continental Law in the Nineteenth Century*, Continental Legal History Series, vol. 11, p. 135.

versality, Duguit's judgments can be true only if the doctrine of solidarity is, in contradiction to his own claims, an ethical imperative. It seems fair to characterize such a position as crypto-idealism. Duguit has not gotten rid of ethics at all, as he proposes to do, but he has agreed not to use the word "ethics" lest his extremely shaky ethical system be challenged.[33]

Although Duguit's aversion to the concepts of ethics may seem to be the product of philosophical *naïveté*, he can claim the support of many philosophers for the faulty method by which he actually builds up his ethical system. Bertrand Russell thus analyzes the method:

> It may be laid down that every ethical system is based upon a certain *non sequitur*. The philosopher first invents a false theory as to the nature of things, and then deduces that wicked actions are those which show that his theory is false. To begin with the traditional Christian: he argues that, since everything always obeys the will of God, wickedness consists in disobedience to the will of God. We then come on to the Hegelian, who argues that the universe consists of parts which harmonize in a perfect organism, and therefore wickedness consists of behavior which diminishes the harmony—though it is difficult to see how such behavior is possible, since complete harmony is metaphysically necessary. Bergson . . . shows that human beings never behave mechanically,

[33] M. Duguit naively confesses to having experienced some disquietude with his ultimate appeal to social fact when German armies vanquished Belgium. But the final punishment of Germany apparently convinced him that social force is its own justification. "Objective Law" (1920-1921) 20 *Columbia Law Rev.* 817, 21 *Columbia Law Rev.* 17, 126, 242, esp. 254-256.

and then, in his book on *Laughter*, he argues that what makes us laugh is to see a person behaving mechanically—*i.e.* you are ridiculous when you do something that shows Bergson's philosophy to be false, and only then. These examples have, I hope, made it plain that a metaphysic can never have ethical consequences except in virtue of its falsehood: if it were true, the acts which it defines as sin would be impossible.[34]

The application of this analysis has been modestly under-estimated by Mr. Russell. For all ethical theories which are extracted from positive thought, scientific as well as metaphysical, show a similar weakness. Everything obeys the law of evolution. Therefore those societies that do not obey the law of evolution are inferior. All commercial transactions take place in accordance with the laws of supply and demand. Therefore every interference with the laws of supply and demand is undesirable. All law springs from the national spirit. Therefore law which does not spring from this spirit (code law, etc.) is bad.[35] It is unnecessary to multiply examples.

34 *Sceptical Essays* (1928), ch. 7 (Behaviorism and Values), p. 91.

35 It is only with the aid of this fallacy that the historical, analytical, metaphysical, and sociological schools of jurisprudence are able to wage civil war. Were the interests of these schools properly confined to the history, the internal analysis, the metaphysical status, and the sociological functioning of law, respectively, conflict would be impossible and we should see, instead, simply a salutary division of labor. But each school has smuggled an ethics into its positive studies. To the argument of the historicists that since law is a product of national custom, the *Rechtsgefühl*, or the *Volksgeist*, it *ought* to follow these lines, the analytical school replies that since law is the command of the sovereign or the ruling of the courts, it *ought* to obey these latter masters. Jurists of metaphysical and sociological persuasion add to the heat of the fray with equally invalid brands of crypto-idealism.

The abduction of law from the domain of morality is defended by Professor Morgan in a slightly different manner. "It must be remembered," he writes, "that the law does not have the same purpose as religion or ethics or morals. It is not concerned with developing the spiritual or moral character of the individual but with regulating his objective conduct toward his fellows. Consequently courts will have to formulate and apply some rules which have no relation at all to morals, some which have to place a loss upon one of two equally blameless persons, some which impose liability regardless of fault and some which refuse to penalize conduct denounced by even the morally blind. It must be apparent that the moral law has no mandate upon the content of the rules of the road."[36]

This position is so representative of the class of theories we are considering, and so generally accepted, at least in our American law schools, that it may be worth while to point out in detail some of the ambiguities and fallacies it involves. In the first sentence we are told that law does not have the same *purpose* as religion or ethics or morals. It is upon the ambiguity of this word that the specious force of the rest of the argument depends. If the word refers to the state of mind of judges or legislators, the assertion that this differs from the state of mind of moralists, ethical philosophers and religious leaders is perhaps true, but it is completely irrelevant to Professor Morgan's ethical conclusions as to what the law ought to do. If by the *purpose* of law is meant that at which law *ought* to aim, the statement is relevant, indeed basic, to his further conclusions, but obviously false. For the law ought to secure the good life,

[36] E. M. Morgan, *Introduction to the Study of Law* (1926) pp. 32-33.

which is the *ideal* purpose of moral and religious rules as well.

In the second sentence of this excerpt we are told that law is *not concerned* with certain noble ends. Again, the same basic ambiguity. If the law is not actually concerned with man's spiritual or moral character, that is an unfortunate fact which we ought to remedy. But if this assertion means that the law ought not to be determined by such factors, it is simply false. Man's moral life is fundamentally moulded by rules of property law, family law, etc., and the refusal to follow the meaning of such legal rules into their ultimate moral or spiritual implications is the essence of legalistic obscurantism.

In the next sentence, we are told that *consequently* courts *have to* formulate rules which have no relation at all to morals, and here the confusion between the *is* and the *ought* bears its first fruits. Thus far Morgan's statements can be justified on a positive interpretation, but if that interpretation be given, the inference of *have to* (apparently ethical) from *does* and *is* is clearly fallacious. Here an ethical interpretation of the foregoing premises is required, and that, we have seen, results in patent error.

Thus the resolution of the foregoing ambiguities leads us to a dilemma. Professor Morgan's inferences are, if valid, based upon false premises, and if based upon true premises, invalid. Their truth, as distinguished from the validity of their inference, can be defended, but only upon the assumption that the word *morality* is severed from reference to objective conduct and even to such problems of "inner belief" as are involved in the distribution of liability apart from fault, etc. Of course, if any one wishes to use the words *morality* and *ethics* in this milk-and-watery significance, no logical objection can be raised. But when such a use of terms results in, or springs from, the belief that judgments of good and bad can legitimately be applied only to man's secret intentions, we are called upon to point out that this is an indefensible theory of morality.

A great many other jurists attempt in one way or another to discover an end of law independent of ethics or morality. Korkunov writes, "Morality furnishes the criterion for the proper evaluation of our interests; law marks out the limits within which they ought to be confined."[37] But obviously law does not actually do this, and if the reply is made that at least law ought to do this, then we must turn to morality for the basis and significance of this *ought*. Vinogradoff writes, ". . . law is clearly distinguishable from morality. The object of law is the submission of the individual to the will of organized society, while the tendency of morality is to subject the individual to the dictates of his own conscience."[38] Berolzheimer supplies the following argument, based, it seems, upon the unpleasant connotations of the idea of *expediency*: "If all law has in view the welfare of society, then law abdicates in favor of administration; the ideal of political expediency displaces the idea of right."[39] It is unnecessary to multiply instances of this juristic attempt to abduct law from the domain of ethics and morality. For the writers who make the ideal end of law independent of morality never refrain from passing ethical or moral judgments

[37] Korkunov, *General Theory of Law* (1894, trans. by Hastings 1909), Modern Legal Philosophy Series, vol. 4, p. 52.

[38] Vinogradoff, *Common Sense in Law* (1914) p. 58.

[39] Berolzheimer, *Rechtsphilosophische Studien* (1903), ch. 6, § 22.

upon law. They have simply rejected particular moral theories, such as that of the infallibility of conscience (Vinogradoff), believing, correctly, for the most part, that these doctrines are useless for jurisprudence, and incorrectly assuming that they are the whole of morality. A more or less unconscious moral standard is made the basis of their valuations of law, and while such a morality has frequently been more nearly correct than the current ethical theory which was rejected, the resulting confusions of thought have been atrocious.

The attempt to free legal criticism from an ethical and moral basis is logically doomed to failure and results practically only in the confusions of crypto-idealism. Law cannot be abducted from the domain and sovereignty of ethics simply because every abductor, in his own person, is bound by that sovereignty, and with his every step, enlarges that domain.

6. NON-MORAL LAW AND JUDICIAL "LOGIC"

Those who admit in general the ultimate responsibility of law to morality frequently insist that there is at least a large part of law in the criticism of which ethics must be quite irrelevant. The boundaries of this non-moral realm are variously drawn and may be either of a substantive character or of an adjective or functional significance. In either view, such a claim is fatal to the soundness of our theory, which denies the ultimate validity of all legal criticism which is not ethical. It is our task, then, to examine and, if possible, to refute these objections.

There is, in the first place, a comparatively trivial interpretation which may be given them, in terms of which no incompatibility with our basic position can arise. By non-moral domains in the law, we may mean sets of equally valuable alternatives. In this sense of the term, law, like every other aspect of human life, may be non-moral, but in these domains there can be no appeal from morality to a non-moral principle (precedent, custom, etc.) to decide which alternative act is better than the other. By the very formulation of our problem we have denied that any alternative is better than the others. It is only the claim that in certain domains of law valid problems of what ought to be done may be solved without any appeal to the concept of the good life that we are concerned to refute.

Such a claim is presented by the theory that a large part of civil law, especially commercial law, constitutes a domain in which some principles other than those of morality must be our guide.[40] What jurists generally mean when they speak of the existence and necessity of non-moral law,[41] is that there are many questions of conduct which would be morally indifferent if there were no law, but which become morally significant under the reign of law, and in regard to which it is morally imperative that the law take some definite stand. That statement can scarcely be contradicted, although its application is often grossly exaggerated.[42] The fact that something is affected by legal sanctions adds certain moral considerations to any problem of conduct. The possibility of being punished and of caus-

40 This is held to be the case especially with such rules as those determining the age of majority, the forms of common legal transactions, the interpretation of standard phrases in deeds and wills, etc.

41 *Cf.* Pound, *Law and Morals* (1924) pp. 73-77.

42 *E.g.*, as in Hobbes' doctrine that morality first arises under the reign of law.

ing consequent harm to friends and dependents, the possibility of harming those who rely upon the law, the possibility of destroying social order, which in some degree is a necessary condition of the good life, all these are pertinent facts in a moral judgment, which may appear only after law is created.

All this, however, offers no ground for denying that in so far as law has any effects upon human conduct, non-moral law (in the sense of law whose existence does not present a moral problem) is impossible. Even the rule of the road, the favorite example of non-moral law, is full of moral values. When there is a law on the subject, my disobedience of it, involving the possibility of injuring myself and others, certainly entails some moral evil. The question of whether or not I ought to obey such a law is therefore a moral question. Finally, the question of whether or not there ought to be such a law is a moral question. It is not generally true that no moral values are involved in the choice between a rule keeping traffic to the left and one keeping it to the right. Where such a choice is enacted into law, there are regularly physiological peculiarities or social habits which make one rule preferable to the other. But even if the choice were morally indifferent the law chosen would not be morally indifferent,—that is to say, the demand that the law enact at least one of the two possible rules would be no less a moral demand because of the indeterminateness of the alternative. The demand that I save a friend's life and the act by which this is accomplished do not cease to be moral if there are a number of slightly different ways of attaining this result, among some of which my choice is morally indifferent. So in a very large portion of the civil law (especially commercial law), the choice of rules, within certain limits, is of negligible moral significance, while the demand that there be a definite choice within these limits is of the greatest moral importance. It is upon such a moral demand that the justification of so-called non-moral law must rest, and such a demand may easily so outweigh all the other factors in the situation that it would be good, say, to keep to the right, that being the law, even though the law ought to have been made, originally, the other way.

A second claim of exemption from the domain of morality is commonly advanced on behalf of the judicial function. The question which a judge faces in coming to a decision, it is argued, is purely legal, not moral. Legislatures may endeavor to decide what the law ought to be, but it is for the judge to decide what, in any particular case, the law is. It is apparently in this vein that Maine, distinguishing the philosophy of law from the philosophy of legislation, says, "The jurist, properly so called, has nothing to do with any ideal standard of law or morals."[43] And in the same vein Dean Pound has said, "The utilitarian theory of Bentham was a theory of legislation. The social theory of the present is a theory of legal science."[44] So, in the general philosophy of the Anglo-American bench and bar, "public policy" (the legal equivalent for "morality") seems to be relevant to the decision of a case only when precedents and statutes fail and the function of the judge becomes "legislative."

43 *Loc. cit. supra* note 1.

44 "Mechanical Jurisprudence" (1908) 8 *Columbia Law Rev.* 605, 613; and see "The Scope and Purpose of Sociological Jurisprudence" (1911) 25 *Harvard Law Rev.* 140, n. 4.

Now it is clearly true that the nature of the good does not determine the decisions of judges. Such a determination, as Santayana remarks, is the essence of magic. It is also true that judges generally come to decisions without thinking about moral principles.[45] But it is not true that the goodness or rightness of a decision can be measured except in moral terms.

It may be the case, again, that the professional disavowal of "moral" considerations refers only to the "conscience" theory of morality exemplified in Professor Morgan's dichotomy between "moral character" and "objective conduct." As such it is a valuable defense against the sentimental theory of justice, now increasingly fashionable, which abstracts from the elements of a case everything but the interests of the two parties, and weighs these by an intuitive application of the judge's code of "fairness."[46] But in its actual use, the theory we are attacking goes far beyond this repudiation of sentimentalism. Its actual effect is to exclude the conscious consideration of ethical issues from the judicial mind and to lend weight to the unconscious and uncriticized value standards by which judges decide what they *ought* to do. Fundamentally it attempts to set up as a standard of legal criticism *truth* or

[45] The judge, of course, makes all sorts of moral assumptions, not only in choosing among competing doctrines but as well in the supposedly logical processes of generalization, classification, and construction by which respectable "rules" are drawn from precedent and statute. In difficult cases such moral assumptions frequently become explicit and may even invite analysis. But the question to which the judge's critical faculties are regularly restricted is: "What decision would an intelligent lawyer familiar with statutes and past decisions expect in this situation?" or, more politely, "What *is* the law?"

[46] See Hutcheson, "The Judgment Intuitive: The Function of the 'Hunch' in Judicial Decision" (1929) 14 *Cornell Law Quart.* 274; Frank, *Law and the Modern Mind* (1930) *passim.*

consistency rather than *goodness*. But neither truth nor consistency can be rivals to goodness, in legal criticism or anywhere else. Truth and consistency are categories which apply to propositions or to sets of propositions, not to actions or events. A judicial decision is a command, not an assertion. Even if any sense could be found in the characterization of a decision as true or false (or, in the nonethical sense of the terms, right or wrong, correct or erroneous), such truth or falsity could not determine what decision, in any case, ought to be given. That is a question of conduct and only the categories of ethics can apply to it. In answering such a question, the ethical value of certainty and predictability in law may outweigh more immediate ethical values, but this is no denial of the ethical nature of the problem. *Consistency*, like *truth*, is relevant to such a problem only as an indication of the interest in legal certainty, and its value and significance are ethical rather than logical. The question, then, of how far one ought to consider precedent and statute in coming to a legal decision is purely ethical. The proposition that courts ought always to decide "in accordance with precedent or statute" is an ethical proposition the truth of which can be demonstrated only by showing that in every case the following of precedent or statute does less harm than any possible alternative.

The ethical responsibilities of the judge have so often been obscured by the supposed duty to be logically consistent in the decision of different cases that it may be pertinent to ask whether any legal decision can ever be logically inconsistent with any other decision. In order to find such an inconsistency we must have two judgments, one for the plaintiff and one for the defendant. But this means that we must have two cases, since a second judgment in the same case would supersede the first judgment. And between the facts of any two cases there must be some difference, so that it will always be logically possible to frame a single legal rule requiring both decisions, given the facts of the two cases. Of course such a rule will seem absurd if the differences between the two cases are unimportant (*e.g.* in the names or heights of the two defendants). But whether the difference is important or unimportant is a problem not of logic but of ethics, and one to which the opposing counsel in the later case may propose contradictory answers without becoming involved in self-contradiction.

The confusion arises when we think of a judicial decision as implying a rule from which, given the facts of the case, the decision may be derived (the logical fallacy of affirming the consequence).[47] That logically startling de-

[47] The periodic attempts of students of the common law to put forward logical formulae for discovering "the rule of a case" all betray an elementary ignorance of the logical fact that no particular proposition can imply a general proposition. Wambaugh, Salmond, Gray, Black, Morgan, and Goodhart agree that the rule of a case (the *ratio decidendi*, the proposition for which a case is a precedent) is a general proposition necessary to the particular decision. See Wambaugh, *Study of Cases* (2d ed. 1894) ch. 2; Salmond, "Theory of Judicial Precedents" (1900) 16 *Law. Quart. Rev.* 377; Gray, *Nature and Sources of the Law* (1909) § 555; Black, *Judicial Precedents* (1912) p. 40; E. M. Morgan, *Introduction to the Study of Law* (1926) pp. 109-110; Goodhart, "Determining the Ratio Decidendi of a Case" (1930) 40 *Yale Law Jour.* 161. Logical objections to this conception are dismissed by Professor Morgan as "hypercritical" and "too refined for practical purposes." But Professor Oliphant, who refuses to be deterred by such warnings (see his reply in "Mutuality of Obligation in Bilateral Contracts at Law" (1928) 28 *Columbia Law Rev.* 997 n. 2 to Professor Williston's charges of scholasticism, "The Effect of One Void Promise in a Bilateral Agreement" (1925) 25 *Columbia Law Rev.* 857, 866), has suggested an alternative conception that is logically sound and practically far more useful. Rules of increasing generality, each of them linking the given

rivation of the "law of precedents" from judicial precedents, Black's *Handbook of the Law of Judicial Precedents*, thus sums up the matter:

> Even if the opinion of the court should be concerned with unnecessary considerations, or should state the proposition of law imperfectly or incorrectly, yet there is a proposition necessarily involved in the decision and without which the judgment in the case could not have been given; and it is this proposition which is established by the decision (so far as it goes) and for which alone the case may be cited as an authority.[48]

But elementary logic teaches us that every legal decision and every finite set of decisions can be subsumed under an infinite number of different general rules, just as an infinite number of different curves may be traced through any point or finite collection of points. Every decision is a choice between different rules which logically fit all past decisions but logically dictate conflicting results in the instant case. Logic provides the springboard but it does not guarantee the success of any particular dive.

---

result to the given facts, spread pyramid-wise from a decision. The possibility of alternative modes of analysis makes a decision the apex not of one but of many such pyramids. No one of these rules has any logical priority; courts and lawyers choose among competing propositions on extra-logical grounds. "A Return to Stare Decisis" (1928) 6 *Am. Law School Rev.* 215, 217-218; and *cf.* Llewellyn, *Bramble Bush* (1930) pp. 61-66; Bingham, "What is the Law?" (1912) 11 *Mich. Law Rev.* 1, 109, 111 n. 31. The picture clearly suggests that the decision bears to the rules the same relation that Professor Whitehead has traced between a point and the lines or surfaces that would ordinarily be said to include the point. See *The Principles of Natural Knowledge* (1919) ch. 8; *The Concept of Nature* (1920) ch. 4 (The Method of Extensive Abstraction).

[48] Black, *Handbook of the Law of Judicial Precedents* (1912) p. 40.

If the doctrine of *stare decisis* means anything, and one can hardly maintain the contrary, despite the infelicitous formulations which have been given to the doctrine, the consistency which it demands cannot be a logical consistency. The consistency in question is more akin to that quality of dough which is necessary for the fixing of a durable shape. Decisions are fluid until they are given "morals." It is often important to conserve with new obeisance the morals which lawyers and laymen have read into past decisions and in reliance upon which they have acted. We do not deny that importance when we recognize that with equal logical justification lawyers and laymen might have attached other morals to the old cases had their habits of legal classification or their general social premises been different. But we do shift the focus of our vision from a stage where social and professional prejudices wear the terrible armor of Pure Reason to an arena where human hopes and expectations wrestle naked for supremacy.

No doubt the doctrine of *stare decisis* and the argument for consistency have a significance which is not exhausted by the social usefulness of predictable law. Even in fields where past court decisions play a negligible role in moulding expectations, courts may be justified in looking to former rulings for guidance. The time of judges is more limited than the boundaries of injustice. At some risk the results of past deliberation in a case similar to the case at bar must be accepted. But again we court fatal confusion if we think of this similarity as a logical rather than an ethical relation. To the cold eyes of logic the difference between the names of the parties in the two decisions bulks as large as the difference between care and negligence. The question before the judge is: "Granted that there are differences between the cited precedent and the case at bar, and assuming that the decision in the earlier case was a desirable one, is it desirable to attach legal weight to any of the factual differences between the instant case and the earlier case?" Obviously this is an ethical question. Should a rich woman accused of larceny receive the same treatment as a poor woman? Should a rich man who has accidentally injured another come under the same obligations as a poor man? Should a group of persons, *e.g.* an unincorporated labor union, be privileged to make all statements that an individual may lawfully make? Neither the ringing hexameters of *Barbara Celarent* nor the logic machine of Jevons nor the true-false patterns of Wittgenstein will produce answers to these questions.

What, then, shall we think of attempts to frame practical legal issues as conflicts between morality, common sense, history, or sociology and logic (logic playing regularly the Satanic role)? One hesitates to convict the foremost jurists on the American bench of elementary logical error. It is more likely that they have simply used the word *logic* in peculiar ways, as to which they may find many precedents in the current logical text-books.[49] Bertrand Russell has warned us:

> When it is said, for example, that the French are "logical," what is meant is that, when they accept a premise, they also accept everything that a person totally devoid of logical subtlety would erroneously suppose to follow from that premise. . . . Logic

[49] See M. R. Cohen, "The Subject Matter of Formal Logic" (1918) 15 *Jour. of Phil.* 673.

> was, formerly, the art of drawing inferences; it has now become the art of abstaining from inferences, since it has appeared that the inferences we feel naturally inclined to make are hardly ever valid.[50]

If we construe the word *logic* in the light of this warning, we may readily agree with Mr. Justice Holmes when he asserts that "the whole outline of the law is the resultant of a conflict at every point between logic [*viz.* hasty generalization] and good sense,"[51] and find some meaning in the statement of Mr. Justice Cardozo that the "logic" of one principle prevails over the logic of another[52] or in his

[50] *Sceptical Essays* (1928), ch. 7 (Behaviorism and Values), p. 99.

[51] *Collected Legal Papers* (1920), "Agency," pp. 49, 50. And see Isaacs, "Logic v. Common Sense in Pleading" (1918) 16 *Mich. Law Rev.* 589.

[52] *Nature of the Judicial Process* ch. 1 (Introduction. The Method of Philosophy), p. 41. Justice Cardozo illustrates (*op. cit.* pp. 38-39) the method of logic or philosophy, which is distinguished from the methods of history or evolution, of custom or tradition, and of sociology, with the rule that one who contracts to purchase real property must pay for it even though, before the sale is actually completed, the property is substantially destroyed. This, he maintains, is the projection to its logical outcome of the principle that "equity treats that as done which ought to be done," a principle which does not apply to the sale of chattels which did not come under the jurisdiction of Chancery. But what sort of principle is this? It is certainly not a logical principle, *i.e.* a proposition certifiable on logical grounds alone, since it is obviously false. If it were true, no plaintiff in equity could ever obtain a judgment, since he could never in the face of such a rule show that the defendant had *not* done what he ought to have done. Would it not be quite as logical for a court to say "equity does not treat that as done which has not been done"? If so, what support does logic give to the rule of real property in question? If a rule is undesirable we do not make it less undesirable by deducing it from another rule too vague to be liked or disliked and then concentrating our critical attention on the process of inference rather than the premise. What is in question in the case proposed is not a logical problem or a choice of judicial methods but a conflict of social interests, and there is much that may be said in favor of throwing upon the party who contemplates future enjoyment of a definite piece of real property the risk of its destruction and the necessity of insurance. But what may thus be said bears no peculiar *imprimatur* of Logic. See also *The Growth of the Law* (1924) pp. 79-80.

pride that "We in the United States have been readier to subordinate logic to utility."[53] We may have to interpret the word "logical" as synonymous with "aesthetically satisfying" in order to understand the statement of Mr. Justice Brandeis and Mr. Warren that a distinction between cases where "substantial mental suffering would be the natural and probable result" of an act and cases "where no mental suffering would ordinarily result" is not logical though very practical.[54] Such an identification of the rules of logic with those of intellectual aesthetics seems to be assumed at times by Justice Cardozo as well.[55] No verbal definition is intrinsically objectionable. But it seems fair to suggest that the use of the word *logic* in the senses exemplified in these typical passages seriously lowers the probability of clear thinking on the relation between law and ethics.[56] Most of us think of logic as the most general

53 *The Growth of the Law* p. 77. This is said with regard to the tendency in recent decisions (of which Judge Cardozo's opinion in MacPherson v. Buick Mfg. Co., 217 N. Y. 382 (1916) is a noteworthy landmark) to extend the scope of a manufacturer's obligations to the ultimate consumer with regard to the quality of the product. Again, the rejected "privity" analysis of the situation seems to be peculiarly "logical" because it permits the deduction of an undesirable rule from another undesirable rule which is too vague to arouse the resentment which the deduced rule arouses.

See also *op. cit.* p. 83, where "adherence to logic and advancement of utility" are balanced in terms of "the social interest which each is capable of promoting."

54 Warren and Brandeis, "The Right of Privacy" (1890) 4 *Harvard Law Rev.* 193, reprinted in *Selected Essays on the Law of Torts* (1924) 122, 126.

55 "If I am seeking logical consistency, the symmetry of the legal structure, how far shall I seek it?" *Nature of the Judicial Process* p. 10. And *cf. ibid.* pp. 33-34.

56 *Cf.* the attacks of Hoernlé, Wu, and Adler on the misuse of the term *logic* in current legal literature. Hoernlé, Review of *Science of Legal Method* (1918) 31 *Harvard Law Rev.* 807; Wu, *Juridical Essays and Studies* (1928), ch. 11 (The Juridical Philosophy of Roscoe Pound), pp. 131-132; Adler, "Law and the Modern Mind: A Symposium" (1931) 31 *Columbia Law Rev.* 99-101.

and formal of the sciences.[57] Upon that basis we may say, paraphrasing a remark of Mr. Justice Holmes, that conformity with logic is only a necessity and not a duty. The bad judge is no more able to violate the laws of logic than he is to violate the laws of gravitation. He may, of course, ignore both. But it is not our purpose to deny that there would be less judicial stumbling were courts more constantly aware of the logical relations between particular and universal, between premise and conclusion, between form and content.

7. CONCLUSION

The theory which denies ethical justiciability to law, in whole or in part, cannot be maintained. Its superficial plausibility arises from the narrow connotation given to the terms *ethics* and *morality* when they are extruded from the field of legal valuation. The falsity of the theory arises from the fact that, along with the promptings of conscience, the principal values of life are banished from the juristic consciousness and an inadequate "practical" ethics substituted. The invalidity of the inference by which this theory is established arises from the fallacy (*quaternio terminorum*) by which the extrusion from law of "ethics" in its broadest sense is inferred from a denial of its legal importance in its narrower connotation. Finally, the confusion of the theory lies in the indeterminate character of the

[57] See Russell, *Principles of Mathematics* (1903) ch. 1, *Mysticism and Logic* (1921) 111-112; M. R. Cohen, "The Subject Matter of Formal Logic" (1918) 15 *Jour. of Phil.* 673; Wittgenstein, *Tractatus Logico-Philosophicus* (1922) *passim*. *Cf.* Tweedledee's statement of this position (*Through the Looking Glass*, ch. 4): "If it was so, it might be; and if it were so, it would be, but as it isn't, it ain't. That's logic."

system of values substituted by our jurists for what they call "ethics" and "morality."

Law is just as much a part of the domain of morality as any other phase of human custom and conduct. It has no special purpose, end, or function, no restriction of moral scope, other than that which its positive and practical nature may impose in the way of limitations of applicability.[58] It is our cardinal contention that whatever can be asserted about the valuation or criticism of law—until its positive characters and capacities are measured—can with equal validity be affirmed of the valuation of shoes, ships, sealing-wax, cabbages, and kings. An essay on the criticism of law must be fundamentally an essay on ethics,[59] with only the added problem of proving that it is an essay on ethics. It may be possible, after reviewing the positive aspect of law, to delineate restrictions upon the domain of ethics applicable to our present subject.[60] It will certainly be possible to show that many suggested restrictions and qualifications of jurally relevant ethics are invalid. Only in these respects, and upon a polar basis of fact and value, can we advance from a general treatment of ethics to the more particular treatment of legal valuation, the part of

58 See Bentham, *Fragment on Government* (2d ed. 1823) ch. 4; Pound, "Jurisprudence," in *The History and Prospects of the Social Sciences* (1925) pp. 474-476.

59 *Cf.* Bentham: "Those who, for the sake of peace, seeking to distinguish politics and morals, assign utility as the principle of the first, and justice of the second, only exhibit the confusion of their ideas. The whole difference between politics and morals is this: the one directs the operations of governments, the other directs the proceedings of individuals; their common object is happiness. That which is politically good cannot be morally bad; unless the rules of arithmetic, which are true for great numbers, are false as respects those which are small." "Principles of Morals and Legislation," ch. 2, 1 *Works* 1, 12.

60 We have, in fact, already restricted the realm of the good applicable to legal criticism to that which appears in human life.

ethics relevant to law. Prerequisite to that advance is the general investigation of the nature and significance of ethics.

We have the right to conclude, then, that the instrumental value of law is simply its value in promoting the good life of those whom it affects,[61] and that any law or other element of the legal order which has effects upon human life can be judged to be good or bad in the light of those effects. The complete valuation of law will include a consideration of any intrinsic legal values by considering the values, intrinsic and instrumental, in the lives of those whose actions constitute the life of the law. Consequently the total valuation of law resolves itself into a judgment upon the life of human beings in so far as it is involved in the law itself or is affected by law. The evaluation of law must be made in terms of the good life, and to demonstrate the nature of this standard is the task of ethics, and, more particularly, of morality. Difficult as that task is and uncertain as its conclusions have been, it is a vicious illusion to suppose that the task of the statesman is less difficult or that his conclusions can be more certain.

61 Since the law may affect those who are not directly subject to it, we cannot limit our ideal to the good life of subjects, although this limitation will be practically accurate when consequences to non-subjects are negligible.

CHAPTER TWO

LEGAL IDEALS AND THE GOOD LIFE

1. THE POSITIVE AND THE NORMATIVE IN THE CONSTRUCTION OF LEGAL IDEALS

THE standard of the *good life* as applied to legal criticism points in two directions. It points to *life* as the material in which the symbolism of statute and court decision must be seen and judged,—to life, that is, rather than to such limited aspects of life as we commonly subsume under the ideas of justice or liberty or peace. It points as well to the *good* as the ultimate ideal of legal activity,—again to something distinguished by its inclusiveness from the limited goods and the still more limited "oughts" which have from time to time been set up as sufficient ideals for the fashioning of the legal order. Are we justified in maintaining that there is no more simple or certain source of knowledge in legal criticism than a jurisprudence which is responsible not only to pure ethics but to all the natural and social sciences that explain the life of man?

We have seen that the attempt of legal criticism to evade the idea of the good is suicidal. What of the converse attempt to eliminate the positive sciences from the apparatus of legal criticism?

A complete science of ethics would afford the answer

to every problem of legal criticism. To suppose, however, that non-ethical science is therefore irrelevant in the valuation of law is to mistake the essential nature of ethical science. It is logically conceivable that men should be blessed with infallible intuitions concerning the value of all things. Without knowing what the effects of a particular lie or a particular legal decision were to be, one might be aware that those effects would be bad. In such a world positive science, while useful in many practical affairs of life, would be irrelevant to our judgments of good and bad in the field of law or in any other field. In such a world ethical science would be independent of economics, psychology, physiology, and every other positive discipline. We should not have to know, for instance, what effect a given medicine might have on the human system. It would be enough to know that under the circumstances the medicine ought to be administered. Many moral philosophers and jurists have believed that we do live in this sort of world. If, however, the ethical intuitions that we do have are limited to the objects of our direct experience, we will have to learn how these scattered and usually trivial objects are related to the larger wholes that we seek to value. And these relations will be disclosed not by ethical intuition but by positive science. We do not in fact have ethical reactions to the real character of a man or the real consequences of a law until we know what that character or those consequences are, and it is to psychology, economics, or some other positive science that we must turn in the endeavor to relate the complex thing that we judge to things of which we do have immediate moral knowledge.

Thus positive science plays in ethics a role similar to that which mathematical science plays in physics. Every proposition about masses and velocities is an empirical proposition which might conceivably be directly verified; and since all the propositions of physics are of that type, mathematics might seem irrelevant to physical science. But we cannot actually verify every empirical proposition of physics, and mathematics supplies the relations between propositions that we can verify and those that we cannot. Thus our direct knowledge of physical events, in itself fragmentary and trivial, is rendered fruitful and capable of systematic scientific development. So the fructifying of our ethical insights through positive science is integral to the development of a science of ethics. The knowledge that happiness is good will not lead us to the conclusion that the abolition of poverty is good without the additional assumption, upon the truth of which ethics throws no light, that poverty is a cause of unhappiness. That the abolition of poverty is desirable will not show that usury laws are good unless the effect of such laws is to reduce poverty, again a purely positive assumption. That portion of ethical science which we have called legal criticism is thus intimately dependent upon non-ethical propositions which it is the function of positive science to verify and organize.

It is important to recognize that the truth of these propositions is in no way guaranteed or illumined by ethics. The type of legal thinking we have called crypto-idealism springs naturally from something that may be called crypto-positivism. Legal philosophers like Kant, Hegel, Stammler, and Kohler, who have insisted upon the basic dependence of legal criticism upon ethics, have often minimized or ignored the equally basic dependence of legal criticism upon positive science.[1] In deducing practical rules as to marriage, slavery, property, and contract from abstract and formal moral postulates, they have regularly failed to make explicit the positive premise involved in every step of the descent from the heaven of ethical axioms to the terrestrial fields of law administration. The result has been that their positive premises are as unenlightened as are the ethical premises of positivistic jurists. And the spectacle of these legal philosophers descending the steps of legal criticism with the aid of a birds-eye map, naively unaware that every step has a positive vertical as well as an ideal horizontal side, and reminded only by their bruises that the steps vary somewhat in height, has implanted in many terrestrial jurists the firm belief that the important thing about steps is, after all, the vertical side. Some have concluded that climbing is an illusion, and have remained in the fields of the actual. Others have tried the ascent and found to their dismay that on the horizontal side the steps of legal philosophy are decorated with holes and slippery places.

The disdain of ethical philosophers for the positive studies which reveal, for instance, the difference between prohibiting adultery and preventing adultery, has ancient roots in the ethics of "conscience." Intuitive or commonsense ethics recognizes no dependence upon positive science. The immediate reaction of conscience to a particular situation demands no intellectual concatenation of the situation judged with other situations. Indeed it seems probable that adhesion to an ethics of conscience, which

[1] *Cf.* M. R. Cohen, *Reason and Nature* (1931) pp. 416-419.

we have seen to be rather fashionable among jurists, is responsible for the legal tradition which regards investigation of the actual effects of legal decisions and statutes as trivial or useless. It is only when a scientific ethics has reduced to a minimum the ultimate elements of value that it becomes necessary to call upon positive science for the delineation of causal connections between these elements and other aspects of the cosmos. Consider, for instance, the question of the proper legal attitude towards incest. So definitely does "conscience" speak on this question that no legal scholar in the last century has found it necessary to look into the social effects of laws dealing with the marriage of relatives. But Bentham was forced by his ethics to delineate the positive nature of such laws in terms of human happiness before passing judgment upon them, and the result is a penetrating, if sketchy, account of the way in which such legal sanctions affect domestic life and the marriageability of women in modern society.[2] By crystallizing the uneliminable substance of moral intuition, scientific ethics delimits its role and makes room for a rational element in moral judgment.

This rational element in moral judgment may always be viewed as a positive definition or analysis of the object of the judgment. A habit of judicial conduct, a legislative act, an administrative ruling, is analyzed into such elements as cost in human energy, pain to a certain number of lawbreakers, etc. It is positive science which presents legal events and institutions in the context of their consequences

[2] *Theory of Legislation* (ed. by Dumont 1802, trans. by Hildreth, 2d ed., 1871), "Principles of the Civil Code," Part 3, ch. 5.

and alternatives, and thus permits the reduction of legal criticism to the pure ethical form *A is intrinsically good.*[3]

But what shall be the terms of analysis in our positive legal science? We cannot hope to trace in every aspect the consequences of legal activity. It is notorious that social science freed from ethical thought produces horrid wildernesses of useless statistics.[4] Ethics will not help us to decide whether social statistics of any given sort are true. It will help us, however, to decide whether they are useful. A conception of the good is essential to the distinction between important and unimportant studies. Sociological jurisprudence, we may venture to predict, will remain a pious hope and a program until its advocates adopt some ethical system which indicates, as does hedonism, a definite variable to look for in tracking down the significance of any legal element.

To this phrasing of our general problem, the anti-utilitarian is likely to raise the objection that we can value events without an interminable calculation of consequences, that if this were not the case ethics would in fact be impossible. And since our general insistence that there is a positive pole in legal criticism is quite independent of any conclusions with regard to the nature of the good, we shall try to show that any non-utilitarian standard of criticism must take account of exactly the same positive elements.

The distinction between intrinsic and utilitarian values

[3] For a proof that all ethical propositions can be logically reduced to this form, see ch. 3, § 2, *infra.*

[4] "Very little experience of using current official statistics is required to convince that statistics gathered for no purpose beyond filling a report with impressive tabulations are seldom valuable for anything else." Pound, "The Call for a Realist Jurisprudence" (1931) 44 *Harvard Law Rev.* 697, 701.

is not in the nature of the value, but in the nature of the thing valued. When I judge an act intrinsically I judge a certain part of the universe in abstraction from other causally connected parts. When I judge the same act from a utilitarian point of view, I am simply passing a judgment of intrinsic value upon everything which that act involves or entails (including itself). Every utilitarian valuation may thus be considered as an intrinsic valuation from another viewpoint,—considering as the object of valuation not the abstracted act or law but the total set of changes in the universe that we bring about when we commit an act or pass a law. We have not considered the law or act intrinsically, but we have considered something else (the causal complex which it identifies) intrinsically. Positive science appears, then, in this role as a means of finding out what it is that we are valuing.

If any one challenges the legitimacy of the utilitarian philosophy and proceeds to make intrinsic valuations of law, we can only reply that he has challenged a vocabulary rather than a doctrine. An example may make this clear. I shoot off a pistol on the Fourth of July. This experience is pleasant and self-expressing and self-developing and free. The opponent of utilitarianism therefore decides that this act is intrinsically good, "regardless of its results." But now note that what is thus valued is only a part of what I have really done. Let us suppose that I have killed my neighbor in this act, that I have deprived the world of a great literary genius, that I have made his children wretched, and put his wife in a position to contract a happy re-marriage. Each of these things is a part of what I did at one particular instant, and each has as much right to be intrinsically valued as the first description of the event, *i.e.* "shooting off a pistol." In judging any one of these descriptions the anti-utilitarian would be judging only a part of the individual event, and if it were his task to evaluate the whole event he would have to weigh one element against the other to reach a final decision. But clearly this procedure would differ only in the terminology employed from the procedure of the utilitarian who values my act as *causing my neighbor's death* (instead of *killing my neighbor*), *causing the world's deprivation*, etc. Although the anti-utilitarian may use different standards of value,[5] the event to which they are applied cannot be different from that regarded by the utilitarian, if both applications are accurately effected.

The only advantage of the utilitarian terminology is that it cautions us against making the popular metaphysical error of considering the abstractions (universals) by which we identify events as the events themselves. The action which we characterize as shooting off a pistol is at the same time an action of causing death, suffering, joy, etc., and the fact that it can be brought under one category does not prevent the application of other categories. The fact that an action is an instance of lying does not prevent it from being also an instance of causing happiness or

[5] Typically, the anti-utilitarian accepts as a criterion of value some attribute of the human will. This would free him from the task of discovering what the effects of a particular volition may be, were it not for the fact that one man's volitions may affect the environment and mould the will of others. At this point one preserves the dogmatic ethical certainty which utilitarianism threatens by invoking the notion of the freedom of the will. Psychology and other positive sciences of human conduct become impossible, and ethics is freed from a degrading dependence upon unstable knowledge.

pain. Similarly a law prohibiting the sale of intoxicating liquors may be also a law impelling people to drink ginger ale or to smoke. Such a law may cause a certain redistribution of wealth, a certain modification of international trade, a certain change of attitude towards law enforcement, etc. All of these characters may be just as relevant to the valuation of the law as its assumed purpose or intrinsic command, and it is the great contribution of the utilitarian philosophy that it has drawn attention to elements in actions or events, legal and non-legal, which are often overlooked. It stresses the undeniable and frequently forgotten fact that in order to value anything intelligently we must know what it is. Any legal action that can be valued is more than the writing of certain words or the issuance of certain commands; it is also the effecting of certain social changes. What law does is part, and the most important part, of what law is, and the indispensable task of positive science in legal criticism is the exposition of the full nature of jural activities.

Our problem, then, is the same, whether or not we profess the name of utilitarians. We are given certain events, actual or possible, to evaluate—events that are designated or identified by characteristics which do not exhaust their nature, and we are required to discover, so far as we can, this complete and manifold nature. A valuation of law which does not take into account this full nature may, as a matter of fact, be true (just as a valuation which does not take into account the nature of value may be true), so that a utilitarian calculation of effects is not a logical prerequisite of any ethical judgment. It is however, a prerequisite of intelligent judgment or valid inference, the first condition of which is that we know what we are talking about.

To discover the full nature (*i.e.*, the intrinsic character and complete causal efficacy) of any juridical act in terms of human life is a task of the utmost difficulty, but though the problems which it involves are for the most part incapable of ultimately satisfactory solution, this complete solution remains a logical ideal presupposed by the ideal of valid ethical judgment upon law. The latter ideal, too, is one beyond human attainment, but a progressive approach to it demands a parallel approximation to the complete understanding of law in its positive sociological aspects. There is this difference, however, between the two ideals: whereas that of positive knowledge is seldom sought for its own sake and is generally recognized to be clothed with tremendous complexity and difficulty, the ideal of valid ethical judgment is the subject of widespread and powerful aspirations. Accordingly there is a general assumption that the latter ideal permits of complete attainment, and that, consequently, it must be independent of the former.

It is easier to admit incompetence in questions that do not seem directly to concern our practical ethical conclusions, than to confess the uncertainty and inadequacy of these conclusions, precisely because our desires are more potent in the latter realm and more impatient of obstacles which we are easily tempted to overlook. It is therefore not surprising that nearly the whole course of legal-ethical thought has been marked by a search for some standpoint of juristic criticism which evades the consideration of interminable problems of positive science. Some short-cut to valid ethical criticism is imperatively demanded, and few indeed are the jurists who have not claimed to discover such a short-cut.

Now although the motives which inspire these claims may be easily disparaged, there is no logical reason why one or more of them should not be valid. True it is that in order to discover whether our short-cut leads to the end of the longer road, somebody must follow that road to discover its end. And so, although some simple principle of legal criticism may be correct, we cannot be sure that it is correct without solving all the problems of positive science the consideration of which it proposed to avoid, and noting whether the complete evaluations of law coincide with those to which our simpler principle points. To know that any such principle is correct and adequate is impossible unless all the positive elements in law are understood, and we may therefore dismiss as untrue all claims for the attainment of certainty in legal criticism which dispense with the arduous task of discovering what law does and can do.

But if it is the truth of such principles, rather than our certainty of its attainment, which we are criticizing, we cannot argue from the psychological motives or logical reasons which impel belief in them. They can be refuted only by showing the incompatibility of their conclusions with the results of a more perfect investigation of cause and effect in the realm of goods. It is this latter labor which must be undertaken if our own general conclusions are to be proved important and useful as well as true. For although it be true that an ethical judgment which takes into account the full nature of legal activity (in so far as that activity is relevant to the good life) must be true (assuming that our purely ethical standard is valid), such judgments would involve needless labor and uncertainty if any shorter route to legal-ethical truth were known. That no such route is known, that the concept of the good life constitutes a necessary as well as a sufficient ethical basis for legal criticism, is accordingly an important point in our thesis, a point which cannot, it seems, be elaborated on any *a priori* grounds, but must involve the criticism of legal principles that have actually been propounded or utilized in the solution of our problems. Our conclusion, then, we must confess in advance, cannot have compelling logical force, since the material to be examined is of indefinite extent and not to be exhausted by any historical treatment. But we shall attempt to establish, with as high a degree of probability as the subject matter permits, the thesis that involved in the ideal of legal criticism is an analysis of legal elements into ultimate terms of that which makes human life good.

2. STANDARDS OF LEGAL CRITICISM

The standards which have been suggested and avowedly or tacitly used as substitutes for the valuation of the complete nature of legal acts all involve some abstraction from this full nature which makes a part of our positive investigation unnecessary and may also make part of the realm of ethical goods irrelevant to our valuation. The mere fact that we are dealing with abstractions, with partial aspects of legal elements, does not suffice to invalidate our valuations, from an ultimate ethical standpoint. Abstraction is necessary in all thought, and even an estimate of law in terms of the good life makes many results of law irrelevant to our criticism. What renders a given standard of valuation inadequate is not its mere abstractness but the fact that the abstraction involved is not exhaustive or representative of all the values implicated in law. And this fault seems definitely ascribable to legal standards of two sorts: those which, abstracting from all the results of law, evaluate either the form or the expressed content or the purpose of law, and those which restrict themselves to such limited aspects of legal results as the maintenance of peace, freedom, justice, "social" interests, or "natural rights."

The standards of legal valuation which have been proposed and utilized as substitutes for the estimate of the complete nature of law in terms of the good life may be defended on four grounds, which must be successively demolished if the standard in question is to be refuted. The evaluation of law in terms of any such ideal or standard will be of final ethical validity: (1) if this standard is the sole good, (2) if it is the only good which law can secure, (3) if it is the only good which law can secure without a greater sacrifice of other goods, or (4) if it is so correlated with other goods that in securing the given ideal law also secures a maximum of goods in general. Only by showing each of these alternative conditions to be unsatisfied can we prove the inadequacy of the standard in question.

A. The Aesthetic Valuation of Law

Simplest of the abstractions which have provided jurists, judges, and lawyers with standards of legal criticism is that which views a body of law as an isolated rational system and examines only the relation between the various elements of a legal order. It may seem absurd to suggest that jurists after examining this bony skeleton have seen fit to pronounce upon the body of law it supports and upon the activity of that body. And indeed no one, it seems, has seen fit to champion openly any such standard of valuation. Yet it is impossible to read the works of jurists and juristic historians without being impressed with the powerful hold which this essentially aesthetic standard has upon the legal mind and with the definite slant it has given to professional criticism of law.

It is difficult, at first blush, to identify law as an aesthetic object. For laymen it frequently has no aesthetic value at all. But jurists have certainly attached such value to the object of their study and contemplation, although they would probably be the last to admit it.[6] Roman law is considered by every writer on the subject to be far superior to Greek law, not because it had better effects upon the social life of the time,—for that is extremely doubtful, and its irrelevancy to the valuation is shown by the failure of jurists to prove it or even to assert it,—but simply because it shows a greater harmony in its explication, a greater emphasis upon analogy and precedent, a greater

[6] Sir Frederick Pollock seems to be an exception among students of the common law. His appreciation of "Law as a work of art" is made explicit in *Essays in the Law* (1922) p. 273.

unity in its content, a greater care throughout for what is called *elegantia juris*. When the *Gelehrten* of the fifteenth and sixteenth centuries in Germany, against the spirited opposition of the common people, threw into the discard the old local law to make room for the *Corpus Juris Civilis*, were they motivated by utilitarian calculations that the Roman law was better fitted to bring about the good life than was the traditional legal order? Or were they not rather impelled to action by their fascination with the elegance of the classical law and by their disgust with the rudeness of the old barbarian order? Even today we cannot read the works of Ulpian or Gaius without marvelling at their technical artistry and subtle beauty. How easy it is still, even for the lay reader of the Roman law books, to translate this aesthetic appreciation into moral approval before attempting to discover whether the artist has worked in the service of Jehovah or Satan.

We need not go to ancient history to appreciate the hold which this concept of *elegantia juris* has upon the legal mind. At almost every bar association convention held in this country, papers have been read in which the interference of legislatures with the judicial development of the law is roundly denounced. An important element in these denunciations seems to be the vague feeling that legislation spoils the harmony and symmetry and unity of law which has been developed by a professional class with a strong care for such matters.

Jurists like to dignify this interest with the name of *logic* rather than *aesthetics*. But this misuse of the word *logic* cannot affect the real state of affairs. The demand for development of law by analogy, the search for a few general principles from which a whole system of positive law can be deduced, the objection to laws which contradict other laws (which is simply the opposition to change), these are not conditions laid upon the law by logic, for no law which has meaning can be illogical. These demands may be justified in view of their social consequences, and indeed a certain amount of harmony and symmetry in legal development may serve the important social purpose of rendering law easily comprehensible and thus facilitating social order and security. But certainly *elegantia juris* is neither the sole ethical good, nor the only good which law can promote, nor the only good which the law can achieve without the sacrifice of more important values.

And finally, this aesthetic ideal can be correlated with only an infinitesimal portion of the goods which may be secured by law. For if this were not immediately obvious we should be forced to the conclusion by the observation that a given aesthetic effect in law can be produced in more ways than one, for instance by transposing all rewards and penalties legally prescribed, or by commanding whatever a legal system prohibits and prohibiting whatever it commands. It would be absurd to suppose that such transpositions could not affect the value of law even when its peculiar aesthetic elegance was preserved. We may therefore conclude unhesitatingly that the aesthetic valuation of law, or as the jurist may refer to phrase it, the "logical" valuation of law, is not valid from an ultimate ethical point of view. Whatever values this ideal may lead to, such as the aesthetic enjoyment of law students and jurists and the social convenience of law that is easily grasped (an element not always correlated with the intricate beauty or the esoteric simplicity[7] which appeal to the jurist), will receive proper consideration in our valuation of law as it involves and secures the good life,—but these values must generally be rather trivial in comparison with the wider and deeper effects of law upon human behavior.

Unimportant as these aesthetic interests are from the point of view of ethics, they are of extreme significance in our positive calculation of legal effects and possibilities. The enforcement and interpretation of law are very largely in the hands of just those men who are most apt to be moved by the aesthetic considerations in question. To neglect the part which these motives play in determining the actual social significance of legal elements is fatal to the accuracy of our legal criticism. The juristic conservatism of bench and bar, the judicial custom, in this country, of emasculating statutes "in derogation of the common law," the shocking neglect of sociological investigation into the effects of law, and the slowness of the law to respond to the pressure of dominant social classes are all very largely determined by the weight of aesthetic standards in the legal mind. And these standards attain supreme directive power in the development of those portions of the law which are far removed from non-professional interest and understanding, such as the greater part of our civil law.[8]

[7] *Cf.* N. Isaacs, "The Promoter: A Legislative Problem" (1925) 38 *Harvard Law Rev.* 887.

[8] M. René Demogue has some interesting remarks on this issue in a section on "The Limitations of Technique as a Recipe for Law." *Analysis of Fundamental Notions* (1911, trans. by Scott and Chamberlain 1916), in *Modern French Legal Philosophy*, Modern Legal Philosophy Series, vol. 7, pp. 407 *et seq. Cf.* the following statement from the original report of the committee on the scope of the current "Restatement of the Law": "Changes in the law which are, or which would, if proposed, become a matter of general public concern and discussion should not be considered, much less set forth, in any restatement of the law such as we have in mind."

It is therefore no less important to appreciate the real weight of this aesthetic attitude than to recognize its ethical inadequacy. And this weight we may better realize when we note the manifestations of a similar viewpoint in other walks of life. We have all heard doctors speak of beautiful cases or operations or dissections, and such beauty is not impaired by any fatal outcome, although the standards by which such beauty is judged may have had originally a partly utilitarian basis. So the printer or "make-up" editor of a newspaper is likely to regulate his own work and to judge that of others by reference to certain standards of type distribution which undoubtedly had original utilitarian value but which have become so deeply ingrained in his aesthetic consciousness that a "dummy" conforming to them appears as right, and any other as wrong. This professional slant is commonly too strong to permit a violation of the accepted canons of the art for the purpose of producing desirable results which these standards, under peculiar or novel circumstances, cannot achieve. We have here simply typical cases of that transformation of means to ends which, far from being a mode of thought peculiar to misers, is at the heart of most human activities. Every technique gives rise to standards of criticism which are only partially correlated with the value of the results secured, and which frequently, especially in the professional

(William D. Lewis, "The Restatement of the Law by the American Law Institute" in *Proceedings of the Academy of Political Science*, vol. 10, no. 3 (*Law and Justice*), p. 7, 13 (1923). By avoiding questions of public interest, free play has been secured for the remolding of the law in accordance with professional aesthetic ideals. The power of these ideals may best be appreciated by comparing the hopes of Professors Oliphant and Llewellyn (see "The Relation of Current Economic and Social Problems to the Restatement of the Law" in *Proceedings*, *supra*, p. 17) with the actual work of the American Law Institute.

mind, completely overshadow those results (as is so generally the case in Art). A religious ritual originally valued as a means of securing communion with God or of obtaining some wish comes to have an overpowering intrinsic beauty and value of its own.[9] A similar process may be noted in the observances of etiquette, the usages of cookery, the practices of opera singers, the progress of philosophy, the conduct of sport, even the activities of armies. A famous general objected to war on the ground that it ruined the discipline of the army.

We need digress no further into the origin and nature of aesthetics. It is enough to have indicated that jurists, like other people, are subject to a perfectly natural and perfectly definite fallacy of valuation due to an excessive preoccupation with technique and a consequent confusion of the aesthetic judgment with the ethical.[10] This general explanation of our adversaries' errors, while it cannot furnish us with respectable arguments for their refutation, at least serves to explain how the self-evident platitudes which form the structure of this essay may possibly possess some originality and importance in juristic literature, and, like all similar psychological explanations of illustrious error, it enables us to end our controversy with a feeling of mental security.

[9] *Cf.* Picard, *Le droit pur* (1908) pp. 311 *et seq.* "On dirait que c'est avec joie que le Juriste de profession invoque alors la *Dura Lex sed Lex!* pour assurer la spoliation de la victime. C'est un hommage, une sorte de sacrifice humain aux Fétiches juridiques." And see M. R. Cohen, "Legalism and Clericalism," 41 *New Republic* (1924) 15.

[10] If the ethical judgment is itself in a sense aesthetic, it is at least more comprehensive than the purely aesthetic judgment, taking into account, as it does, not merely immediate values but potentialities of further goods and evils not directly perceived.

B. The Valuation of Law in Terms of Its Expressed Content

A second fallacy of illicit abstraction in legal criticism, which, like the aesthetic judgment, is more used than championed, is that involved in the attempt to pass final ethical judgments upon consideration of the immediate content of legal decrees. A rule of law commanding or permitting a good thing or prohibiting a bad thing is held to be good, and a rule commanding or permitting a bad thing or prohibiting a good thing, bad. All questions of the actual extent to which law will secure obedience and of the actual nature and results of this degree of obedience are held to be irrelevant to our value judgments.

This is perhaps the commonest error that appears in legal criticism. Popular arguments on legal and political questions are frequently couched entirely in this framework, and juristic theories of natural law or abstract right (*Recht*) usually rest squarely upon this inadequate and fallacious base. Those who have talked the language of natural law and abstract right have continually confused two very different questions, namely "Is it right for people to act in a certain way?" and "Is it right for the state to command such action?" In appealing to "universal conscience" the advocates of natural law have put such questions as "Is it right to steal?", "Is it right to murder?", "Is it right to break a promise?" Important as it is to ask questions of this sort in building a system of legal criticism, the answers to these questions are not, as such, valid answers to questions concerning the proper application of political force. For questions of the latter sort demand a consideration of evils inherent in the legal process itself (*e.g.* the suffering caused by punishment and the social cost of legal machinery), as well as those evils which the law attempts to prohibit.

Even those jurists who reject as "unhistorical" belief in natural law and reject or radically qualify belief in an abstract right are prone to overlook as obscene the facts of law resistance. The political fiction that legal sovereignty is identical with the power to compel obedience is still offered as an excuse for the blindness of legal criticism to the discrepancies between law-in-books and law-in-action. But without a clear vision of these discrepancies, law dissipates its forces in hopeless attacks upon uncontrollable evils, and stimulates new evils equally impregnable to the new laws they invoke, but wholly obscene and insignificant to political purists.

The valuation of law in terms of its expressed content is, in short, inadequate and fallacious. It is inadequate as a framework of legal criticism, because it offers no guide to the morality or immorality of that portion of law which commands or prohibits acts that are morally indifferent before the reign of law, and because in dealing only with the rightness or wrongness of commands it neglects such important legal-ethical problems as the character of the sanctions that should be attached to these commands, the nature of their enforcement, and the morality of obedience and disobedience to law. And finally, this type of criticism is erroneous because neither one of its two claims is true.

It is not true, in the first place, that all rules of law

commanding or permitting good things or prohibiting bad things are good. Certainly there are many goods (*e.g.* wisdom, love, heroism) which the law ought not to *command*, either because such commands could not be enforced and would constitute mere dead weight in the legal order, or because such enforcement could not avoid overwhelming injustice and inconvenience, or because the fact of command would rob the activities in question of part of their value. And it is almost as obvious that rules of law *permitting* activities that would be good in the absence of a legal rule may be bad. An important set of such instances arises from the necessity of economy in the law, a necessity dictated by the social value of peace and security and the intellectual and mnemonic limitations of the human mind. Economy demands that the distinctions drawn in the law be not too fine. It may therefore be morally desirable for the law to refuse its sanction to good activities of minor importance rather than attempt to set up a legal distinction between such activities and a larger class of closely related activities which ought to be prohibited. Thus it may be a good thing to drink wine occasionally, but if no convenient distinction can be drawn between such drinking and drinking that is socially harmful, then it may become right for the law to prohibit all liquor traffic, whether harmful or innocent. Under almost every legal category we can find some cases where the application of the general rule works undoubted evil to the parties immediately concerned, but where this evil is itself demanded by a wider good. Unfortunate as this state of affairs may be, we shall not cure it by pretending that it does not exist and that law permitting good actions is always good. Similar arguments may be adduced to show that law prohibiting evils is frequently bad. Such prohibition may be absolutely unenforceable or its enforcement may involve great moral evil, or the prohibition, though good in its immediate effects, may be bad simply because it sets up dangerous precedents for similar laws in less justifiable situations. This last consideration attains obvious importance in problems such as that of censorship.

The converse contention involved in the standard under consideration, namely that rules of law prohibiting goods or sanctioning or commanding evils are bad is open to exactly the same objections. There are many good acts that ought to be prohibited either because they cannot be clearly distinguished in the law from more important evils, or for any of the other reasons suggested above. And for the same reasons of general expediency and security the law must permit and even command acts that are bad. Thus at every point, the valuation of law in terms of its expressed content breaks down in crucial cases, simply because the actual effects and limitations of these legal decrees are ignored. Without attempting to deny the large measure of truth attained by such evaluations, we need have no hesitation in denying the ultimate ethical validity of this standard.

C. The Valuation of Law in Terms of Its Purpose

Many of the foregoing objections can be reasserted with regard to legal criticism which abstracts from everything but the purpose of laws in evaluating them. Now it may be a good thing, frequently, to praise or blame people according to their intentions rather than on the basis of the actual goods or evils they have brought into being. Such praise or blame, reward or punishment, may be ethically justified as encouraging motives which are productive of good in the long run, or discouraging those of the opposite tendency. But purposes may be praiseworthy when the acts in which they culminate are not, and the acts themselves may be praiseworthy (*i.e.* of such a nature that it is good to praise them) even when they are really bad (provided such praise will encourage repetitions or imitations that miss the peculiar, possibly accidental, element that makes the given act bad). Thus there is no need of confusing the question of whether law-makers and their laws merit praise or blame for their good or evil purposes with the question of whether these laws are actually good or bad. And while it is perfectly proper to evaluate juristic purposes, only confusion results when such valuations are put forward as applying to actual law. For since it is human to err, the value of legal intentions and aims must frequently differ considerably from the value of legal results.

The errors natural to a valuation of law in terms of purpose arise from four main sources. In the first place, this formula assumes that there is a uniquely determined purpose in every legal act. This is manifestly untrue, as even a cursory reading of legislative debates or judicial opinions[11] will show. In the second place, the principle assumes that those who make law are wise enough to adopt a proper technique for securing any given end, a flattering assumption, to be sure, for judges and statesmen, but one

11 The opinions of the English appellate courts, delivered seriatim by the individual judges, are particularly illuminating in this connection.

which cannot withstand criticism. Omniscience, even in the narrow field of legal technique, is denied to man, and numerous indeed are the cases where jural purposes have completely miscarried through miscalculations of legal technique. In the third place, those who evaluate law in this way must assume that lawmakers have the power, as well as the wisdom, to secure desired results. And although legal thought is peculiarly inclined to the hallucination of omnipotence, this assumption that lawmakers, unlike other mortals, get what they want is refuted on every page of history,—a fortunate thing, perhaps, for these other mortals. Finally, it is not true that legislators accomplish only that which they wish to accomplish. Every law or judicial decision has effects which reverberate far beyond the sphere envisaged by its author. And it would be truly strange if these unforeseen effects did not sometimes alter the value of the contemplated result.

Consider, for instance, how the French code's stand against primogeniture, by making it difficult to have a large family without breaking up one's estate into portions too small for efficient exploitation, has affected the modern French attitude to marriage and procreation. Indeed, to create a law is to summon from another world a power whose form, with all our magic, we see only dimly. Whether it will follow our bidding or not, whether it will bring us unforeseen gifts or unforeseen harm, we hardly know. But to those who counsel us then to leave all this wonder-working and to exile those who tempt us with the names of new spirits, one may reply that whenever we do not create a law we imprison a spirit that may be the Messiah himself, and perpetuate the rule of those fairies, goblins, demons, and genii whom, with all our past experience, we can scarcely yet distinguish and classify.

The ethical fallacy which confuses the purpose and the effect of an act is not restricted to the field of law. Most people, being more confident of their goodness than of their wisdom, prefer to be judged by that phase of conduct which least involves scientific calculation, by their choice of ultimate ends, their final motives or purposes. But this moral assurance is neither good nor wise. Distant as is our knowledge from the ideal of truth, our ultimate purposes, if only because of their mutual inconsistencies, must be as far from the ideal of goodness. And even when they most completely approximate this norm, our particular, immediate purposes or intentions, being determined by calculations of causality and possibility as well as by ultimate ethical choice of ends, must suffer from the inadequacy of our science as well as of our morality. The road to hell is said by travellers to be paved with good intentions. And judgments upon purpose in law, *das Zweck im Recht,* will pave a road only to a foolish and unreal *juristischer Begriffshimmel.*[12]

We must conclude then that while it is perfectly proper

[12] It is unfortunate that von Jhering, whose whole legal philosophy was a protest against the valuation of law in terms of "concepts" and an insistence upon the ethical primacy of actual legal *results*, should have formulated this philosophy in terms of "purpose." It is true that "purpose" is often conceived in objective terms (*cf.* the legal presumption that a man intends the natural consequences of his acts), and is generally so understood by von Jhering. But there are confusions inherent in this conception which von Jhering and his modern followers have not completely avoided. To identify result and purpose is to dim our vision of that omnipresent human fallibility which separates hope from achievement. It is not far from this assumption of human divinity to the notion that the purpose of any act affords an infallible criterion for its valuation. Such a notion enslaves legal (or, for that matter, literary or artistic) criticism to the interests it ought to judge.

to evaluate legal purposes or intentions, the identification of such judgments with ethical evaluations of law is founded upon an inexcusable confusion and is pregnant with those errors which the neglect of positive inquiry into the full nature of legal acts always involves.

D. The Valuation of Law in Terms of Peace

The three non-utilitarian standards of legal valuation already examined agree in making scientific inquiry into the potentialities and consequences of law irrelevant to legal criticism. What is judged is some abstract phase of the actual legal command, either its formal relation to other commands, or its bare content, or its intended purpose. Each of these abstractions we have seen to be illicit in this sense, that while the phase of law thus considered may properly be valued, its valuation is not a universally correct index to the goodness or badness of law.

The standards of legal criticism which remain to be considered all involve a similar fallacy, but one based upon a less narrow abstraction in the subject of our judgments. Investigation of the results of legal activity is not completely ignored, but only those aspects of such activity are to be considered which involve some particular "end of law" that is less than the total of human goods. Thus our problem of legal values is to be simplified by reducing the extent of the positive inquiries that demand our attention and by rendering a substantial portion of the domain of ethical values irrelevant to our legal criticism. Standards of this sort can be rationally justified only by showing that these simplified evaluations always correspond to the more tedious evaluation in terms of the law's full positive nature and the relation of this nature to the total domain of ethical goods.

There is a popular substitute for such a demonstration, which, because it is difficult to understand, is not easily refuted. The advocate of peace (or justice, or liberty, or anything else) as the "end of law" may tell us that this is simply the proper purpose or function of law, and that if there are other goods which the law can secure, it would nevertheless be improper to secure them. This contention is, as it stands, quite ambiguous, and susceptible of refutation only upon successive consideration of several different meanings which it may have. If we are told merely that the securing of peace, for example, is the *actual purpose* for which law is instituted, and that any other good, say the redistribution of wealth, is alien to this original purpose, then we need not be disturbed. When tools are made for bad or inadequate purposes, it may be very desirable to put them to new uses, *i.e.* to "pervert" them. So we need not fear to take an instrument originally constructed to secure peace and beat it into a form in which we can use it for the attainment of general well-being.

But the contention in question may be taken to mean that peace is the ethical ideal which law *should* approach, and that it is wrong for the law to do good in other ways. As thus baldly stated, such a principle is too obviously absurd to be dangerous. For either the law cannot do any real good outside the realm of the suggested end of law, in which case the latter point of the contention is without significance, or the law can do some such good, in which case the former point is false. But this principle frequently appears in conclusions when only the interpretation treated above was admitted in the premises. And this Protean character of our formula makes it a most difficult adversary in combat, so that many juristic discussions and judicial decisions have embalmed this mode of reasoning. This is indeed the first argument that one hears whenever there is a proposal that the law take under its purview some new field of conduct. We may admit the assertion that it is not the business of law to engage in charity, but this will not justify the natural inference (frequently made without a change of wording) that such activity ought not to be the business of law.[13]

The principle we are considering may be given a third interpretation, as meaning that it is impossible for the law to secure good except in so far as it approaches the ideal of peace (or whatever else is the "proper end of law"), and that in approaching this ideal it secures the greatest possible amount of good. Exhumed from the preceding ambiguities, this is a perfectly clear statement, which can be refuted only by showing that a maximum attainment of the given ideal, in some legal situations, is not correlated with a maximum of general ethical value. This is the issue already set up as our final test of the adequacy and correctness of jural ideals.

On this basis we may examine the first of our quasi-utilitarian value standards, the ideal of peace or general security as the norm of legal activity. Maintained most explicitly by Thomas Hobbes, this ideal has always exerted a powerful force in political thought, and it is not with any intention of disparaging its importance that we wish to

[13] *Cf.* Pollock, *Essays in the Law* (1922) pp. 265-266.

suggest its inadequacy as a final standard of law. Indeed no greater service can be performed on behalf of noble ideals than to free them from the extravagant pretensions with which they have been encumbered by followers more loving than wise.

The ideal of peace or general security is the most primitive end to be sought and achieved through the legal order. Not only is this ideal always of the utmost importance for human well-being, but it constitutes a purpose which the law is peculiarly adapted to fulfill. Thus, when the political organization possesses extremely limited power, the ideal of peace is the only end which it can effectively pursue. Attempts at social reform, the equalization of economic opportunities, the redistribution of power, etc., will be not only ineffective but also destructive of the general support which enables law to secure its great end of peace. Peace must be bought at the price of a legalization or tacit ignoring of great social evils, and the bargain may be well worth while. The relevance of these considerations to international politics is obvious. Never has peace been a more pressing need of mankind than at the present time, and no one whose ideals are more than verbalisms or glittering superficialities can fail to see the frequent moral necessity of suppressing noble aspirations, legalizing injustice, and accepting iniquity, in order to achieve peace by means of an international polity too weak to enforce the best peace.

But the value of international peace, for which we are, or should be, willing to sacrifice so many other goods, is no greater than the value of civil peace. Accustomed as we are, however, to an extraordinary level of domestic security, we tend to forget its precarious dependence upon the reign of law. It is therefore most instructive to find in the works of Hobbes a wholly sympathetic treatment of the ideal of peace as a norm of law and a consideration of the effects of political pluralism upon the attainment of this ideal,—points which, in the *bellum omnium contra Hobbes* waged by political scientists for three centuries, have been much obscured. Hobbes has been severely attacked as a champion of despotism, but what he really argued for was simply the coordination of political power in a single sovereign,—either an individual, a restricted group, or a determinate organization of the whole people. What he attacked was the division of power between state and church ("The Kingdom of Darkness"), and between state and individual conscience, divisions which, in his own times, exhibited so clearly their pragmatic *reductio ad horribile.*[14] There are other divisions of political power treated by Hobbes, such as those involved in the absolute right of property or in the "separation of powers", which are still of extreme importance as obstacles to social security.

In a characteristic epigram Hobbes sums up his basic position. ". . . in matter of government, when nothing else is turned up, clubs are trump."[15] This is not a blind glorification of force. It is simply a clear recognition of the fact that in every orderly activity, whether card playing or social intercourse, there must be a recognized supremacy or sovereignty, and that the power which controls the army must exclusively occupy this place in society if the evils of anarchy and civil war are to be avoided. This is a truth the recognition of which is, at all times, so important that

[14] *Cf.* Laski, *Foundations of Sovereignty* (1921) pp. 233-234.

[15] Hobbes, *Dialogue Between a Philosopher and a Student of the Common Laws of England* (1681), "Of Punishments".

we may forgive some of the exaggerations with which it has been clothed. But we cannot with intellectual integrity ignore them. In his compelling analogy of the state to an animal, which has been a starting point for "organic" political theories ever since, Hobbes offers a symbol in which are implicated at once the strength and the weakness of his political philosophy. On the one hand, the state, no less than the animal, is an entity upon whose harmonious and coordinated activity the well-being of each part depends. But on the other hand, the state exists for the happiness and virtue of its members, while the members and organs of an animal (no less than the state itself) know neither happiness nor virtue and can justify themselves only through the whole organism. The reign of law and order is therefore not an intrinsic good, but an instrumentality for the achievement of the good life, and, like every other tool, it must be discarded or mended when it fails to accomplish such an end.

There are limits to the ethical sacrifices which may be rightfully made in the struggle for order and security. And moralists like Hobbes do no honor to the cause of peace by shutting their eyes to these limits. After all, none but the dead are as secure as the caged convict,—who is not an attractive incarnation of the good life. To sacrifice successively the elements of life that make peace good in order to achieve peace is like burning up the house in order to light it. Even when peace is the only good which a political organization can achieve, its maximum attainment, achieved by a discreet legal deference to dominant social forces, may not be desirable. But when, through added physical and psychical strength, the state reaches a point where it can effectively legislate for other ethical goods, there must be many cases where legal-ethical questions irrelevant to the ideal of peace call for settlement in the light of some other norm, and further cases where the risk of organized resistance ought no longer to stay the hand of social reform and where the ideal of peace ought to be sacrificed to other human ideals, such as those of equality or freedom.

We must conclude, then, that although peace is an enduring human ideal, a first requirement of the good life and one particularly susceptible of achievement through law, and although a good deal of law must pursue peace at great costs in order to achieve a maximum of ethical values, there is no truth in the supposition that peace or security constitutes a valid and adequate norm for all legal activity.[16]

E. The Valuation of Law in Terms of Liberty[17]

The word *liberty*, as Madame Roland suggested, is a dangerous one, as is, indeed, any term that combines a strong eulogistic flavor with a wide ambiguity of meaning. It is therefore most important, in considering the adequacy of liberty as a supreme standard for the valua-

[16] A more adequate treatment of security as the ideal of law, which, although made from a slightly different viewpoint, reaches similar conclusions, is to be found in Demogue, *Analysis of Fundamental Notions*, in *Modern French Legal Philosophy*, pp. 418-470. *Cf.* also Bentham, *Theory of Legislation* (ed. by Dumont 1802, trans. by Hildreth, 2d ed. 1871) "Principles of the Civil Code," Part 1, ch. 7 *et seq.*

[17] A brief critique of current American liberalism following the general lines of the two succeeding chapters appears in an essay "More Notes on Freedom" by the author in collaboration with L. M. Kramer, published in *The New Student*, February 1929, p. 21.

tion of law, to disentangle the various principles which are fused or confused in a constant formula.

In the widest sense given to the term in ethical or political discussion, liberty is simply freedom from external human regulation. This freedom is at once too broad and too shallow a concept to afford a satisfactory index of human values. On the one hand it includes the freedom to do evil, to suffer, and to interfere with the freedom of others, as well as the freedom to attain moral excellence and happiness. The domain of liberty or freedom thus contains many things which everybody recognizes to be bad. On the other hand, freedom is never the sole or even the finally determinative element in human goods. The presence or absence of external human restraints is an immaterial and unimportant issue when one has not the power within himself or in his relation to the non-social universe, to bring about that which he desires. Liberty, then, in this broad sense, can make no plausible claim to supremacy among political ideals. It is only when social conditions involve striking and needless restraints upon desirable and desired courses of conduct that men are sufficiently attracted to the torch of liberty to be blinded by its glare or burnt in its flames. That this torch has led great crusades it is not our purpose to deny. That it is not a sufficient guide to moral conduct even in the realm of law is too obvious, when our analysis is clearly made, to call for further argument.

But this, it will be objected, is setting up a man of straw to knock down. Those who claim for liberty the supreme place in the hierarchy of political values are not thinking of as loose and negative a concept as is here defined.

Granting this, however, it is still important to realize that the various uses to which the word *liberty* is put all involve restricted realms of this wider whole, and that those who speak the language of liberty assume the obligation of tracing these restrictions and limitations. For a good deal of the appeal which the ideal of liberty exercises is based upon the fact that each of us understands by *liberty* primarily the liberty to do the things he likes to do. As Bayard Taylor described a similar situation,

Each heart recalled a different name,
But all sang "Annie Laurie."

The agreement as to the value of liberty reached in this manner must be purely verbal, and when taken as anything more must be misleading. The only alternative to inconclusive argument about ambiguous terms is a more careful distinction and definition of meanings. What, then, are these ideas, narrower than the one already considered, yet held to be sufficient for the ethics of law?

Perhaps the most popular of the restricted notions of liberty used in legal and political philosophy is that involved in the phrase "the liberty of each in so far as it is compatible with the like liberty of all."[18] What does this mean? I kill John Smith, and somebody tells me that this

[18] *Cf.* Carter: ". . . there is a guide which, when kept clearly and constantly in view, sufficiently informs us what we should aim to do by legislation and what should be left to other agencies. This is what I have so often insisted upon as the sole function both of law and legislation, namely, to secure to each individual the utmost liberty which he can enjoy consistently with the preservation of the like liberty to all others. . . . Whatever tends to preserve this is right. All else is wrong." (*Law: Its Origin, Growth, and Function* (1907) p. 337.) This is essentially the Kantian doctrine, and is developed by Stammler and other neo-Kantians in legal philosophy. *Cf.*, also, Spencer, *Justice* (1891) § 27.

is inconsistent with John Smith's liberty to kill me. I have therefore violated the principle of equal liberty and done a wrong. But if I answer that I have not simply killed John Smith, that I being a good man have killed John Smith who is a bad man, then can any one say that this action is incompatible with the like liberty of all others? Again, someone may tell me that studying law is wicked because in view of the limits to the number of law students the world can support, this act of mine interferes with the like activity of all others. But again I reply that there is some narrower description of my activity which can be made universally applicable. Or, to attack the problem from the other side, does the fact that slapping my neighbor's face is compatible with, and even conducive to, the like liberty of all prevent the act from being wrong? These are simply trivial cases of a fundamental truth that is regularly ignored by those who speak of "like" or "equal" liberties. No two things are absolutely alike or equal. Similarity has meaning only on the background of diversity. Things are similar as they partake of identical universals, but they are not constituted by these universals. Thus we can significantly talk of similarity only in respect to this or that consideration. It is metaphysical nonsense to talk of equal liberties without specifying the respects in which this equality applies or the dimensions along which the magnitude of liberty is to be measured.

The liberty of a miner to contract is equal, in certain formal and legal aspects, to that of the mine-owner. In respect to other considerations the liberties of the two parties are fundamentally and widely diverse. The judge who talks about equal liberties in such a case is invalidly assuming that an aspect of conduct that happens to appeal to him is *the* correct index of equality. This logical fallacy (in the technical jargon, "fallacia a dicto secundum quid ad dictum simpliciter", or, in its converse, "fallacia accidentis") is probably the chief intellectual obstacle to legal reform in this country today.[19] All legislation tending to equalize wealth or happiness is condemned as violating the principle of equal liberty. We must not prescribe limits to the industrial bargain because this would upset the "equal liberty of employer and employee." We must not equalize the inheritances of the new generation because the "equal liberty of all to bequeath whatever they possess" is thereby endangered. What is to happen when equal liberty to bequeath what one owns interferes with equal freedom to inherit what one needs, when equal liberty to sign a paper excludes equal liberty to live a decent life, these are problems whose solution the very formulation of the doctrine in question precludes. How bitterly ring the words of Anatole France: "The law, in its majestic equality, forbids the rich as well as the poor to sleep under bridges, to beg in the streets, and to steal bread." The philosophy of equal liberties, which our American courts insist on resurrecting from its timely English grave, is as illogical as it is mischievous. The whole conception is simply a disguise with which personal preferences ashamed of their

[19] Especially depressing examples of this fallacy are to be found in the numerous decisions of American courts upon the constitutionality of statutes regulating hours, wages, and conditions of labor. For a summary and analysis of cases and tendencies in this field of law, see Frankfurter, "Hours of Labor and Realism" (1916) 29 *Harvard Law Rev.* 353; Pound, "Liberty of Contract" (1909) 18 *Yale Law Jour.* 454. *Cf.* collection of Spencerian aphorisms in judicial opinions in Legislation Note (1931) 31 *Columbia Law Rev.* 686.

nakedness assume the aspect of transcendental dignity. From such a source legal philosophy can receive no adequate nourishment.[20]

Similar to the foregoing conception of liberty and equally inadequate as a supreme standard for legal philosophy is the ideal of political liberty, *i.e.* freedom from legal or political restraint. Of course, this ideal is a valuable one when its limitations are recognized. It is chiefly through the balancing of security and liberty that a wise legal order can be constituted. What men want and need in order to live the good life is neither the stultifying security of despotism nor the boundless legal freedom of anarchy.[21] But the proper equilibrium between these poles cannot be attained so long as either is supposed to be supreme. This is too patent a fact for the advocates of the supremacy of liberty wholly to ignore. The *laissez faire* doctrine, therefore, although leading in its logical extension to anarchy, is always limited implicitly by certain accepted legal restrictions, especially those relating to property[22] and to direct fraud or force. Thus it is made practicable, but not good.[23] For the legal restrictions upon

20 An analysis of the conflicts inherent in the legal ideal of liberty will be found in Professor Robert L. Hale's contribution to the discussion of the "Restatement of the Law," *Proceedings of the Academy of Political Science,* vol. 10, no. 3, pp. 50-54 (1923).

21 An excellent illustration of the balancing of these poles, rendered with true practical political wisdom is to be found in Bertrand Russell's *Proposed Roads to Freedom* (1919).

22 See R. L. Hale, "Coercion and Distribution in a Supposedly Non-Coercive State" (1923) 38 *Pol. Sci. Quart.* 470; M. R. Cohen, "Property and Sovereignty" (1927) 13 *Cornell Law Quart.* 8.

23 The ringing denunciation of Dr. Arnold is still worthy of our attention: "This neglect to provide a proper position in the state for the manufacturing population is encouraged by one of the falsest maxims which ever pandered to human selfishness under the name of political wisdom—I mean

liberty which it sanctions, since they are inconsistent with the apparent direction of the doctrine, are covertly and therefore uncritically accepted. A legal rule requiring respect for a given economic system is no less an interference with liberty than one which changes that system. Only by shutting their eyes to restrictions that already exist do those who profit by such restrictions convince themselves that they are championing the cause of political freedom in advocating *laissez faire*. The moral to be drawn from this, however, is not that *laissez faire*, as actually advocated, is wrong because it is a perversion of liberty, but that liberty itself is an inadequate political ideal which even its staunchest champions must patch up in secret ways.

Freedom from legal restraint, if laws serves any valuable end in society, is incompatible with the only sort of freedom that is worth preserving, the freedom to lead a good life, and therefore cannot possibly serve as a final ideal for the valuation of law. The doctrine of political liberty points to the incontrovertible fact that there is evil inherent in restraint, legal or otherwise, but it ignores several equally important facts. Its advocates forget, too frequently, that legal restraint is often the only available alternative to the narrower and harsher restraints of eco-

---

the maxim that civil society ought to leave its members alone, each to look after their several interests, provided they do not employ direct fraud or force against their neighbors. That is, knowing full well that they were not equal in natural powers, and that still less have they ever within historical memory started with equal artificial advantages, knowing also that power of every sort has a tendency to increase itself, we stand by and let this most unequal race take its course, forgetting that the very name of society implies that it shall not be a mere race, but that its object is to provide for the common good of all, by restraining the power of the strong and protecting the helplessness of the weak."

nomic, social, and professional groups.[24] The obvious fact that restraint is good for those whose injury it prevents is obscured by this doctrine. Finally the advocates of liberty as the supreme political good regularly display a notable ignorance of the value which restraint has for those who are restrained. It is a fact too basic to be obscured by bigoted and exaggerated formulations that every valuable realm of human conduct demands a certain discipline, a certain narrowness, in short a definite system of restraints, —which are usually too complicated for the individual to invent and too inscrutable for him to accept unless he is governed by that set of social pressures we call culture. Without such infringements upon liberty, the human soul would be a formless and powerless liquid. Man's need and desire for the regulation of his conduct by accepted authorities is the most fundamental fact to be observed in all his associations, in church, state, university, family, and the lesser organizations of industry and social intercourse. And this elementary human demand for authoritative direction is enough to invalidate any theory which sets up as the norm of legal activity the absence of law.

Freedom, then, in each of these senses, is an inadequate legal ideal. Neither freedom in general, nor an essentially indeterminate "equality of freedom", nor the anarchist ideal of freedom from legal restraint can serve to indicate the goodness and badness of law. It is the freedom to do and enjoy good things that is valuable. It is this freedom

24 See M. R. Cohen, *Reason and Nature* (1931), pp. 396-398. For a legal study of the shifting domain in which the state has asserted its power over the internal affairs of labor unions at the instance of dissatisfied minority groups, see "Elements of a Fair Trial in Disciplinary Proceedings by Labor Unions" (1931) 31 *Columbia Law Rev.* 847; "Judicial Resolution of Factional Disputes in Labor Unions," *ibid.*, 1025.

that gives moral prestige to the related doctrines already discussed. And this ideal constitutes a statement rather than a solution of the fundamental legal-ethical problem. There must be an appeal to a higher principle in order to decide what elements in life are good. Thus in its most directly ethical interpretation, our doctrine of freedom cannot be a supreme material norm for legal philosophy. But there is a further inadequacy in this doctrine, arising from the fact, already alluded to, that liberty (*i.e.* freedom from human interference) to live the good life is not a sufficient, although a necessary, condition for that life. For one to lead a worth-while existence, it is not enough that others respect this activity. There is needed also the internal or non-societal capacity for such a life. Thus it is as valuable to educate men, to create proper aptitudes and desires, as it is to secure an external tolerance. And since the legal order is not without consequences upon the first of these issues, the ignoring of that aspect will render any ideal of liberty inadequate as a legal norm and possibly, in critical cases, untrue as well. If, for instance, we are called upon to restrict the realm of non-interference with good activities in order to stimulate the good life more directly (*e.g.*, by compulsory education), we must actually go counter to the ideal of liberty in order to achieve the greatest possible good.

We are forced to conclude, then, that even under its most directly ethical interpretation, the doctrine of liberty is inadequate, materially and formally, to serve as a supreme standard of legal criticism.[25]

25 Dean Pound suggests some of the real legal evils consequent upon the unqualified pursuit of liberty as a legal ideal in the following passage: "Law was a device to secure liberty, its only justification was that it pre-

F. The Valuation of Law in Terms of Social Interests

Impotent as is the ideal of liberty to provide a final norm for law, there is a more plausible view which regards individual liberty as the limit, rather than the aim, of ideal law. The liberty of the individual is regarded as a domain into which the law must not enter, except in so far as one man's freedom conflicts with another's. Law is to be restricted to a settlement of conflicts among individuals in accordance with *inter-individual,* or *social,* interests. The position is clearly stated by Mill in his classic *Essay on Liberty,* from which we quote the following paragraph:

> The object of this essay is to assert one very simple principle as entitled to govern absolutely the dealings of society with the individual in the way of compulsion and control, whether the means used be physical force in the form of legal penalties, or the moral coercion of public opinion. That principle is that the sole end for which mankind are warranted, individually or collectively in interfering with the liberty of action of any of their number is self-protection.

---

served individual liberty, and its sole basis was the free agreement of the individual to be bound by it. . . . But on the side of law it [this doctrine] has given us the conception of liberty of contract, which is the bane of all labor legislation, the rooted objection to all power of application of rules to individual cases, which has produced a decadence of equity in so many of our state courts, the insistence upon and faith in the mere machinery of justice which makes American legal procedure almost impossible of toleration in the business world of today, the notion of punishing the vicious will and of the necessary connection between wrongdoing and retribution, which makes it so difficult for our criminal law to deal with anti-social actions and to adjust itself in its application to the exigencies of concrete criminality." "Do We Need a Philosophy of Law?" (1905) 5 *Columbia Law Rev.* 339.

> That the only purpose for which power can be rightfully exercised over any member of a civilized community, against his will, is to prevent harm to others. His own good, either physical or moral, is not a sufficient warrant. He cannot rightfully be compelled to do or forbear because it will be better for him to do so, because it will make him happier, because, in the opinions of others, to do so would be wise or even right. . . . The only part of the conduct of any one for which he is amenable to society is that which concerns others. . . . Over himself, over his own body and mind, the individual is sovereign.

Although this principle is not propounded by Mill as an absolute norm for all law, being meant to apply only to mature members of modern civilized communities, it constitutes an important limitation upon the realm of goods which law ought to secure, and as such demands careful consideration.

There are so many important truths involved in this principle, truths the recognition of which is a fundamental ethical necessity, that the task of elucidating the theory's inadequacies and errors is by no means a pleasant one. For a simple principle which contains only a small amount of error holds our attention to facts that are easily forgotten when, by elaborate correction, the theory is made accurate and unmanageable. Thus erroneous theories in ethics, law, and even physical science, may be more useful or moral than true theories. But we shall attempt to show that however useful Mill's views on the limits of justifiable legal activity may have been when they were first set forth, and however useful they may be today, they are not ultimately true and there is no reason to suppose that a belief in them will always be useful.

The first point to be noted in regard to this theory of the sanctity of individual liberty is that, as strictly stated, the suggested exemption from legal control applies only to a small and unimportant set of actions. The number of ways in which a man can harm himself without indirectly harming other members of the community is extremely limited. In all the instances where Mill suggests that the state ought not to interfere with individual liberty, *e.g.* in the consumption of liquor or opium, the actions under consideration involve many interests besides those of the agent. There are questions of the treatment of dependents, of temptation or offense to others, of stimulus to crime, etc., all closely implicated in the problems raised by these activities. To take Mill's fundamental example, freedom of thought and expression, can anybody doubt for a moment that thought and its expression have profound effects upon society? Ironically enough, Mill devotes a whole chapter of his essay to demonstrating the importance of these effects. It seems then that the exemption from social control of acts involving only the agent is much too narrow a principle to validate either the conclusions that Mill wishes to draw or any others that are not purely trivial. Indeed, since the application of law to an event is *prima facie* evidence that more than one person is interested in it, we may say that the exemption of purely individual interests from direct legal control (and Mill seems usually to ignore indirect legal controls in this connection) is, in the words of Holmes, "only a necessity and not a duty."

The principle of respect for liberty takes two other allied forms in Mill's treatment. One is that acts "in which it is chiefly the individual that is interested" are to be exempt from legal control. And this principle, although perhaps a good rule in many cases, cannot possibly have ultimate ethical validity. A crime very frequently affects the agent more than the rest of society, but this should not render the former immune to punishment. A third interpretation of this theory, nearer than either of the others to the paragraph quoted in this section, though less adapted to the actual uses for which Mill invokes the principle, is that in determining the extent to which any action is to be encouraged or condemned by law, we ought to consider merely its effects upon those who have not actually performed or consented to it. Again, we are forced to admit a profound truth in this doctrine,—for the law rarely succeeds in making men happy by frustrating their desires. But can we say that the law *never* succeeds in adding to the intrinsic values of a life by opposing desires, perhaps, momentary, that bring prolonged suffering in their train? Is not a law which secures a man from the lasting misery and degradation of the drug addict by interfering with his liberty to buy opium, to that extent, a good law,—wholly apart from its effects upon dependents, neighbors and associates? Do laws that prevent me from selling myself into slavery or contracting to work for starvation wages or authorizing my own destruction really hurt me? In all these cases the principle of absolute legal respect for individual liberty appears to be invalid. Political liberty is not the sole human good, and it may frequently be kept from a given individual in order to secure for him more important intrinsic values. That cases of this sort are rare is due not so much to the fact (insisted upon by Mill) that we have become civilized and able each to judge what is best for us, as to the less assuring fact that we are still painlessly ignorant of how to make other people happy. Liberty, in this sense, as Demogue says, is a doctrine of despair.[26]

If it be said that liberty to sell oneself into slavery, to enter an improvident contract, or to authorize one's own destruction is not "really" liberty but rather a destruction of future liberty, the whole basis of political individualism fades away. The exercise of freedom, like the actualization of any possibility, always limits the choices which the future presents. If it be said that "freedom free to slay herself" is not really freedom, and if John Smith, *aet.* 25, has enforceable duties towards John Smith, *aet.* 50, the "sovereignty of the individual over himself" becomes an empty and trivial concept. For in every important aspect the relation between two periods of a man's life is a social relation, springing from the social ties of sympathy and community of interest, subject to the corrosion of selfishness, and susceptible to control by third parties. Political individualism is based upon an arbitrary distinction between the relations that bind men into society and the relations that bind ephemeral creatures into men. If this arbitrary distinction be rejected, the basis of the claim that the individual's good is not a proper subject for legislation vanishes into thin air.

In a more modern formulation of this theory of respect for liberty (or personality), law exists to effect *social* in-

[26] *Analysis of Fundamental Notions,* in *Modern French Legal Philosophy,* p. 509.

terests (*i.e.* interests affecting more than one person), or to delimit interests, the valuation of which is a matter of ethics beyond the realm of law.[27] To this statement our previous criticisms still apply. The fact is that law actually does exist only when a problem of social interests, a problem of conflicting demands requiring delimitation, is raised. But it is simply a fallacy to infer that the settling of such disputes is the sole norm of law. It is the right settling of conflicts, the right delimitation of interests, which the law ought to secure. And since the problems raised by litigation are always parts of larger wholes in which individual values and values beyond the spheres of the opposed parties are involved, this rightness will depend upon factors beyond the immediate conflicting interests which the law adjusts. Thus although law is limited in its direct application to outward conduct, it must take into account the spiritual values it calls into being. And although it cannot live except where interests of different individuals collide, it must be judged equally by its further effects upon elements of life that engender no social conflicts.

A failure to recognize the responsibilities of legal criticism to those human interests which do not assume litigious form leads legal philosophy, even in the able hands of a Kohler or a Pound, to a somewhat complacent acquiescence in the economic and political demands of dominant social groups.[28] The "jural postulate of the civilization of the

[27] Korkunov, *General Theory of Law.*

[28] See, for instance, Kohler's defense of the violation of international agreements when they conflict with a state's "vital interests." *Philosophy of Law* (1909, trans. by Albrecht, 1914), Modern Legal Philosophy Series, vol. 12, § 31.

time" is commonly conceived as a function of demands asserted by groups that are economically and politically able to formulate and fight for their interests.[29] A more humane legal philosophy must search painstakingly for the human goods that are not self-consciously arrayed in the arenas of social controversy.

No doubt the criticism will be raised that a doctrine which involves the whole individual life in the norm of state activity favors and furthers autocracy, paternalism, and the unjust interference of law in matters that should be left to individual discretion. Life becomes intolerable, it is urged, when the state can interfere in every matter where it expects to do a little good, and an ethical theory which sanctions such activity must be false as well as wicked.

We have given this objection a rather bland and unprecise expression because it is usually made in about this form. But by paring down the irrelevant implications it involves, we shall see more clearly the falsity of the only charge which applies directly to our ethical conclusions.

In the first place, our position does not sanction political activity wherever the state *expects* to do good. Such activity is justified only when it actually *does* good. And if the nasty question—"But who is to be judge?"—is raised, we must point out its complete irrelevancy to the point at issue before vouchsafing it a reply. The proposition that the state ought to do good is not the same as the proposition that the state ought to do what I (or anybody else, or the state itself) may think is good. There is as

[29] *Cf.* Judge Hough's criticism of Dean Pound's *Spirit of the Common Law*, quoted *supra* p. 20, note 27.

much difference between the two statements as there is between the assertion that of two angles of a triangle the larger is opposite the larger side, and the assertion that of two angles of a triangle the larger is opposite the side that Mr. Jones thinks is the larger. Moreover the first proposition is absolutely true, the second quite probably false. The state ought to do good, anywhere and everywhere and under all circumstances,—even though nobody knows what that good is. And now to the question of who is to be judge of the state's ability to do good, we can give an answer no more indefinite than the question, namely, that whoever is best able to see the effects of law upon the good life will make the most accurate judge. Of course if legislators, judges, and jurists fall prey to the easy hallucination of ethical omniscience and political omnipotence they will be emboldened to interfere with men's activities in ways productive of real evil, hoping to bring about the good life. But they will no doubt make equally unfortunate mistakes in applying any other ethical theory,—certainly they are guilty of moral atrocities in applying the opposite doctrine of respect for individual liberty. And in any case the evil uses to which a true theory may be put by the ignorant or malicious do not afford an argument against the truth of the doctrine. We are thus driven from a new angle to the point we have made before,—that our theory is not bad, but that even if it were it would still be true.

When the confusions thus indicated are avoided, the invalidity of the criticism under consideration becomes manifest. The law in any situation can do good or it cannot. If it can, within the realm proposed for individual discretion, then it ought, and the demand for non-interference in the individual life reduces to the absurdity, "It is not good for the law to do good." If it cannot, then this demand is invalid as a refutation of our theory, which does not maintain that the law should do good when it cannot.

The real truth which gives intellectual solidity to the specious garments of this objection is that actually, in all societies, there are a great many situations where the law's interference to promote an obvious good actually accomplishes harm rather than good. The evils inherent in law,—the suffering inflicted upon those on whom the sanctions of the law fall, the burden upon the mind of the citizen, the social cost of legal machinery, the discouragement of experiment and free cooperation in the solution of social difficulties,—are easily overlooked by the legislator. The aesthetic valuation of law takes a peculiar form in the mind of the administrator of actual or imaginary states. He is professionally prone to estimate the value of law in terms of completed rhythms and harmonies.[30] Gaps in the domain of law are aesthetically intolerable, although there are many realms of life which are more responsive to non-legal instruments of social control than to the direct pressures of law. Plato's Republic exemplifies the work of the political artist at its freest. It is a state to contemplate with deep satisfaction—but who would desire to live in it? The "administrator's fallacy" is perhaps curable only with the purgatives of liberalism. But those purgatives are poor food for a legal philosophy that values its intellectual integrity.

The material evils in law-making which the "administra-

[30] See Bertrand and Dora Russell, *The Prospects of Industrial Civilization* (1923) pp. 147-149.

tor's fallacy" engenders, our formal ethical principle cannot deny. They must be taken into account in every calculation of the effects of law upon the good life, in every determination of the possibilities of legal action, and therefore in every application of the theory that the value of law depends upon this life. To seek a more transcendent justification of liberty than that involved in the recognition of these simple and one-sided evils is a process as useless as it is popular.

We conclude then, that there is no justification for the principle that the law ought to concern itself purely with "social" interests, or that legal philosophy need not look beyond the necessity of "delimiting" realms of conflict.[31]

G. *Justice as the Standard of Legal Valuation*

Of all the standards by which law has been measured, none has been more widely urged than the ideal of justice. But while most jurists will agree that law is good in so far as it is just, this agreement is to a large extent merely verbal, so various are the meanings with which the word *justice* is currently endowed. We shall attempt to show that when this meaning is not simply identical with *the good which law is able to achieve*, justice, although a useful and important concept, cannot furnish a final standard for the evaluation of law. In order to proceed to this point, we must distinguish as carefully as may be, the various ideas which the word *justice* has been used to symbolize.

In its narrowest sense, justice is simply the fulfillment

[31] *Cf.* von Jhering's classical criticism of the views of Mill and Humboldt in *Law as a Means to an End* (*Das Zweck im Recht*, 1877, trans. by Husik 1913), Modern Legal Philosophy Series, vol. 5, pp. 399-409.

of the positive law. We speak of courts of justice in this sense, and we frequently mean by just obligations, rights, demands, etc. simply those that are guaranteed by law. But in this sense of the term, justice cannot be significantly put forward as a standard for the valuation of law itself. It is therefore inadequate for our present purposes, and if conceived as a supreme standard of legal criticism must lead to error.

At the opposite extreme from this narrow meaning is the identification of justice with human goodness. Unlike the former positive definition, this is one from which the imperative or ideal character of justice can be analytically derived. The distinction is an important one. If we define justice in terms of goodness, either as identical with goodness in general or as a limited portion of the realm of goodness (*e.g.* goodness in external action), then our task is to find, by a positive examination of legal elements and an ethical evaluation of them, what things are just (*i.e.* what things in this realm are good) and, if possible, what further secondary criteria are available for the determination of this question. That is essentially the task which we have laid down on the constructive side of the present essay, which may, in this sense of the word, be considered an inquiry into the nature of justice. But on the other hand we may start off with a purely positive definition of justice such as the strictly legal concept first mentioned, and then our task must be to determine how far the attainment of justice is a good. These procedures cannot be confused without serious error, although their purpose is the same, namely to discover what the law ought to do. To return to our definition of just law as the law that ought to be, we may say that in this sense justice provides a valid ethical standard, but one which is identical with the standard we have already insisted upon, a standard which demands the complete calculation of legal activities in terms of the good life. And this fact is not altered if we restrict the term *justice* to that realm of goods which applies to conduct in society, to outward conduct, or to conduct which affects other people than the agent, since the immediate effects of law fall under all of these categories. Further consequences of legal activity upon other realms of conduct will not be ignored in this way, since they receive treatment under the head of instrumental values involved in the conduct primarily affected by law. We have seen, similarly, that if the law can effect goods outside of human life, these goods may nevertheless be considered as endowing the good life with instrumental values. Thus with each of these normative definitions of justice, our essential problem and our general formulation of its solution remain unaltered.[32]

But there are alternative conceptions of justice, primarily positive in their nature, whose ethical validity cannot be analytically deduced from their definition. They present us with material formulae for the just solution of legal problems, and leave us with the significant task of deciding to what extent *justice* is a desirable end. Thus when people

32 This conception of justice appears very clearly in the following phrase from A. E. Taylor's, *Problem of Conduct* (1901): "that law of justice, which bids us treat every member of the whole community with just as much consideration and perform for him just such services as are most desirable in view of the good of the community as a whole." (p. 202) *Cf.* Picard, *Le droit pur* (1908) pp. 315 *et seq.* And, from Aristotle, "The political good is justice; for this, in other words, is the interest of all." (*Politics,* Book 3, ch. 12.)

say that in certain cases justice should be sacrificed to mercy or to expediency, they cannot mean by *justice* "that which ought to be (in the realms under consideration)," although they may think that justice is one of the desiderata that should be taken into account. That is to say, if I define *justice* as equality, or distribution of goods in proportion to moral excellence, or distribution according to the principle of need, I must be prepared to consider the logical possibility that just activities will not be good. With such definitions, our primary problem is not to work out their positive content (as is the case with normative definitions), for this is already given, at least in outline. It is rather to determine the adequacy, from an ultimate ethical standpoint, of these principles. And when we find that any of these conceptions of justice is in some respect inadequate for ethical criticism, we may conclude that its content does not provide the ultimate standard for which we are searching.

The classical formula of justice, "to give every man his due", is frequently interpreted in a non-ethical sense, although the ease with which this meaning can be shifted to one that is analytically normative perhaps accounts for its great convenience and popularity. The nub of the problem lies in the word *due.* Are we told to give every man what ought to be given to him, or, on the other hand, what, by law or custom, he is protected in demanding? The two principles are distinct in meaning, although in most cases they may point to identical conclusions. The first principle being analytically normative does not give any definite content to our ethical standard. We have always to ask what it is that is due to each man. And since every legal action may be phrased in terms of giving something (a right, privilege, power, or immunity, if not a more material entity) to somebody, we are still left with the general formal principle that the law ought to do as much good as it can, which is only expressed in a new language under the terms of this theory. But if the second interpretation is given to our present formula, its ethical inadequacy is obvious. Certainly it is not always good to protect or to fulfill the demands that have been traditionally protected. In many cases such protection or observance achieves, immediately, certain elements of human well-being. In other cases, although no such benefit is conferred upon the parties most directly concerned, a certain amount of social security or personal discipline is produced by the observance of socially accepted obligations. But only a mystical and unscientific deification of the state or society can lead us to believe that such observance constitutes a legal norm of universal validity. And if this is not such a norm, then it remains a limited ideal, coordinate with other limited ideals already examined, and demanding for its application a final court of appeals in which all such standards may be weighed, one against the other, in the light of some more fundamental ethical principle.[33]

There is another conception of justice, which sets up as its supreme principle the maxim, "to each according to his

[33] Of all the jurists who have dealt with the problem of *suum cuique*, Tourtoulon is the only one who has carefully distinguished between the positive conception of justice in terms of this formula, and the ethical ideal of law. The former principle is, in his view, the basis of metaphysical law or *just law*. But this will frequently differ from *good law*. An unjust law may be justified. See *Philosophy in the Development of Law*, ch. 14, and Professor Husik's review of the volume in 71 *U. of Pa. Law Rev.* 416 (1923). But, as to the value of this "metaphysical law," *cf.* Professor M. R. Cohen's editorial preface to this work, especially pp. xxxvi *et seq.*

merit." The distribution of rewards and punishments in "proportion" to merit and demerit has a philosophical pedigree dating back to Aristotle.[34] In criminal law it is the basis of the retributive theory of punishment,[35] and in civil law it serves in one way or another to provide a philosophical basis for the general theories of liability (*i.e.* tort and contract) and property.

We may ask two questions of this theory of justice. In the first place, what is meant by *proportion* between merit and reward? In the second place why should such a proportion be realized?

It appears that in no rigorous sense of the term can a proportion or ratio be said to exist between merit and reward. For such a relation to exist it would be necessary that both entities should be capable of a quantitative expression in terms of each other or in terms of some common denominator. That this is not the case is possibly a rash assertion, but it is certainly true that there is no known reduction in this case. What is meant, then, by the principle, "to each according to his merit", must be simply that in any two instances the greater merit should be recognized by the greater reward, and, negatively, the greater demerit by the greater punishment.

This principle, however, appears to be both inadequate and fallacious. It is inadequate because it offers no determination of the extent of reward or punishment appropriate to a given merit or fault. All we are told is that this

34 Aristotle, *Nichomachean Ethics,* Book 5.

35 A critique of this theory with especial reference to criminal law is offered in Tarde's *Penal Philosophy* (1903 (4th ed.), trans. by Howell 1912), Modern Criminal Science Series, vol. 5. See especially §§ 5, 90, 97. *Cf.* also Demogue, *Analysis of Fundamental Notions,* in *Modern French Legal Philosophy,* pp. 480 *et seq.*

should be greater or less than in certain other cases, and we have a set of variables with no constant, which is clearly indeterminate. But even this inadequate formula seems to involve error. To repay evil with good, is certainly not, as this theory would imply, the blackest of sins. Nor is it true that equally grave offenses merit equally severe punishment. Some offenses, such as stupidity, are generally incapable of cure by punishment. Punishment can then be justified only as an intrinsic good, and we must make the further assumption that the value of punishment is in no way dependent upon the human welfare or happiness which it achieves, if we are to hold the theory that equal offenses merit equal punishments.

Such a doctrine we cannot, of course, disprove. But it appears to be repugnant alike to civilized common sense and to all philosophical thought that is not based upon logical fallacies. Its limited application in law, in the form of the *lex talionis,* is generally regarded as a mark of barbarism. While the fundamental and almost universal aesthetic appeal in the "eye for an eye" doctrine may be great enough to justify certain concessions to the principle for the sake of legal economy, certainty, and popular support, no plausible reason can be given for the doctrine except on the basis of this immediate aesthetic appeal. It must therefore be considered as coordinate with other limited and equally immediate interests, such as the interest of the wrong-doer in his own happiness, and it remains the task of ethics to formulate some wider principle by which these various intuitive value judgments may be weighed together and unified.

There are various other conceptions of justice which it

will not be necessary for us to examine. Such are those which, on the basis of the Kantian morality or some other system of pure ethics, give a content to the normative definition of justice. These we shall examine in our analysis of ethical systems.[36] There are other theories of justice which we treat in other parts of the present chapter, under such headings as "natural law" and "liberty". There are still other theories which we are unable to understand and shall not, therefore, attempt to criticize.

But we must turn, at parting, to a final conception of justice which is perhaps the most popular of all, a conception which refuses to be bound by any formula and which finds its roots in a peculiar sentiment or instinct. As Geny says, "It is a kind of instinct which, without appealing to the reasoning mind, goes of its own accord straight to the best solution, the one most conformable to the aim of all juridical organization."

Clearly there is some such sentiment in the human soul, but is there any ground for supposing that it always or generally provides a correct solution for social problems? It does not seem to us that this question can possibly receive an affirmative answer. For even assuming that this instinct begins to work only when all the positive data of our problem have been collected (or are statistics also gathered by an inner feeling?), the sentiment of justice, working upon such materials, is, like all moral sentiments, largely a composite of accepted moral doctrines. It is thus as variable as the theories from which it springs, and this fact alone would show that it cannot serve as an ultimate standard of valuation. Furthermore, if this sentiment is a

[36] See Chapter Three, *infra.*

complex of implicit moral beliefs, it is no more impregnable to intellectual criticism than the beliefs upon which it is based. To refine this sentiment of justice by a critical examination of its foundations is as much the task of legal philosophy as the refinement of common sense, in general, is the task of philosophy and science. To make such a sentiment the supreme arbiter of our legal-ethical problems is simply to assign ultimate authority to our moral ignorance.

H. Natural Law as the Standard of Legal Valuation

The ideal of natural law is one of the most powerful concepts that has motivated juristic thought. Through the great development of Roman jurisprudence the Stoic ideal of a law of nature exerted its humanizing force, and this standard was still accepted as the supreme ethical norm of law in the European development of international law, in the evolution of English equity and Common Law, and in the constitutional organization of most modern states. Even today, in spite of a passing eclipse, the ideal of natural law in one form or another is maintained by many of the most eminent continental jurists.

It is not remarkable, then, that in so long and adventurous a history the doctrine of natural law should have been subject to widely divergent interpretations. In general, we may distinguish two main ingredients in this concept, ingredients which have been mixed in all proportions. There is first the notion of value. Natural law is primarily the law that ought to be. The second ingredient in the concept of natural law is the element of universality. Not only have these two elements been united in various ways, but occasionally one or the other has appeared alone in the natural law doctrine. It is with these extremes that our analysis of the theory can best begin.

Natural law as the law that ought to be is obviously entitled to a supreme place in the hierarchy of jural standards. It is unnecessary to reiterate the arguments by which we have attempted to show the importance of this concept, however named, for juristic thought. It must be noted, however, that the ideal thus identified is a formal one, which provides as yet no material standards of legal criticism. No substitute can be found within this doctrine for the arduous investigations into ethics and positive science which the establishment of such standards demands. This limiting form of the natural law theory is simply a framework for legal-ethical thought. Yet it is a solid one, sufficient to maintain the whole superstructure of legal criticism. If the language of natural law and natural rights is completely forgotten the lessons taught by this theory will endure. Its defenders have persistently maintained the distinction between positive fact and ideal law, which is the first condition of rational thought on jurisprudence. Whatever their attitude to existent law,—and they have been more often innovators and revolutionists than conservatives,—they have insisted upon one fundamental fact which the wielders and courters of power have always attempted to obscure,—the fact that decrees of courts and kings are acts, not ideals, that positive law has, as such, no claim to obedience, that law is not to be judged in its own courts.

Such is the doctrine of natural law in its purely ethical interpretation. What do we find upon the purely positive side? In its connotation of generality a natural law is simply a widely applicable description of natural phenomena. It is apparently in this sense that Ulpian speaks of mating and caring for offspring as accordant with natural law.[37] Clearly, such a notion cannot serve as a valid standard of legal criticism. The difference between what is usual and what is right is not abolished by calling the former class *natural*. To attempt to show by argument the impropriety of valuing objects on the basis of their universality would be a fruitless undertaking. If it is not immediately obvious that there are natural evils in the world, no amount of argument can bring this "accordance with nature" ideal to a *reductio ad absurdum*. But, in the belief that ethics means something, we shall assume that what is natural (in this positive sense) is sometimes bad. And this assumption seems justified whether we think of natural law as the description of usual human activities or, in its more common significance, as the usual political prescription of human activities (*ius naturale* as *ius gentium*).[38]

Finally we have to consider the great body of natural law doctrine in which the two elements thus separately considered are fused or confused. This union of value and universality has been justified along three lines. In the first place, universal acceptance has sometimes been regarded as a criterion of good law. In the second place, universality has been regarded as a distinguishing mark of those phases of human activity (natural rights) which law ought to pro-

[37] Dig. i. 1. 1. 3.

[38] Dig. i. 3. 32, 1.; Gaius, i. 1.; etc.

tect. In the third place, it has been believed that the law that ought to exist is universally applicable.

The first of these theories, we have already suggested, is implicit in the intellectual process by which the *ius gentium,* the law supposed to be common to the various Italian communities, was transformed into a *ius naturale,* which became, through the Praetor's Edict, the leaven of equity in Roman jurisprudence. In this country similar practical needs have found a similar rationalization. Under the rule established by Justice Story in *Swift v. Tyson,*[39] the federal courts, in cases where they are required by the Judiciary Act to apply the law of a particular state, will disregard local peculiarities in the judicial development of the common law and assume that the "true rule" in that state is to be found "not in the decisions of the local tribunals but in the general principles and doctrines of commercial jurisprudence." The scope of the doctrine which *Swift v. Tyson* inaugurated is dubious, and its recent extensions have been valiantly attacked in several dissenting opinions of Mr. Justice Holmes,[40] but it is probable that the natural law or general jurisprudence which the doctrine invokes will play a growing role in the development of American common law.

In one form or another the assumption that universality is a mark of "valid" law has worked through all modern legal history, exerting a most important influence in the reform of peculiar local institutions and formalities endowed merely with historical prestige. Such prestige is,

[39] 41 U. S. (16 Pet.) 1 (1842).

[40] Kuhn v. Fairmont Coal Co., 215 U. S. 349 (1910); Southern Pacific Company v. Jensen, 244 U. S. 205 (1917); Black & White Taxi Co. v. Brown & Yellow Taxi Co., 276 U. S. 518 (1928).

of course, like the prestige of inherited religion, greatly weakened when people realize that in other places and times different customs have prevailed. And since law which can justify itself only by the fact of inertia is likely to be bad, the stimulus of a wider perspective in jurisprudence, popular and scientific, has been of considerable value. But when seriously considered as a scientific guide to right legal activity, the principle under consideration is quite inadequate. Not only is the value of universality limited, as Mr. Justice Holmes has insisted,[41] by the experimental value[42] of diversity, but the amount of universality to be found in positive law decreases with great rapidity as we extend our view of political institutions. On any adequate anthropological perspective, the constant material of positive law is obviously too meager to furnish a true or useful guide to legal criticism. It is therefore unnecessary further to justify the rejection of this theory by pointing out that evils are sometimes as universal as any goods.

The second attempt to fuse the elements of universality and value in a normative theory of natural law takes the form of a theory of natural rights based upon natural instincts or modes of behavior. Everybody, the argument runs, will defend himself against attack. Therefore self-defence is a natural right which the law ought to recognize and protect. Similarly we may deduce natural rights to hold property, to make agreements, to pursue happiness,

41 See cases cited *supra*, note 40.

42 This value, of course, is limited by the amount of thought directed to such diversity. The unparalleled opportunities of comparative legal research which accidental state boundaries to legal rules present in this country have been very sporadically explored.

and so on through the list of basic human activities. The inference of value and claim to legal sanction from the premise of universality is of course palpably invalid, but this does not prove the conclusion false. It may be the case that what is generally done is right, as it may be the case that what is generally believed is true. To test either assertion we must examine general activities or beliefs, in the light of moral or scientific principles. When this is done, it is as obvious in the former case as in the latter that the suggested criterion is hopelessly inadequate. Ritchie's detailed and penetrating analysis of natural rights has demonstrated too clearly for further question or argument the ultimate inadequacy of this theory.[43] Without going into the argumentative material so compellingly laid out by this author we may affirm the sufficiently obvious conclusions that these various natural human tendencies are frequently conflicting and therefore not competent courts of last appeal, that they are usually incapable of precise formulation or application, and that they frequently cover obvious evils or fail to comprehend equally obvious goods.

The final theory by which the "law of nature" school attempts to combine the two implications of the doctrine consists in the contention that ideal law is universally applicable. But this statement in its abstract form means nothing.[44] Any rule can be made universally applicable by expressly incorporating in it all the empirical conditions

43 Ritchie, *Natural Rights* (1895). *Cf.* Bentham, "Anarchical Fallacies —An Examination of the Declarations of Rights Issued During the French Revolution," 2 *Works* 491.

44 See Bentham, "The Influence of Time and Place in Matters of Legislation," ch. 5, § 2, 1 *Works* 171, 192-193.

of its applicability. Thus a rule that all Frenchmen alive in 1918 shall have certain rights is just as truly a logical universal as a rule that all people injured through the negligence of others shall have certain rights. It is abstractly possible to put together in logical form all the bodies of law which for various communities are ideal, and, by maintaining the necessary restrictions upon the content of each rule, to have a body of law that ought to be universally applied.

The real problem here is one of degree. How much uniformity is there between the ideal law for various communities? That is a question which can be answered only after a consideration and comparison of the needs, powers, and social conditions of different societies. And here the defenders of the old natural law theory have been wont to err on the side of undue insistence upon uniformity, through a failure to realize the extent and importance of actual social diversities. It is amusing to read the elaborate arguments by which jurists have attempted to set up the positive law of their respective states as universally applicable ideals. The process is carried to its *reductio ad absurdum* by Kant, Fichte, and Hegel, in whose works we may find the most amazing transcendental justifications for the peculiar legal system of the Prussian state in some of its most trivial details.

Kant, for instance, vouches the eternal principles of reason in support of the landowner's right to all ownerless things that come upon his property[45] (except through ship-

[45] Kant, *Science of Right* (1796-7, trans. by Hastie 1887) pp. 97. *Cf.* a criticism of the Kantian approach in some recent eminent domain cases in (1929) 29 *Columbia Law Rev.* 1155.

wreck[46]) and the principle that sale of stolen goods in market overt passes valid title to the *bona fide* purchaser.[47] Fichte asks no aid from empirical science in deducing from the fundamental irrationality of determinism the principle that prostitutes must be punished by exile.[48] Hegel, although he criticizes Fichte for the latter's *a priori* justification of passport photographs,[49] finds that the eternal world-reason requires the passage of title to goods at the moment a contract to sell is concluded.[50] All three agree in condemning on *a priori* grounds, democracy,[51] polygamy,[52] and "petticoat government."[53]

Today a wider historical perspective and a more modest conception of the role of metaphysics in the solution of social problems has led the "natural law" school of jurisprudence to a very conservative estimate of the constant element in ideal law.[54] The position is well summed up by Saleilles in the following words:

[46] Kant, *op. cit.*, p. 98.

[47] *Ibid.*, p. 150.

[48] Fichte, *Science of Rights* (1796, trans. by Kroeger 1869) p. 429.

[49] Hegel, *Philosophy of Right* (1820, trans. by Dyde 1896) p. xxviii; Fichte, *op. cit.*, p. 379.

[50] Hegel, *op. cit.*, pp. 82-83.

[51] Kant, *op. cit.*, pp. 167-169; Fichte, *op. cit.*, pp. 243-244; Hegel, *op. cit.*, p. 317.

[52] Kant, *op. cit.*, p. 111; Fichte, *op. cit.*, pp. 406-407; Hegel, *op. cit.*, pp. 172-173.

[53] Kant, *op. cit.*, p. 167; Fichte, *op. cit.*, p. 444; Hegel, *op. cit.*, p. 172.

[54] This trend is presaged by Montesquieu, who writes, in the *Persian Letters*: "There is no one best form of state or constitution: no law is good or bad in the abstract. Every law, civil and political, must be considered in its relation to the environment . . ." Bentham's tribute to Montesquieu is worthy of note: "Before Montesquieu, a man who had a distant country given him to make laws for, would have made short work of it. 'Name to me the people,' he would have said; 'reach me down my Bible, and the business is done at once. The laws they have been used to, no matter what they are, mine shall supersede them; manners, they shall have mine,

What does not change is the fact that there is a justice to be realized here below, the sentiment that we owe to all respect for their right, according to the measure of social justice and social order. But what shall be this measure, what shall be this justice, what shall be this social order? No one can say *a priori.* All these questions depend upon certain social facts with which the law comes in contact. These facts change, evolve and are transformed. But that depends in turn upon the conceptions one forms as to justice and order, as to authority and liberty, as to the right of the community and the rights of individuals, as to the proportion to be established in the incessant strife between these opposing forces, and this proportion varies and alternates.[55]

Norman Wilde expresses a similar sentiment:

The modern doctrine of natural rights is realistic and historic. It knows nothing of humanity as such and its abstract rights, but finds only a varying body of traditions as to what are the essential conditions of social welfare. . . . In every growing society there is as much need for the revision and reinterpretation

---

which are the best in nature; religion, they shall have mine too, which is all of it true, and the only one that is so.' Since Montesquieu, the number of documents which a legislator would require is considerably enlarged. 'Send the people,' he will say, 'to me, or me to the people; lay open to me the whole tenor of their life and conversation; paint to me the face and geography of the country; give me as close and minute a view as possible of their present laws, their manners, and their religion.' " "The Influence of Time and Place in Matters of Legislation," 1 *Works*, 171, 173.

[55] Saleilles, "L'Ecole historique et droit naturel d'apres quelques ouvrages recents" (1902) 1 *Revue trimestrielle de droit civil* 98-99.

of its rights as there is in the growing child for the alteration of its clothes.[56]

Stammler and Demogue have expressed substantially similar views on this "natural law with changing content."[57] Our own arguments are all in essential accord with this view. It is only because of the unfortunate connotations and ambiguities of the phrase "natural law" that we have sought to present our own position in a different terminology. For in addition to the alternative interpretations of the doctrine already criticized, there is in the natural law terminology a confusing reminiscence of noble savages, a suggestion of the competence of the untutored conscience to deal with all jural problems, a vague implication of a law-giver in the sky who is more powerful than terrestrial legislators, and a confusing double use of *law* in its normative and positive meanings. "The gravest objection to the whole theory of natural rights," concludes Ritchie, "is, that it is always tending to confuse the two sets of notions, by representing what may on occasion be moral duties as legal or quasi-legal rights, and by concealing under such ambiguous terms as 'can' and 'cannot' the difference between 'ought' and 'is,' or between 'wish' and 'power'."[58] It is therefore simply for reasons of meth-

56 Wilde, *Ethical Basis of the Modern State* (1924) pp. 82-83.

57 Stammler, *Theory of Justice* (1902, trans. by Husik, 1925), Modern Legal Philosophy Series, and *Wirtschaft und Recht* (1896) p. 685; Demogue, *Analysis of Fundamental Notions*, p. 403. The phrase "changing content" is a questionable concession to the modern prejudice against absolutes. What actually changes is not the body of principles which constitute ideal law, but the selection of those principles which are pertinent to the contemporary social scene. The content of one's map does not change as one journeys—if the original map is comprehensive enough to include one's whole itinerary.

58 Ritchie, *Natural Rights*, pp. 242-243.

odological convenience that we prefer to substitute a formula in terms of positive law and the good life for one in terms of natural law or natural rights.[59] In substance the two standards are equivalent when natural law is taken to mean ideal law; and the alternative interpretations of the natural law theory are all to be rejected as unjustified in their claims to a supreme place in legal valuation.

J. Conclusion

Such, then, are the proposed short-cuts to legal criticism. Some, we have seen, end abruptly in vile swamps and blind ravines, others, no less abruptly, in pleasant and fertile fields far from our journey's end. Still other trails lose themselves in thick woods or on barren rock. A few paths reach our final goal, but these are not short-cuts, for, at a little distance, they run parallel to the long road. It is to this road, then, that we must return, pursuing the effects, the complete nature, of law with the compass of pure ethics.

On this road, each of the material juristic ideals whose inadequacy we have attempted to establish,—security, liberty, justice, and the rest,—serves as a valuable guide when its limitations are clearly recognized. We have tried not to disregard or minimize the values implicated in these norms. But there is room for only one absolute in a given system. Conflicts between these various ends are at the heart of most social problems and we must find some common denominator for their treatment. That common stand-

59 For a general discussion of the problem of legal criticism in terms of natural law, see M. R. Cohen, *Reason and Nature* (1931), Book 3, ch. 4.

ard must be, in general, the good life, which, if our foregoing criticisms are sound, is a necessary as well as a sufficient ethical basis for the valuation of law. And here legal philosophy calls to ethics for a living concretion of this abstract principle.

CHAPTER THREE

THE GOOD

1. SCIENTIFIC METHOD IN ETHICS

WE HAVE seen that the value of law depends upon the efficacy of law in promoting the good life. It follows that legal criticism must be based upon an adequate description of what this life is, and that all the uncertainties and inaccuracies which attend our formulation of this ideal are likely to reappear in our valuation of law.[1] We are therefore constrained to proceed to the careful investigation of the nature of this ideal before we can give substantial content to the abstract formula of evaluation we have reached.

There is no need to minimize the difficulty of this search or the unsatisfactory character of the oracles that it has discovered. The typical jurist, coming inevitably to this point in his inquiry, feels that he has passed the borders of civilization and scientific method. Shutting his eyes and holding his nose, he makes a wild dash into the jungles of ethics and, grabbing the newest idol he can find in the huts of the natives, he returns with it to more enlightened domains. There the jurist tries to forget that his oracle is,

[1] "He who proposes to make the fitting inquiry as to which form of government is the best, ought first to determine what manner of living is most eligible; for while this remains uncertain, it will also be equally uncertain what government is best." Aristotle, *Politics*, Book 7, ch. 1. *Cf.* Rottschaeffer, "Jurisprudence: Philosophy or Science?" (1927) 11 *Minn. Law Rev.* 292, 298-305.

underneath its new legal attire, a trophy from lands where neither the canons of scientific method nor the rules of evidence are revered,—and he usually succeeds. But a greater intellectual integrity and a less firm faith in the unchallengeable character of the juristic conclusions that can be attained must impel us to enter the domain of ethics with open eyes, to find, perhaps that scientific method is not as impossible of application there as has generally been supposed.

Few will deny that ethics can be scientific to the extent that it incorporates materials from psychology, sociology, and the other disciplines which help us to analyze the possibilities and the consequences of conduct. But can the distinctive concern of ethics with things valued for themselves be subjected to the canons of scientific method?

Certainly the history of ethical thought offers no basis for an affirmative answer to this question. Spinoza, of all moralists, came nearest to giving his ethical insight scientific form, yet one has only to attempt the task of throwing his demonstrations into rigorous logical form to realize how far his "system" is from even its Euclidean model. And anyone who does not share the specific moral prejudices of Kant and Hegel finds their "systems" outrageously unsystematic and their "deductions" hopelessly illogical. For the rest we have scarcely a pretense at introducing into ethics the clarified logical structure that characterizes a developed science.

But we cannot rest with the judgment of history. We do not doubt that psychology and meteorology are sciences, although the portions of these disciplines which have already assumed the distinctive form of science are exceedingly minute. What, if anything, distinguishes ethics from these other disciplines which, in hope rather than summary of achievement, we call scientific?

The most common attempt to distinguish the field of ethics from the field of science is based upon the assumption that there is a fundamental distinction between fact and value, between the *is* and the *ought*. For does not ethics, without such a distinction, lose its identity in psychology, anthropology, or history? And if we accept this distinction, what ground have we for expecting that the rational technique that has proved fertile in the realm of facts will be equally applicable to the realm of values?

The dilemma thus framed is vitiated by a confusion between absolute and relative distinctions. Certainly the question of whether a given thing exists is quite different from the question of whether that thing ought to exist. But it does not follow from this that the field of what ought to exist is distinct from the field of what does exist. For the proposition that something ought to exist may be equivalent to the proposition that something else exists. Just as the distinction between being and non-being, valid for any given quality or relation, is impotent to create distinct realms of being and non-being, so the distinction between *is* and *ought*, valid in a given context, fails to create distinct realms of fact and value.

Thus the absolutistic hedonist may maintain that the proposition, "Peace ought to exist among nations," is identical with the proposition, "Peace among nations does actually produce a greater amount of happiness than the alternative, war." The ethical relativist will maintain that the former proposition is equivalent to the proposition that somebody has a certain psychological attitude toward peace or the consequences of peace which he does not have toward the alternative to peace. In either case, and in the many ethical systems of which these are logically typical, we affirm the equivalence of an *ought* proposition with an *is* proposition that has a different subject, *i.e.*, a complex of pleasures and pains or a human attitude rather than an international state of affairs. And even those who hold that an *ought* proposition can never be identical in meaning with a proposition in "natural" terms do maintain that such an identity can be found between the proposition that something *ought* to exist and the proposition that that thing *does actually* have, or produce consequences which have, a peculiar, objective, unanalyzable property—goodness—and that the alternatives to that thing do not have this property in a similar degree. *Ought* propositions are thus always reducible to *is* propositions. The distinction between *is* and *ought* is valid only for propositions about the same subject, and this relative distinction cannot ground an absolute distinction between the whole field of the *is* and the field of the *ought*. Objections to the possibility of ethical science must find some other basis than the alleged distinction between the realm of fact and the realm of value. Values are facts, and if they are facts of a peculiar sort, so too are colors, sounds, and intervals of time.

The possibility of a science of ethics rests upon the applicability of scientific method to those facts, whether "natural" or non-natural, whether discovered by introspection or by external observation, which form the substance of ethical knowledge. Are goodness and its related concepts less susceptible to scientific analysis than largeness, heaviness, yellowness, or cheapness?

In a survey of the ethical theories of the past we are struck by the prominence of "self-evident first principles," a prominence equalled only in the realm of religion. It is, in fact, as a branch of religion rather than as a scientific pursuit that the historic course of ethical reasoning can best be appreciated. Now an essential distinction between religion and science is the fact that religion demands dogmatic certainty, while science, to the extent that it is not purely formal, is content with hypotheses eternally subject to empirical refutation and never claiming *a priori* certainty.

Science does not proceed from self-evident principles or dogmas. Even in mathematics, the only part of the science that is above question is the mechanism of questioning, that is logic. The fact that Euclid's postulates are to many people self-evident is an interesting datum for psychology, but it has no particular significance for mathematics. Science can begin with any set of assumptions that does not involve logical inconsistency, and the ultimate appeal to obviousness or empirical verification, which no concrete science—not even applied mathematics[2]—can escape, is an appeal involving the whole set of related propositions, and not merely the sub-class of them which, for reasons of convenience, has been used as a starting point.

If a science of ethics rests upon the possibility of ethical knowledge, it rests no less upon the possibility of ethical

[2] For an analysis of the distinction between pure and applied mathematics, see M. R. Cohen, *Reason and Nature* (1931) Book 2, ch. 1.

error. For science, dynamically conceived as a process of verification, is obviously inapplicable to a field in which we are divinely blessed with infallible wisdom. The mere systematization of our certainties is an intellectual *tour de force* which does not require the scientific refining of our observations, our generalizations, and our inquiries.

Now intuitive or common-sense ethics recognizes no scientific liabilities. Conscience or intuition is supposed to supply immediate and unchallengeable answers to all ethical problems. Thus ethical science, the systematic verification of ethical knowledge, can be a meaningful ideal only to those unfortunate individuals who have not been divinely blessed with infallible moral intuition.[2a]

Even philosophers to whom the manifest inconsistencies of intuitive or common-sense ethics are a sufficient index of fallibility have commonly supposed that there may be found within the body of common ethical intuition the axiomatic seeds of all ethical knowledge. Thus the traditional treatment of the subject discovers certain indubitable truths, from which all sorts of deductions are made that are assumed to be beyond question, owing their validity to the strength of the original premises. This method involves two erroneous assumptions and a larger number of most unfortunate results. In the first place, it is assumed that there have been discovered fundamental general propositions of ethics which no sensible man can doubt, and this is obviously untrue, since there is no basic

2a *Cf.* the saying of Moto-ori, the divinely inspired teacher of Shintoism: "Systems of morals were invented by the Chinese, because the Chinese are a people without morals. But in Japan there is no necessity for a system of morals; for every Japanese will do right if only he consults his own heart."

ethical doctrine upon which all sensible philosophers have agreed. Kant's categorical imperative, the naturalistic correlation of value with interest, the supremacy of the life of reason, the freedom of the will, the supreme goodness of that which is most "real,"—all these doctrines involve the most dubious assumptions and cannot with any plausibility be regarded as in themselves self-evident or indubitable.

More important is the objection that even if philosophers had discovered basic propositions which, considered in propositional vacuum, seemed to be self-evident and immediately obvious, this fact would not guarantee the truth of apparently false conclusions deduced from such premises. One of the tests of the certainty of a proposition is the certainty of the conclusions that can be derived from it. Thus an ethical assumption loses its indubitable character as soon as it gives rise to dubious implications. The assumption that any entities could be combined to form a class seemed perfectly self-evident to logicians until it was shown that this led to the paradoxes of self-containing classes. Then it was clearly recognized that this assumption had to be modified, and the theory of types was offered as a modification of the traditional logical premises. Similarly, if Hegel's original ethical premises sound reasonable, *in vacuo*, and we find that he derives from them such highly doubtful conclusions as that the punishment of death is necessarily due to murder, that a man ought to marry but not primarily for love, that economic imperialism is the proper destiny of a civilized state, that war preserves the ethical health of a people, and that the only form of government approved by reason is a hereditary constitutional monarchy,[3] we can no longer argue that these propositions must be true because they follow from indubitable premises, for the premises are no longer indubitable when they have produced doubtful conclusions.

We cannot show all the misfortunes which have followed upon ethical dogmatism, and it would be a preposterous exaggeration of the influence of philosophy to ascribe human intolerance to the dogmatic ethics of philosophers. The dogmatism of ethical philosophers has primarily reflected rather than caused the dogmatism of human morality in general. But on the other hand, the aid which such philosophies of morals have furnished to selfish and reactionary social programs must be written large in the book of human misery.

The cure for dogmatism in morals is not, as is very popularly supposed today, to be found in the dogma that absolute tolerance is a supreme good. Such tolerance is, in the first place, impossible in any society where most human acts appreciably restrict the freedom of other individuals. In the second place, the dogma of tolerance is neither less doubtful nor less dangerous than other ethical dogmas.

The cure for dogmatism, in ethics as in any other field of human knowledge, is to be had, not through a substitution of new dogmas for old or a general rejection of all general propositions, but rather through the development of a scientific technique of questioning (*i.e.* "verifying") our fundamental general propositions. In order to question a fundamental proposition of ethics, we must see its

[3] Hegel, *Philosophy of Right* §§ 101, 161-162, 246, 273, 324. *Cf.* pp. 107-109 *supra*. *Cf.* Rogers, *Morals in Review* (1927) p. 384.

possible alternatives. Science is always a broadening of our intellectual horizons toward the ultimate limits of logical possibility or being. Our intellectual ideal in the development of a scientific ethics must be the clear consideration of all meaningful answers to our basic ethical problems in the light of a systematic elaboration of the logical consequences of these various answers.[4]

Ultimately the systems we thus derive must face the scientific test of empirical confirmation. They must fit into our immediate moral observations just as a scientific physics must fit into our immediate physical observations.[5] We have no more logical right to reject our moral observations at the behest of moral theories than we have to reject our physical observations because they conflict with physical theories. But as the student of physics learns to distinguish what he actually sees in the physical phenomena before him from a mass of improper expectations and inferences, so the student of ethics may hope to refine his ethical observation by viewing the realm of abstract ethical possibilities and examining the interconnection of propositions in that realm.

What is perhaps more important, the questions we put to the moral sense in gathering the observational material on which a science of ethics must rest may differ as much from men's common moral questions as do the problems of the physical laboratory from the naive cosmic queries

[4] *Cf.* Russell, *Our Knowledge of the External World as a Field for Scientific Method in Philosophy* (1914), Lecture 2 (Logic as the Essence of Philosophy), esp. pp. 58-59.

[5] *Cf.* Russell, *Mysticism and Logic* (1917), ch. 8 (The Relation of Sense-Data to Physics).

The term "observation" is here used to refer to such simple judgments as "This is brown, larger than that, round, ugly, intrinsically good, etc."

of the child. Our humanly vital ethical problems commonly involve complicated questions of natural causation and of the malleability of human habits and desires, questions which are not in themselves ethical. The search for simpler starting points and testing points of ethical theory may lead us to realms as remote from every-day life as are the behavior of decerebrated dogs and the activity of light rays in an interferometer, where psychology and physics find simplicity. This means, no doubt, that ethical science will not quickly offer satisfactory solutions to our humanly important ethical problems. It means that ethical philosophers will continue to court simplicity in the vital problems of Robinson Crusoe, Socrates, and the pig (not to mention less honorable denizens of the traditional moral menagerie), while the poignant cry of the children of the world goes unanswered.

Let us not forget that in every science we must begin with problems and materials that common sense regards as foolishly trivial. Patience to consider such problems is as fundamental a need in ethical science as is the perseverance which will carry us beyond them.

In the end our ethical judgments will not be infallible. Human certainty in material realms is never perfect. But the method of science seeks to bring ethical theory to rest upon the broad basis of all relevant ethical knowledge rather than upon the small selection of fundamental axioms on which moralists have commonly tried to rest their theories. This is the most we can ask of any scientific theory, whether it be of celestial mechanics or of the norms of human conduct.

Scientific ethics, in this sense, is not a Spencerian study

of the trend of evolution in human customs. Neither is it an anthropological investigation of the sort that M. Lévy-Bruhl has called for in his reduction of ethics to a "science des moeurs."[6] Neither of these studies is part of ethics, although, like most other sciences, they may shed light on its problems. The moral observations of primitive individuals cannot be excluded from a universal science of ethics any more than the astronomic observations of such persons can be excluded from the science of astronomy. But while modern anthropology has given us invaluable exhibitions of the functioning of customs, incentives, and institutions, the notion that a distillation of primitive tabus will prove a fruitful method of attaining ethical truth is rather naive. The difficulties of discovering the moral beliefs of those most closely united to us sympathetically and intellectually, of separating judgments of ultimate value from non-ethical judgments of causation, of defining the precise objects towards which approbation or disapproval is expressed, and of separating the observational kernel of a moral opinion from the husk of conventional doctrine—these difficulties are multiplied a thousandfold in intercourse with primitive people. What one may learn with some definiteness is that a Zuni husband should not speak to his mother-in-law. But whether this is a matter of utilizing an arbitrary convention to express a personal attitude (as we use the collection of letters t-h-a-n-k-s or the motion of removing one's hat from his head) or a matter of ethics, and, if the latter, whether the act condemned is regarded as intrinsically evil or simply a wise precaution against the activities of ghosts, insects,

[6] See *Ethics and Moral Science* (1904, trans. by Lee, 1905).

fungi, or fathers-in-law, these are questions to which no reliable answers have ever been given.

The science of ethics is simply the application of scientific method to the data of ethics. The two cardinal aspects of scientific method are (1) the logical explication and systematic development of possible hypotheses, and (2) the testing of these hypotheses and implications in the light of immediate observation. In each of these aspects ethics is eminently capable of scientific treatment, and the difficulties that exhibit themselves are shared by every other science which deals with a highly complex subject matter. An ethical theory is an attempt to coordinate and systematize certain primitive observations and to eliminate the inconsistencies and inaccuracies involved in them. There is an assumption here that our primitive observations are not indubitable, and such indeed is the case, not only in ethics but in every other body of empirical knowledge. All observation, as Kant insisted, is more than the pure perception which, not being given in propositional form, is immune to falsity and inconsistency (as well as, *stricto sensu*, truth). The simplest ethical observation that can be expressed involves a conceptual element, an element of inference or generalization, which introduces the possibility of error (and of truth). Thus in ethics, as in other sciences, our simplest and most fundamental observations will be subject to refutation;[7] but this refutation will assume the truth of other ethical observations, so that we always come down to the test, which science shares with common sense, of "immediate obviousness."[8] Of course

[7] See M. R. Cohen, *Reason and Nature*, Book 1, ch. 3, § 1.

[8] The phrase and its implications are Professor Whitehead's.

there are many conclusions of science which are not directly verifiable but these are accepted only because they are necessary presuppositions or implications of what is verifiable, or because they are purely logical and therefore again indubitable and obvious. Thus the ultimate appeal of an ethical system is to the immediate obviousness of its intelligible conclusions.

Proceeding, then, from a logical explication of possible ethical systems, we shall attempt to consider each of these systems in the light of the relevant data of ethical observation, rejecting those theories whose accordance or explanatory power is lacking or inadequate. If we find, for instance, that a given hypothesis implies that nothing which has existed in the past and nothing which we now possess can be good, and if it is very clear that some such things are good, then we shall be justified in rejecting that hypothesis.

It would be very convenient if we could succeed in showing that all ethical theories but one must be rejected, from which we could infer that that theory is the only true ethical doctrine (assuming our array of possibilities to be logically exhaustive). But there is no reason to suppose, either on *a priori* grounds or from any analogy with the more exact sciences, that such a conclusion will be established. There are two more possibilities.

First, we may reach mutually incompatible theories which explain the same facts in so far as the facts are known and agreed upon, but which would conflict as to other facts that are not yet known and perhaps never can be known. This is the situation of applied geometry at present, where only one of the three incompatible parallel postulates of Euclid, Lobatchewsky, and Riemann can (as applied geometry and on the basis of a uniform interpretation of the indefinables,—*line*, *point*, etc.) be true, where each explains the known data, and where it is possible that the three hypotheses will never produce observably different results and thus permit of final choice. In the conflict between the wave theory of light and the old corpuscular theory, optics faced a choice which, until Fresnel and Young devised their crucial experiments, was incapable of solution. Numerous other examples from the natural and social sciences might be adduced.

In the second place, we may arrive at more than one system, differing in postulates, definitions, and undefined terms, yet reaching the same conclusion in every possible question, and therefore logically equivalent. This is again found to be the case in geometry, where the various systems of euclidean geometry developed by Hilbert, Pieri, Veblen, and Huntington differ absolutely in their choice (and even number) of postulates, definitions and undefined terms, and are yet of such a nature that every assertion in one system may be translated into a corresponding assertion in each of the others. In mathematical logic, too, the system of Whitehead and Russell developed in the *Principia Mathematica* differs in its choice of undefined terms from the stroke-function system of Sheffer and Nicod, yet every proposition in one system can be transformed into a corresponding proposition in the other, by means of a simple formula of translation. If one system is true the other is true, and the choice of which we are to use is simply a matter of practical convenience.

Unless, then, there is some *a priori* reason for assuming

ethics to be more free from uncertainty and multiplicity of interpretation than physics, geometry, or logic, we must be prepared for the possibility that different ethical theories will prove logically equivalent and equally valid, or that incompatible theories will appear which agree in their verified conclusions and await some critical experiment of observation (which may be humanly impossible to conceive or carry out) before a final choice is possible. Unless we view the establishment of a theory of ethics as a problem framed in the language of probability and governed by the same canons of piece-meal, tentative verification that obtain in every other science (peace to the shades of Kant!), we cannot hope to escape the universal illusions which the quest for religious certainty has engendered in this as in every other field of human thought.

2. THE SUBJECT MATTER OF ETHICS

It is an important task of every science and a task seldom satisfactorily accomplished in the early stages of the study to delimit its scope or subject matter. A science may be usefully defined as a set of propositions whose truth or falsity is to be established.[9] What is the peculiar property of those propositions which constitute the science of ethics?

The word *ethics* is commonly used to designate one or the other of two scientific or philosophical disciplines which ought to be carefully distinguished. Ethics is some-

[9] *Cf.* Russell's definition of mathematics: "Pure mathematics is the class of all propositions of the form 'p implies q', where p and q are propositions containing one or more variables, the same in the two propositions, and neither p nor q contains any constants except logical constants." *Principles of Mathematics* (1903) p. 3.

times considered to be the set of propositions involving the concepts *good, bad, better, worse, best, worst, right, wrong, duty*, and the more complex functions of these terms, in so far as they are applied to man's voluntary activity. Again, ethics has been considered as dealing with the sum total of such propositions, whether or not they refer to voluntary human action. As the former, more narrow study is accurately designated by the words *science of morality* or *moral philosophy*, we shall use the term *ethics* exclusively in its second connotation. Ethics as thus conceived includes the entire domain of morality as well as all further judgments of *good, bad, etc.* that are applied to non-human entities and to human experiences which do not involve the will.

We have noted that the propositions with which ethics is concerned are those utilizing the concepts of *good, bad, better, worse, best, worst, right, wrong, duty*, and any other complexes which involve these terms as an element in their analysis. But this provides a rather arbitrary and unsatisfactory definition of our subject matter. Can we find in these concepts a single peculiar quality in terms of which our study can be more simply defined? If that can be done we shall possess not only a clearer notion of our subject matter but an important guiding thread for its scientific investigation.

Otherwise, our logical development of possible ethical systems and our empirical testing of these theories will have to be repeated for each of the concepts with which ethics must deal,—and even at the end of such a series of investigations, the inter-relation of the different ethical concepts will be unexplored. To trace these inter-relations is a task involving some philosophical interest on its own account, but its chief value in the present thesis is purely methodological. If we can show that all ethical judgments presuppose an identical concept, and, in so far as they are ethical, only this concept, then we shall be justified in restricting our treatment of ethics to an analysis of the meaning and extension of this idea. As a matter of fact, most writers on ethics have assumed that a theory either of the good or of duty covers the whole field of ethics. But this assumption has never been defended logically.

It is clear that our task may be accomplished in one of two ways. We may look for a simple quality of which all our given ethical concepts are complex constructions, or else we may take one of the given terms as undefined (for the present, at least) and show how all the other concepts may be reduced to complexes in which this term appears as the only ethical constituent. The former method of procedure involves the assumption that *all* of the ethical concepts under investigation can be analyzed into simpler elements, whereas the latter method does not require this assumption. Since there is some question as to the legitimacy of this assumption we shall proceed according to the latter line of inquiry.

The choice of what terms in a given system are to remain undefined is ultimately an arbitrary one, resting simply upon dictates of scientific convenience and historical usage. It is customary to accept the *point* as an undefined concept in geometry, but it would be just as logical to accept, say, the *sphere* as undefined and to define *point* in terms of *sphere* (which Professor Huntington has actually done in his system of euclidean geometry). Professor Brogan has shown how various ethical concepts may be defined in terms of *better*, and his analysis seems to be fundamentally correct.[10] But it would seem to be a simpler and more convenient procedure to define all our ethical concepts in terms of *good*, if this is possible. For most ethical theories are stated as theories of the good, rather than of the better, and in order to meet such theories face to face in our systematic explication of possible ethical theories, it is needful that we concern ourselves primarily with the nature of *good*, defining all other ethical terms as logical functions of this one. If we can succeed in this task we shall have the right to define ethics as the class of all propositions of the form *A is good.* For we assume that propositions are constituted by meanings rather than by words, that different sentences, whether in diverse languages or in distinct terms of a given system, state the same proposition if their meaning is identical. Thus every statement which can be translated into the form *A is good* does actually assert a proposition of that form.

We propose then to define *bad, better, worse, best, worst, right, wrong,* and *duty* without introducing any ethical no-

[10] Brogan suggests the following definitions: *A is worse than B* means *B is better than A*; *A is good* means *A is better than the non-existence of A*; *A is bad* means *A is worse than the non-existence of A*; *A is as good as B* means *A is not better than B and B is not better than A*; *A is ethically indifferent* means *A is not better than its non-existence, and the non-existence of A is not better than A.* Although definitions of *right, wrong,* and *duty* are not offered, their construction in terms of *better* offers no difficulty, at least if the general conclusions of G. E. Moore on this point, which are elaborated in the following pages, be acceptable. See Brogan's essay "The Fundamental Value Universal" (1919) 16 *Jour. of Phil.* 96, for a fuller presentation of this system and some *a priori* arguments, which appear to us invalid, against the possibility of basing ethical definitions upon *good.* See also A. P. Brogan, "Urban's Axiological System" (1921) 18 *Jour. of Phil.* 197.

tion other than that involved in the concept *good,* that is to say, as purely metaphysical or logical functions of this term *good.* These definitions, in order to serve their intended purpose, must be analytical rather than verbal or symbolic. A mere resolution to use the word *bad* instead of some complex of *good* cannot prove that the actual concept generally denoted by *bad* can be explained in terms of *good.* What we must do is to take the concepts which we really mean by *bad, better, etc.,* and show by building up complex functions of *good,* that such functions can be constructed which are identical in meaning with the concepts to be defined.

It is necessary, first of all, to make a distinction between intrinsic and utilitarian value judgments. An entity is intrinsically good when it is good in itself, abstracted from its *causal* connection with other entities.[11] An entity is said to be a utilitarian good when the conjunction of the entity and its effects is intrinsically good. It is sometimes held that there is a real ethical problem involved when we ask whether an entity is good which has good effects but which is intrinsically neither good nor bad. This is a mistake. The position that an action otherwise indifferent is good or bad in virtue of the intrinsic goodness or badness of its consequences is self-contradictory if it asserts intrinsic goodness of an intrinsically indifferent entity, and tautologous if it uses the word *good* to mean *either intrinsically good or productive of what is intrinsically good.* In neither case is ethical argument relevant to the "prob-

[11] The notion of intrinsic goodness is not excluded by the theory that goods are relative to time, place, or person. Even under such a theory it is necessary to distinguish between means and ends.

lem" of utilitarianism. The question of whether the word *good* ought to be used in the broader sense is of course open to philological argument, and in such argument the utilitarian seems to have the support of popular usage and scientific convenience. What is of interest to the ethical philosopher, however, is the distinction between two sorts of propositions, each of which is ethical. *A is intrinsically good,* is clearly a different proposition from *A with its effects is intrinsically good.* But the form of the two assertions is identical. *A with its effects* is itself an entity, which we may call B, and every utilitarian judgment of goodness can thus be expressed as an intrinsic judgment. In a similar way, utilitarian judgments of badness, betterness, duty, etc. can be expressed as intrinsic judgments upon the act judged with its results. Similarly, purely extrinsic valuations, of the form, *The results of A are good,* may be expressed as judgments of intrinsic value upon these results. We may therefore, for the sake of simplicity, consider in the remainder of this section only intrinsic value judgments and their inter-relations.[12]

The simplest application of value categories seems to be to events or sets of events, actual or logically possible, and the valuation of universals (qualities, relations, objects,[13] etc.) can always be expressed as judgments upon the sets of events which they determine (*e.g.* a valuation of kindness is a valuation of kind acts in so far as they are kind, or in so far as alien ethical elements cancel each

[12] For a more detailed analysis of the anti-utilitarian position in legal criticism, see pp. 48-51, *supra*.

[13] Professor Whitehead's analysis of objects as universals revealing a continuity of manifestation rather than unanalyzable individual things is here followed. *Cf. Concept of Nature* (1920) ch. 7.

other out). By an event we mean a particular entity with a definite space-time location. Thus the life of Caesar, the next war, and the existence of the United States Constitution during the last decade are typical events. Whether the conjunction of two events can itself properly be called an event we need not here decide, since in any case the application of ethical predicates to sets of events seems to be similar to the application of such terms to single events.

Accepting as the undefined starting point of our definitions the ascription of (intrinsic) goodness to an event or set of events, we must show that the remaining concepts of ethics require no further ethical element in their definition. Let us begin by examining the concept *better*. We may define the proposition *A is better than B* (where A and B refer to events or sets of events) as meaning: *There is an event, C, such that the logical conjunction of C and A is good, while the conjunction of C and B is not good.* For example, keeping a hundred children from spinal meningitis (A) is better than keeping a thousand dogs from vivisection (B) if, and only if, there is some third event, say the sickness of fifty children (C), which, taken with the preserved health of the hundred children (A.C) constitutes a series of events that is on the whole good, but taken with the rescue of the thousand dogs (B.C) does not form a good whole. Or, to take an example where it may be easier to focus attention on intrinsic values, the enjoyment of Beethoven's Seventh Symphony on a given evening of the reader's life (A) is better than the conversation of a friend (B), if there is some third event (C) such as the waste of an hour in travelling which, taken with the concert (A.C), is good, with the conversation (B.C), not good.[14]

It should be noted that the definition offered does not assume the existence of actual goods or evils in the world, for although it is put in the form of an existential proposition, the entity whose existence is affirmed is only a possible event. Just as in mathematics we do not need to assume that there are really ten entities in the physical world in order to assert existential propositions about the number ten, so in ethics existential propositions about possibilities must not be taken to assert physical actuality. In other words, since our definition need involve only logical possibility, it cannot be overthrown by an absolute pessimism which denies the real existence of good, or by an absolute optimism which denies the existence of evil, or by the more plausible claim that two entities of which one is better than the other may be so close in value that no third

[14] A consideration of the five cases in which we apply the comparative value concept will help to make the significance of this definition clear, although it cannot be regarded as an integral or necessary part of the definition itself, under penalty of involving certain vicious circles in our further definitions. A may be better than B because A is good and B is bad. In that case we can always conceive an indifferent event, the conjunction of which with A would produce a good, though its conjunction with B would not produce a good. In a second case, A and B may both be good. But if A is better than B there will be some bad event which will in conjunction with B constitute a total that is not good (*i.e.* either bad or indifferent), although it is not bad enough to make the conjunction A.C not good. Similarly, in the third case, where A is better than B although both are bad, there will be a good event, C, sufficient to make A.C good, yet not adequate to make B.C good. In a fourth case, A may be better than B because the former is good while the latter is indifferent. Here we may add a third independent event either indifferent or slightly evil, so that A.C will remain good, while B.C is indifferent or bad. In the fifth case, A will be better than B because it is indifferent, while B is bad. Here a third event may be conceived good enough to make A.C good, while B.C remains bad or moves up to the level of indifference. Thus our definition is shown to apply to all the uses of the value-comparative *better*.

existent can be found such that its conjunction with the former would be good and its conjunction with the latter not good. Nor can our definition be overthrown by a denial that goodness or badness are matters of degree. The definition advanced will be found to explain the relation of a good entity to an indifferent entity, or of an indifferent entity to a bad entity, or of a good entity to a bad entity, if there are only these three levels of value in the moral world.

The objection may be raised that when we think of the concept *better* we have nothing in mind as complicated as our suggested *definiens*. This is quite true, but it is not a valid objection to what purports to be an analytic definition. When we think of gold we think of gold, not of a subject of a long list of physical and chemical properties. Yet the analysis of gold which such a definition performs may be quite correct. Similarly in the realm of mathematics we need not think of a point as a complex function of ordered solids or surfaces in certain arrangements, although such a function (*e.g.* that developed by Professor Whitehead[15]) may identify what we mean by *point* and, for logical, metaphysical, or scientific purposes, offer definite advantages. Thus the only claim for our definition of *A is better than B* is that it adequately represents what is actually meant by the simpler phrase and that it does this in terms of a single ethical concept, *good,* and a number of simple logical constants.

The only serious objection to this definition is that which appears to be raised by Moore's principle of organic

15 Whitehead, *Concept of Nature* (1920) ch. 4 (The Method of Extensive Abstraction).

unities.[16] It is argued that the value of a whole may have no regular relation to the value of its parts. Thus, a bad event, say taking a man's life, and another bad event, say taking the murderer's life, might together constitute a good whole. On the other hand, one of these events might, together with a perfectly indifferent event, constitute a bad whole. Thus we would seem to be led to the absurd conclusion, on the basis of our present definition, that a bad event may be better than an indifferent event, (since the conjunction of the bad event with another event is, apparently, good, while the conjunction of the indifferent event with this other event is not good). If this is the case, our present definition must be abandoned, and with it the greater part of ethical speculation,—for if there is really no constant relation between the values of wholes and parts we shall never be able to determine the value of anything. This inference is, of course, no argument against the principle of organic unities, although it is a fair index of its practical importance.

It is our contention that there are limits to the applicability of the theory of organic wholes which make the suggested objection to our definition of *better* invalid. To trace these limits is an extremely difficult problem. We are face-to-face with the ancient riddle of unity and diversity, which, in a form very similar to that under present consideration, is at the heart of all the difficulties of modern logic with regard to the nature of classes. We shall not apologize, therefore, for entering debatable realms of metaphysics in the solution of this question. After all, every moralist has solved the question of the relation of

16 See G. E. Moore, *Principia Ethica*, pp. 27-36.

goodness to betterness, and our only peculiar misfortune is to have become conscious of its difficulties.

There is no doubt a partial truth in Moore's doctrine. To repeat his own illustration, it may very easily be admitted that neither mere consciousness nor the existence of a beautiful object is intrinsically good, and that the two factors together, constituting the vision of beauty, are a good whole. The example already considered is essentially similar. But in both of these instances, it must be noted, we are dealing with the analysis of wholes into abstract constituents (aspects, factors, ideas, concepts, phases, external objects). The vision of beauty is not a mere logical conjunction of consciousness and beauty. Nor is the punishment of murder viewed in the first illustration merely a logical conjunction, a set, of two killings. In both these cases, the whole is not a logical conjunction of the suggested parts, but an emergent entity in which the suggested parts are united in spatio-temporal existence and maintain a separate existence only in analysis. Thus we may admit that the value of a whole is not simply the value of a set of parts when the whole is not simply a set of the given parts. But Moore has offered no arguments or examples to show the applicability of the organic doctrine to wholes which *are* simply sets of parts, *i.e.* to combinations of independently existing entities.

It is not our present purpose to investigate the extent of the realm in which division or separation is "real" rather than analytical, and in which the principle of organic unities therefore fails to apply. That the logical conjunction of events falls within the former realm is our only contention. An event is an ultimate particular and *ex hypothesi* cannot change. The logical conjoining of events is an ideal and not a temporal process. If A were changed by its addition to B, there could be no such thing as addition. The numerical addition of two stars does not bring new gravitational forces into existence, nor does the addition of six bananas create a stomach-ache. So, the logical conjunction of two human acts does not bring new moral values into existence. The conjoined events which are involved in our definitions remain independent, and, such being the case, none of the objections to our present definition on the basis of Moore's organic doctrine or of the examples which that doctrine covers can be relevant. And this is true even if, as some philosophers believe, it is impossible for two different events to be completely independent of each other. If absolute independence has no incarnations in the empirical world, it may yet be regarded as an ideal, to be approached (like the ideals of frictionless engines and bodies not acted upon by other forces) within any required limit of accuracy.

Having defined the concept *A is better than B*, it is a simple matter to define *A is worse than B* as a logical converse. *A is worse than B* means simply *B is better than A*. And since we have already shown how this last assertion may be expressed in terms of good, a definition of *worse* in terms of *good* has been effected.

The concept of ethical indifference may be defined as follows: To say that *A is indifferent* is to say that *if any event is good, the conjunction of that event with A is good, and, vice versa, if the conjunction of any event with A is good, then the event is good.* For instance the eruption of a volcano on a desert island is indifferent if and only if it can be truly said of every class of events which contains the volcanic eruption and an additional event: The class of two events is good if the additional event is good, and the additional event is good if the class of events is good.

The concept *A is bad* may now be defined as equivalent to the following complex: *Every indifferent event is better than A.* For instance, the next war is bad if any indifferent event (*e.g.* our volcanic eruption) is better than it.

To say that *A is best of a given set of events* is simply to say that *it is a member of that set and is better than any other member of the set.* Since we have defined *better* in terms of *good,* this definition can be reduced, like all the others, to a complex of *good* and certain logical terms.

A is worst of a given class may be defined similarly to mean *A is a member of that class and any other member of that class is better than A.*[17]

[17] That the definitions given above involve no concept other than *good* and the formal relations of logic can be clearly demonstrated by putting these definitions in the chaste language of symbolic logic, where ϕ, the only non-logical term used represents the predicate *is good.* Using the notation of the *Principia Mathematica,* but using the dot (.) between letters to represent the conjunction of events instead of the product of propositions, and considering the class of events and sets of events, actual or non-actual, as the range of entities for which ϕ has significance, this tabulation may be given, as a summary of our analysis of ethical concepts:

A is better than $B. = .(\exists x).\phi(x.A). \sim \phi(x.B)$
A is worse than $B. = .(\exists x).\phi(x.B). \sim \phi(x.A)$
A is indifferent $. = :(x):\phi x. \equiv .\phi(x.A)$
A is bad $. = : .(x): .(y): \phi y. \equiv .\phi(y.x): \supset :(\exists z):\phi(z.x). \sim \phi(z.A)$
A is best of class $K. = : .A \epsilon K: .(x):x \epsilon K.x \neq A. \supset .(\exists y).\phi(y.A). \sim \phi(y.x)$
A is worst of class $K. = : .A \epsilon K: .(x):x \epsilon K.x \neq A. \supset .(\exists y).\phi(y.x). \sim \phi(y.A)$

An instructive analogy to this set of definitions, constituting an alternative interpretation for our symbols, is to be found in the realm of mathematics. Let ϕ mean *is a positive number,* and let A.B mean *the algebraic sum of A and B.* It will be found, then, that our six symbolic propositions define, respectively: (1) A is greater than B, (2) A is less than B, (3) A

We have thus defined what may be called the pure concepts of ethics, since it will be found that our remaining terms, *right*, *wrong*, and *duty*, involve a further notion, that of possibility, which is not strictly a concept of logic. Judgments of good and bad are ultimately irresponsible to the brute contingency of existence, but we recognize that every assertion of *right*, *wrong*, and *duty* involves an assertion of *can*. These latter concepts further differ from those that have already been analyzed in that they are, in their commonest ethical significance, applied only to voluntary human action. They are therefore significant only within that sub-domain of ethics which we have called moral philosophy. It is our purpose to show that they involve no other ethical concept than that expressed in our primary ethical proposition, *A is* (*intrinsically*) *good.*[18]

Right (the adjective), like most of the other terms we have considered, has various non-ethical meanings with which we are not concerned in this discussion. But when we say that a given mode of action is right, we are clearly asserting an ethical proposition. In this sense, an action is right when it is not worse than any alternative action (regarding abstinence from positive activity as itself a kind of action) which can be substituted for it. If a man in a given set of circumstances can do only one of two things and must do at least one, and if one action is better than the other, we say that it is right for him to accomplish the former action. We should say this even if the former action

is zero, (4) A is a negative number, (5) A is the greatest number in class K, and (6) A is the least number in class K.

18 The following analysis is essentially that offered by G. E. Moore. See *Ethics* (1912), ch. 1, 2.

were bad, since this would at least be better than any other possible action. And, on the other hand, we should say this even if the second action were good, provided only the first were better. But it is not even necessary that an action be better than all possible alternatives in order to be right. For if a man is faced with three (and only three) alternatives, A, B, and C, of which A and B are equally good, each being better than C, we should say that performing A was right and also that performing B was right, —in other words that two incompatible actions, neither of which was better than all possible alternatives were each right. It appears, then, that in calling a given act *right* we say simply that *it is a possible act which is not worse than any possible alternative*, and in calling a given act *wrong* we assert that *it is a possible act which is worse than some possible alternative.*[19] When the act in question is possible, these statements are logical contradictories, so that one and only one is true of any given act.

We have finally to show how the concept of *duty* or *ought* can be defined in terms of a complex built upon the concept *good*. When we say that a man ought to act in a certain way, or that it is his duty to act in this way, or that this action is obligatory (morally), we mean not only

[19] Having reduced the concepts of right and wrong to those of better and worse, it is a simple matter to put them in the form *A is good. A is right* will be interpreted to mean: *A is possible, and if any incompatible action is possible, then, for every third entity, the conjunction of this with the alternative to A will be good only when the conjunction of this with A is good. A is wrong* will mean: *A is possible and there is some possible incompatible action for which it will be true that a third entity exists whose conjunction with the alternative to A is good and whose conjunction with A is not good.*

The term *incompatible* is here applied to entities the conjunction of which is not itself possible.

that the act is right but that it would be wrong to perform any of the other incompatible alternative acts.[20] We hold, then, that *A is the object of a duty*, or *A ought to be done*, or *A is obligatory* means *A is possible and is better than any possible alternative.*[21]

Other ethical concepts do not present serious difficulties of analysis, although the interpretation of language used

[20] Thus when there is one alternative better than any other it will be right, and will at the same time constitute one's duty, but if there are several right alternatives, all equally good, we cannot say that each of them is one's duty. We do say, however, that it is a man's duty to choose one (*i.e.* at least one and not more than one) of the right actions. If for instance, A is just as good as B and each is better than C, and the trio constitute an exhaustive set of possible incompatible actions, then we may state the following propositions: (1) A is right; (2) B is right; (3) C is wrong; (4) A is not one's duty (this is of course not the same as the proposition "It is one's duty not to do A",—a confusion which the phrase "ought not" would engender if it were ever taken grammatically); (5) B is not one's duty; (6) C is not one's duty; (7) It is one's duty not to perform C; and (8) It is one's duty to perform A or B (the dilemma of alternatives is now between the disjunction "A or B" and C, of which the former is "better than any incompatible alternative").

[21] In terms of *good* this definition will read: *A is possible, and if any incompatible action is possible, then there will be a third entity such that its conjunction with the alternative to A will not be good and its conjunction with A will be good.* The definitions here arrived at may be put in symbolic form, but they require the addition of a new non-ethical concept which does not seem to be purely formal, namely the concept of possibility. We have seen that judgments of right, wrong, and obligation involve an assertion of possibility and a comparison with other possible incompatible (*i.e.* not compossible) actions. And while there are serious difficulties involved in the interpretation of this concept, they are certainly not ethical in nature, so that we may regard the thesis of the present chapter as realized with the symbolic statement of our last three definitions. Let ψ represent the predicate *is possible*, and with the aid of our fundamental ethical predicate ϕ (is good) and the terms of formal logic, we can represent our definitions in the following form (where the range of significance of the entities involved is the realm of human volitional events and collections of such events):

$$A \text{ is right } . =: : \psi A : : (x) : . \psi x . - \psi(A.x) . \supset : (y) : \phi(y.x) . \supset . \phi(y.A)$$
$$A \text{ is wrong } . =: . \psi A : . (\exists x) : \psi x . - \psi(A.x) : (\exists y) . \phi(y.x) . - \phi(y.A)$$
$$A \text{ is obligatory } . =: . \psi A : . (x) : \psi x . - \psi(A.x) . \supset . (\exists y) . \phi(y.A) . - \phi(y.x)$$

to express these concepts may be a Herculean task. Such concepts are either complex logical constructions of the terms already considered (*e.g. the greatest good*) or applications of these terms to an empirically limited subject matter (*e.g.* the various virtues, which may be defined in Aristotelian fashion as habits of right action, thought, feeling, etc., under various circumstances). None of these concepts can be regarded as either fundamental to general ethical theory or immune to the analysis illustrated in the foregoing definitions. We may, therefore, define the science of ethics as the class of propositions of the type, *A is intrinsically good.*

It would be absurd to suppose that we have eliminated ambiguity from ethics by defining the various concepts of ethics in terms of a single, thus far undefined predicate, *good.* Radically different ideas may be evoked in different minds by the word *good,* though each of these ideas may be logically related in a uniform way to other ideas evoked by the words, *bad, better, etc.* So long as we are seeking to analyze an idea rather than a notoriously ambiguous word, any historical inquiry into the various meanings which the word has had, in English or in any other language, must be irrelevant to ethics. It may be the case that different uses of this word present no material inter-relation, and that the idea which we have been representing by the symbol *good* is only one of a number of ideas commonly symbolized in that way. But we cannot by further definition completely eliminate the possibility of misunderstanding. Symbolic or conventional definition (à la Humpty Dumpty) merely adds to the ways of representing a given idea. And analytical definition, or explanation will not help us, since the analysis of goodness is in fact the fundamental problem of the science we call ethics, and cannot be used, without involving a *petitio principii*, to identify the subject matter of this science. We must, in short, be prepared to question every proposition about goodness, and we can do this only if no such proposition has been used in defining goodness.

It is our assumption that the concept which we have denoted by the word *good* is one which many other English-speaking people similarly denote. Only upon some such basis of common understanding can ethical discussion between different people be significant. Whether our assumption is valid the reader will determine for himself in the light of our further analysis. But whether or not we shall be understood, and whether or not what we say will be relevant to the issues which others think of as "ethical," (inscrutable problems, common to all discourse), it is this single concept to which we shall apply our inquiries. It is this concept whose nature we shall attempt to analyze, and whose empirical applicability we shall attempt to determine. In this procedure, when we inquire into the meaning of *good,* we shall be investigating the significance of an idea, not of a word.

Finally, the definitions we have offered are not presupposed by the following outline of possible ethical theories, although they are presupposed by the claim that this *is* an outline of possible ethical theories. If the foregoing analytical definitions are false, what follows may be only a small part of ethics, namely that part which deals with the concept of goodness. If they are, as we believe, substantially correct, they provide an adequate base for the most general inquiries of ethical science.

3. ANALYSIS OF POSSIBLE ETHICAL SYSTEMS

The valuation of law, we have seen, presupposes the ethical standard of the good life. In our criticism of traditional legal ideals, we have made a number of rough assumptions as to the actual content of this abstract standard. The non-verbal agreement of men as to the content of the good life, whether determined broadly for a civilization or narrowly for a particular class or community, offers the only practical starting point for a legal criticism conscious of its ethical responsibilities. But if our valuations of law are ever to exhibit the precision and systematic fruitfulness which distinguish science from common sense, there must be a continued refinement of this common moral opinion through the critical analysis of possible ethical systems. In order to understand the nature of the good life one must face the more general problem of the nature of goodness. The good life is only a part of the good, and it may be that we shall, in considering the wider problem, introduce truth and error irrelevant to our narrower inquiry. But this risk is the inevitable price of all explanation, and of all thought.

Ethical science is essentially incomplete until it has produced a criterion by which, without further ethical assumptions, the value of anything may be determined. Such a criterion we may most simply achieve by analyzing intrinsic goodness (from which, as we have seen, all other ethical concepts may be derived) into its components, which must, upon penalty of introducing a vicious circle, be purely positive or non-ethical elements. But the achievement of a satisfactory analytic definition of intrinsic goodness leaves ethics an austere and abstract science. To bring its general principles to a useful particularity and to afford a recognizable picture of the good life, ethics must look to empirical materials that are equally within the domains of ethics and of positive science. If, for instance, we discover that the concept of intrinsic goodness is identical with the idea of happiness, we must enter the realms of economics, anthropology, psychology, physiology, even biology and physics, to determine what factors actually determine the presence or absence of happiness, before we can decide what sorts of human conduct are desirable. In these realms we shall be dealing with materials that vary greatly in nature from one society or generation to another, and all conclusions made in this field must bear the qualifying label of a controlling social milieu. We do not propose, in the present volume, to venture further into these latter realms than topographers and field generals are required to venture. Our set task is the determination of standards of legal criticism valid for every time and place. We shall have accomplished this task if we have achieved a definition of the universal ethical constant and indicated the factors which, by varying from one society to another, endow our ideals of good law and the good life with new content in every country and generation.

It may be that we can achieve the ethical criterion we seek without strictly defining the ultimate nature of intrinsic goodness. The modern hedonist may maintain, for instance, that whatever the essential nature of goodness may be, it is something that we actually find where we find human happiness. Such a theory, correlating the psychological entity, happiness, with the ethical entity, intrinsic goodness, is as complete an ethical doctrine as a theory of the analysis of goodness itself. Armed with such a doctrine one omniscient in all the positive sciences might answer every ethical question.

The foregoing considerations point to three questions as the object of our investigation in the field of pure ethics: (1) Is intrinsic goodness definable in natural or positive terms? (2) If so, what is its definition? (3) If not, what natural or positive entities may we find so correlated with intrinsic goodness as to serve as indicia or criteria of value? It will be found helpful to preface the investigation of these three problems with an inquiry into the basic question of relativism and absolutism. Is there a single "goodness" to the analysis of which our further investigation may be directed, or is the object of that investigation irreducibly and absolutely a variable?

To these four basic ethical questions, then, we shall attempt to apply the canons of science. What are the logically possible answers that may be given to these questions? How do these various answers accord with the available data of ethics?

Our task is not the criticism of historically accepted ethical theories. Such an attempt would indeed be pretentious and foolhardy on our part, in view of the vast historical learning which has been and must be expended in such an endeavor. Moreover, that task would be utterly insufficient to establish the outlines of possible ethical doctrines. We shall at times go beyond the domain of historical ethical systems, and at other times wc shall lump together a number of distinguishable systems for our treatment, either because we believe that certain criticisms are valid against a common presupposition of the class of theories or because we are unable to bring valid criticisms against any one of them. We do venture to assert, however, that any theory of ethics (that is, any set of answers to the four fundamental questions we have propounded) which has been or will be believed by any one will find some place within our analysis, however inadequate our present criticism of it may be.

A. The Logical Nature of Goodness

.0[22] Either *A is intrinsically good*[23] has no meaning (.1) or it has a constant meaning (.2) or it has a variable meaning (.3).

One of these views must be correct, since the three propositions are logically exhaustive. The first view we shall term ethical nihilism, the second ethical absolutism, the

[22] The possible answers to our four problems are numbered with one, two, three, or four place decimals, according to the problem considered. Zero is used to denote a set of logically possible answers. Thus .0 denotes an exhaustive set of possible answers to our first problem. An answer to a later question will generally presuppose a particular answer to an earlier question. Where this is the case the number of the earlier answer will appear in that of the later. Thus the number .2203 will designate an ethical theory which assumes the truth of the second answer to our first problem (that of the logical nature of goodness) and the second answer to our second problem (that of the definability of goodness), disregards the third problem (the definition of goodness), and proposes a third answer to our fourth problem (the criteria of goodness).

[23] It has already been noted that this is to be read as a typical proposition, *e.g.* "The reader's life is intrinsically good." The assumption is thus made that a typical ethical proposition is possible, that intrinsic goodness does not change its meaning if we change the object of valuation.

third ethical relativism. In the first view, *A is intrinsically good* and *A is not intrinsically good* are both meaningless and neither true nor false (since the denial of what is meaningless is also meaningless). In the second view, *A is intrinsically good* and *A is not intrinsically good* are propositions which are mutually contradictory, so that one of the two must always be true, the other false. In the third view, *A is intrinsically good* and *A is not intrinsically good* are incomplete expressions and therefore neither true nor false. These expressions are not themselves assertions but rather, when their incompleteness is recognized, questions or propositional functions.[24] Thus while they are not themselves true or false, their answers or values will be true or false. What the values of these propositional functions may be will be discussed under the heading of ethical relativism (.3).

.1 *A is intrinsically good* has no meaning. This view, which we have termed ethical nihilism, is a theory of ethics only in the sense that anarchism is a theory of politics and scepticism a theory of knowledge. It may be distinguished from pessimism in that the latter states either that the universe as a whole is bad or that no existent thing is good. The present view is that nothing at all, existent or logically possible, is intrinsically good. From this it follows that the concept of intrinsic goodness is meaningless, since there is nothing to which it can have reference.

[24] "is president" and "equals 2" are incomplete expressions. When the incompleteness is recognized we write "Who is president?" and "x equals 2," which logicians call propositional functions and other people call questions or problems. See F. S. Cohen, "What is a Question" (1929) 39 *Monist* 350. Thus when we read "Socrates is good" as equivalent to "Socrates is good from the reference x" we recognize a propositional function.

Apparently no philosopher has ever maintained this position, yet it deserves consideration as a logically possible alternative in the array of possible answers to our fundamental question. Moreover it is noteworthy because it is the only basis upon which the possibility of an affirmative ethical system can be denied. Many philosophers have assumed that if goodness is a relative term, or a definable term, or a psychological entity, there can be no such thing as ethics. Even stranger assumptions in this regard have frequently been made. The belief has been expressed that if there is no such thing as free will, or no such thing as a divine or transcendental will, or no possibility of estimating instrumental goodness except by a calculation of consequences, or no possibility of disinterested ethical judgment, ethics must be impossible. None of these propositions, however, can show an affirmative ethics to be impossible unless they imply the proposition under present consideration, which is certainly not the case.

There can be no *a priori* refutation of this position, but in the test of comparison with immediately obvious data, the view proves to be unsound. It is about as clear as any empirical fact can be that this concept of intrinsic goodness does, in the experience of the author and in the experience of others, have some application. We may reject this position with as much confidence as we should reject a theory of physics which denied the possibility of color.

.2 *A is intrinsically good* has a constant meaning. This view may also be expressed by affirming that *A is intrinsically good* is a complete proposition, that it is therefore either true or false and not both. If two people disagree as to whether a particular entity is good, then one must be wrong and the other right.

In maintaining that the ascription of intrinsic goodness to an entity has a constant significance, we are not constrained to deny that many different things or events or universals may be good. The view is simply that intrinsic goodness itself is always the same thing, that the proposition, "The life of Socrates is intrinsically good," has a constant meaning. The fact that this event is good does not preclude other events from being good, and the fact that one universal, say beauty, is good does not imply that other universals, say pleasure or love, cannot be equally good.

Nor does this viewpoint of ethics imply any intolerance or narrowness of ethical judgment. Though goodness be one, its appearances may be many, and the fact that monogamy or democracy or truth-telling is good at one time and place does not imply that it is good under all circumstances. Where circumstances are part of the events to be judged, or where they affect parts of such events, their variation will mean simply that we are in the two cases evaluating two different things, and of course these things may be of different value. Consequently the so-called relativism of ethics to time and place is perfectly consonant with our assumption of absolutism in respect to the nature of the value predicate.

This view may be combined with various concepts of the meaning of *good*. Whether goodness is a simple indefinable quality, as G. E. Moore maintains, or whether it can be defined as pleasantness or accordance with the will of God, we are still in the realm of ethical absolutism.

On any of these definitions or denials of definability, *A is intrinsically good* is either true or false and not both.

Similarly, the acceptance of ethical absolutism does not prejudge the question of what is good. It merely asserts that there is a single unequivocal (though perhaps unknown) answer to this question. The absolutist may hold that pleasure is the only good, or that following one's sense of duty is the only good, or that pain is the only good, or that a combination of these or other elements is the only good, and in any case retain absolutism.

It will be seen, then, that absolutism in this sense is the assumption of practically every ethical system that has been constructed. Nevertheless, no recognition of the fact that this assumption is only one of several possible alternatives has ever been clearly expressed by the upholders of ethical absolutism, and arguments in its favor are not to be found. We have been equally unable to discover or invent any conclusive *a priori* arguments against the position. Our consideration of it must therefore await the further development of the possible forms which this theory may take and of the possible alternatives which may be proposed.

.3 *A is intrinsically good* has a variable meaning. By this we mean simply that the concept *A is intrinsically good* is not a complete proposition, although it is significant. When this incompleteness is recognized, we have a propositional form or function,[25] the values of which are statements of the form *A is intrinsically good* where the

[25] *I.e.*, *ARx*—A has the relation R (a constant) to x (a variable).

variable *good* has been given a definite value and a complete proposition has thus been attained.

On this view *A is intrinsically good* will not contradict *A is not intrinsically good*, since neither is a proposition and only propositions can contradict each other. If we assume a single value of the variable term *good* under each form, the two resultant propositions will be contradictories. Such a relationship between two propositional functions may be called formal contradiction, but this relationship is quite distinct from the relation of contradiction which applies between propositions of which each implies and is implied by the other's falsity.

Good is considered to be a variable like the mathematical x, from which it differs only in the range of its significant values. It becomes complete, or takes a value, only when a reference or point of view is assumed. Since varying points of view may be assumed, there is no such thing as absolute goodness. The difficulties of ethics, the relativist claims, have mostly arisen from the failure to make explicit the reference or perspective of our value judgments. One person says that the American constitution is good, another that it is not good, and an argument ensues. This, says the relativist, is absurd. It is as if one person were to say, "These apples are mine," and another were to say, "They are not mine," and the two were to proceed to argue as if they had made incompatible statements. The two statements are actually not incompatible, for in each instance *mine* involves a different reference. With no reference, *mine* would be a variable, and it attains definite meaning only when some reference has been supplied. *A is mine* abstracted from a personal reference is not a proposition and is neither true nor false. It has meaning, indeed, but this meaning does not constitute a complete proposition and is in fact a propositional function. It may again be noted that we are dealing with concepts, not words. *This is mine* as a sentence may be merely an ambiguous expression, tempting us to ascertain the identity of the speaker. But the abstraction of meaning which is attained by the elimination of any particular reference is a definitely denoted concept, a form the validation of which gives propositions.

We can make significant statements about what is *mine* and what is not *mine* only when the incompleteness of the concept *mine* is supplemented and a constant value is thus produced. To speak of "absolute mineness" is senseless. Similarly, the relativist denies determinate significance to goodness in any absolute sense.

The position of the ethical relativist may be made clear in the following form of relativism (which should be taken as an illustration rather than a necessary form of the doctrine). Let us suppose that when anyone passes the ethical judgment, "A is intrinsically good," he means, "A pleases me." In the particular instance, *me* is perfectly definite, since a reference to the speaker is established. Anybody who repeated the words with a new reference implied would be affirming another relation or quality of A. And the denial of the second affirmation would be consistent with the assertion of the first, so that, of a single event or object, one person could affirm and the other deny its goodness without disagreement. Their references would be different but there would be no sense in speaking of one point of view as better than another, except in reference to a third point of view, which had no more validity than either of the other two. At this point we cannot, consistently with the assumption of relativism, introduce the principle that what pleases, or is intrinsically good from the viewpoint of, many people has more goodness than what pleases few. This would be like saying that what two people own in common, being "mine" from two points of view, has more absolute mineness than what is owned by one man. The relativist may admit no absolute standard for the evaluation of different viewpoints. Every ethical judgment stands in its own right and can be contradicted only when the viewpoint upon which it rests is accepted.

It is not necessary to relate the essential reference of ethical concepts to human desires or to human life at all. Concepts like *near*, *upper*, *early*, and *warmer* all involve a variable reference apart from any human relationship or existence. It is abstractly possible that *good* resembles these terms rather than a term with a personal reference like *mine*.

It must be noted that the popular absurdity that *A is good* means the same as *S thinks that A is good* is not a form of relativism. Through the infinite regress involved in making the whole a part of itself (the object or content of the thought being made identical with the thinking) we should be reduced to the position of moral nihilism, which we have seen to be untenable.

On the relativist hypothesis, there is a clear distinction between *A is good*, which is a propositional function, neither true nor false, and the proposition *A is good from some (at least one) point of view*. The distinction is that between the propositional function, "the variable x has the constant property ϕ", and the existential proposition, "some value of the variable x has the constant property ϕ". A proposition of the latter form may always be significantly denied (though it may be the case that our range of possible ethical references is so great that anything is good from at least one point of view, in which case such a denial, though significant, would always be false). We cannot even falsely deny the propositional function *A is good*, for it is no more possible to deny a propositional function than it is to deny tables or *multiples*.

A final misinterpretation of the relativistic position is that which is widely maintained today as the doctrine of tolerance. Those who deny that there is an absolute ethical code seem frequently to say, "Any ethical code or judgment is as good as any other, and it is wrong to impose one concept of the good upon individuals with different ideals." This is either self-contradictory or simply the expression of a personal preference on a par with other "intolerant" preferences. It is self-contradictory if the value of tolerance is absolute, since it denies all absolutes. On the other hand, it cannot fulfill its claim to supremacy in the realm of ethics if there is no difference in ethical validity between the proposition, "It is wrong to impose one concept of the good upon individuals with different ideals," and the proposition, "It is right to impose one concept of the good upon people with different ideals." Respect for personality finds no valid support in ethical scepticism. We cannot logically derive an ethical system from our ethical ignorance.

This may serve as a sufficient explanation, for the time

being, of what relativism is and what it is not. What are the arguments for and against the position thus delineated?

To answer this question is a most difficult task, in which we can find little help from any ethical thinker. Among classical philosophers, Spinoza and Hobbes, perhaps, came closest to a defense of ethical relativism, but the one escaped to a refuge in God, and the other found relief in the supremacy of the state. Today Santayana has more or less consistently maintained an ethical relativism, but without offering any grounds for its support. We may confess at once that we have seen no conclusive arguments for or against this position. We can only trace its implications and its possible forms in the hope that some point of distinction will appear upon which a rational criticism of the theory in question may rest. It is necessary, however, before attempting this task, to dispose of a few inconclusive arguments on the issue that are likely to cloud our final choice.

The doctrine of relativism in ethics is, of course, an immoral doctrine. It is the assertion of a real anarchy in the moral world, and an acceptance of it may well lead to a good deal of moral anarchy in the real world. This may be a good reason for not saying anything about the doctrine, but it is of course irrelevant to the question of whether the doctrine is true.

A more serious argument against the doctrine is that which G. E. Moore[26] and Bertrand Russell[27] have raised, the point, namely, that under ethical relativism there can be no significant argument upon the locus of intrinsic value.

[26] G. E. Moore, *Principia Ethica. Ethics.*
[27] Russell, *Philosophical Essays* (1910), ch. 1 (Elements of Ethics).

Santayana's reply to this attempted *reductio ad absurdum* presents the relativistic position so clearly that it is worth quoting at some length:

> Mr. Russell and Mr. Moore . . . imagine that the truth of a proposition attributing a certain relative quality to an object contradicts the truth of another proposition attributing to the same object an opposite relative quality. Thus if a man here and another man at the antipodes call opposite directions up, "only one of them can be right, though it may be very hard to know which is right."
>
> To protect the belated innocence of this state of mind, Mr. Russell so far as I can see, has only one argument and one analogy. The argument is that "if this were not the case, we could not reason with a man as to what is right." "We do in fact hold that when one man approves of a certain act, while another disapproves, one of them is mistaken, which would not be the case with a mere emotion. If one man likes oysters and another dislikes them we do not say that either of them is mistaken." In other words, we are to maintain our prejudices, however absurd, lest it should become unnecessary to quarrel about them! Truly the debating society has its idols, no less than the cave and the theatre. . . .
>
> An ethical proposition may be correct or incorrect, in a sense justifying argument, when it touches what is good as a means, that is, when it is not intrinsically ethical, but deals with causes and effects, or with matters of fact or necessity. But to speak of the truth of an ultimate good would be a false collocation of

terms; an ultimate good is chosen, found, or aimed at; it is not opined. The ultimate intuitions on which ethics rests are not opinions we hazard but preferences we feel; and it can be neither correct nor incorrect to feel them.[28]

To sum up, the relativistic doctrine maintains that *A is good*, apart from a particular reference, is not a constant but a variable, that the values of the variable presuppose a definite reference, and that the reference or point of view may be either personal or relative in some impersonal dimension. An acceptance of relativism leaves undetermined the question of what constitutes the range of variation of the variable *good*. In one view which we have suggested, the range of the basic propositional function of ethics, *A is good*, is the range of the function *A is approved by x*, where the values of *x* constitute the class of persons capable of the approving attitude. Other forms of the relativistic doctrine will be later considered. For the present we leave the issue of the present section, unable to bring any valid argument to bear upon the alternative which remains between absolutism and relativism. We must look then to the further development of each system for some ground of rational choice. And the next question that we may properly turn to is, "Can *A is good* be (analytically) defined?"

[28] Santayana, *Winds of Doctrine* (1913) ch. 4 (The Philosophy of Mr. Bertrand Russell), pp. 143-144. This essay is perhaps the only piece of philosophical criticism which has caused another philosopher to change his views. Bertrand Russell, since its publication, has turned to ethical relativism. *Cf.* his *What I Believe* (1925) and a recent preface to *Mysticism and Logic* (New York, 1929).

B. The Definability of Goodness

Having rejected the theory of ethical nihilism (.1), we shall consider the problem of the definability of goodness upon the assumptions of absolutism (.2) and relativism (.3).

.20 Either *A is intrinsically good* is identical with some natural proposition (.21) or it is a proposition which is not identical with any natural proposition (.22).

By a natural proposition we mean any proposition which can be defined without reference to the concepts of pure ethics (*good, better, etc.*). The question before us is, then, whether the predicate *good* is unique or whether it is identical in meaning with some natural term or complex of terms, such as *actual, desired, willed,* or *pleasurable*, falling within the domain of positive science. Any ethical theory which attempts to define an ethical concept in such terms may be called naturalistic. Theories which maintain a fundamental distinction between the realm of values and the realm of natural objects we shall refer to as non-naturalistic, there being apparently no recognized positive appellation for such systems.

It should be noted that this question as to the meaning of *good* is not identical with the question of what things are good. In the present section we shall face only the question of whether *good* has a natural meaning or not. And if a positive answer to this question is found to be tenable we shall proceed, in the following section, to investigate what this natural meaning may be. On the assumption that *good* has no natural meaning the attempt to define *good* must be useless. For *good* will not be reducible to any non-value term, and we have already seen that every value term may be defined in terms of *good*. To avoid a vicious circle we should then have to accept *good* as a concept known by acquaintance (intuition) rather than by description or definition.[29]

.21 *A is intrinsically good* is identical with some natural proposition.

Naturalism in ethics has been more commonly combined with relativism (.31 *infra*), than with absolutism, but examples of naturalistic absolutism are to be found. Professor Perry's definition of *good* as "object of positive interest"[30] is clearly both naturalistic and absolutistic, naturalistic because these terms do not presuppose the existence of non-natural values but are explicable purely in terms of psychology or biology, and absolutistic because the statement that such and such a thing is intrinsically good is simply true or simply false, regardless of any variant reference or point of view. Bertrand Russell has maintained a theory of this type,[31] and proponents of hedonism have often put their theories in these terms although such a formulation is not presupposed by hedonism.

There is obviously no formal inconsistency in the proposition under present consideration, but it has been argued by Moore that the naturalistic hypothesis (whether

[29] Or, to be strictly accurate, as a logical construct of some such concept, since it is possible that badness or betterness is psychologically primary.

[30] Perry, *General Theory of Value* (1926).

[31] *Philosophy* (1927) ch. 22.

absolutistic or relativistic) involves consequences which are manifestly impossible and absurd, and this argument we must consider in some detail. Moore, upholding the view that *good* is a simple indefinable known immediately in intuition, attacks the "naturalistic fallacy" in the following terms:

> The hypothesis that disagreement about the meaning of good is disagreement with regard to the correct analysis of a given whole, may be most plainly seen to be incorrect by consideration of the fact that, whatever definition be offered, it may be always asked, with significance, of the complex so defined, whether it is itself good. To take, for instance, one of the more plausible, because one of the more complicated, of such proposed definitions, it may easily be thought, at first sight, that to be good may mean to be that which we desire to desire. Thus if we apply this definition to a particular instance and say "When we think that A is good, we are thinking that A is one of the things which we desire to desire," our proposition may seem quite plausible. But, if we carry the investigation further, and ask ourselves "Is it good to desire to desire A?" it is apparent, on a little reflection, that this question is itself as intelligible, as the original question "Is A good?"—that we are, in fact, now asking for exactly the same information about the desire to desire A, for which we formerly asked with regard to A itself. But it is also apparent that the meaning of this second question cannot be correctly analysed into "Is the desire to desire A one of the things we desire to desire?": we have not before our

minds anything so complicated as the question "Do we desire to desire to desire to desire A?"[32]

But obviously it is a simple *petitio principii* to offer as a reason for the contention that good is indefinable the proposition that "whatever definition be offered it may be always asked, with significance, of the complex so defined, whether it is good." For this is merely another way of stating that good cannot be defined, and Moore has shown no reason why an adequate definition of *good* is impossible, why, that is, *good* should be simple and unanalyzable. If *good* can be defined (in natural terms), then to ask whether the *definiens* of such a definition is good is simply to question the truth of a tautology. If *good* means "ministering to pleasure" then to ask whether what ministers to pleasure is good is not a significant question.

Moore, then, has shown no reason why, on *a priori* grounds, every definition of *good* must be inadequate, since he has not shown that it will always be significant to ask whether the complex of such a definition is good. He can prove his point, only by showing that every possible analysis of *good* is incorrect, and this he has not attempted to do.

But Moore has not even shown that the one definition he considers is incorrect. He says simply that when we ask whether it is good to desire to desire A "we have not before our minds anything so complicated as the question, 'Do we desire to desire to desire to desire A?'" But if we always thought in terms of the defining complex what sense could there be in defining terms? For we should

[32] Moore, *Principia Ethica*, pp. 15-16.

never think in terms of the defined word, but always substitute the *definiens (ad infinitum?)*. When we think about horses, we have not before our minds anything so complicated as the list of biological characters by which the horse is defined, but that does not show the biological analysis to be incorrect. When the *Principia Mathematica* uses the sign of equivalence, ≡, to mean *either not the left-hand term or the right-hand term, and either the right-hand term or not the left-hand term*, the analysis (assuming it to be real rather than symbolic) is not shown to be false by the fact that when we ask whether A is equivalent to B we have not before our minds anything so complicated as the question, "Is it the case that either not-A or B, and that either not-B or A?" It is just to save our minds this labor that we use definitions, and it may be the case that *good* is convenient mental short-hand for some complex of natural terms.

It is our contention then, that no persuasive reason has been produced to show that every attempt to define *good* analytically must be doomed to failure. We can only examine in detail the types of natural definition that can be advanced and endeavor to consider in each case whether the suggested *definiens* really means what *good* means.

.22 *A is intrinsically good* is a proposition which is not identical with any natural proposition. On the assumption of absolutism (.2) this proposition is the contradictory of the preceding, so that one and only one of the two hypotheses can be true. This view of the unique character of the value predicate has been stated with particular force and clarity in G. E. Moore's *Principia Ethica.*

According to this view, the quality *good* is a simple predicate, like *yellow*, in which no component parts can be distinguished. One recognizes goodness in an object as one recognizes yellowness, without being able to analyze the essential property in virtue of which some things are yellow or good. But although we cannot by analysis define *good*, we can define *the good, i.e. that which is good*, and this is the real task of ethics. We may find that pleasure and wisdom and love are the only things which are good, just as we find that things which have a certain wave-length of light are the only things which are yellow, and we should then be able to define the good as *that which is either pleasure or wisdom or love.* It is a consequence of Moore's view that every proposition of the form, *The good is such and such,* is synthetic in form.

The only proof of this assumption that has been attempted is that given by Moore in the form of a *reductio ad absurdum* of its contradictory. This we have seen[33] to be invalid, but the question of whether this hypothesis is true is, of course, distinct from the question of whether it can be proved.

On the other hand, no strict disproof of this view is known, and our criticism must be restricted to the philosophical foundations of the view and to the ethical conclusions in which it culminates.

The position in question involves a fundamental dualism between the realm of actual or possible existences and the realm of values. It asserts not merely that *A is* and *A ought to be* are distinct propositions, but that *B is* (e.g. *polygamy is the will of Allah*) is always distinct from *A*

[33] See pp. 162-164, *supra.*

ought to be. It refuses to admit that purpose, will, desire, or any other psychological, social, physical, or metaphysical entity is sufficient to explain the notion of ultimate value. All these things, according to this theory, may themselves be valued, and our ultimate standard of valuation is of a radically different nature. But value cannot be wholly removed from contact with existence, since only natural objects can have value. We must find value in the natural world, as we find logic in the natural world, without making either of these things natural entities. The problem then resolves itself into this question: "Is there some quality which we observe in the world of nature which cannot be explained in terms of psychology or any other positive science and which is adequate to furnish the basis of what we can recognize as ethics?" Moore, answering this question in the affirmative, asserts: "Every one does in fact understand the question, 'Is this good?' When he thinks of it, his state of mind is different from what it would be, were he asked 'Is this pleasant, or desired, or approved?' It has a distinct meaning for him, even though he may not recognize in what respect it is distinct. Whenever he thinks of 'intrinsic value,' or 'intrinsic worth,' or says that a thing ought to exist, he has before his mind the unique object—the unique property of things—which I mean by good. Everybody is constantly aware of this notion, although he may never become aware at all that it is different from other notions of which he is also aware." [34]

In order to controvert this position we are required to show that what people really think of in the circumstances

[34] Moore, *Principia Ethica*, pp. 16-17.

indicated is not something distinct from such notions as pleasure and desire. We come down to a problem of introspection, upon the solution of which the empirical confirmation of either alternative hypothesis as to the meaning of good rests. And as we have seen no way of settling this question *a priori*, we can only proceed to the various attempted psychological definitions of this element in our judgments and ask whether any of them adequately represents the predicate that must be the basis of ethics. Needless to say, this is so difficult a question that we shall not be justified in attaching a great degree of certainty to any answer we may reach. If we find no complex of natural factors which appears adequate to explain value, then our acceptance of the unique predicate view can base its finality only upon the ultimacy of our ignorance. On the other hand, if we succeed in formulating some such definition which provides an accurate translation for all the value judgments we have examined, we can accept it as final only on the assumption that these cases are representative of the whole field of ethics. A color-blind individual might define color to his own satisfaction in terms of lightness and darkness or in terms of physical wave-lengths, and he might find that such a definition enabled him to make roughly the same color judgments as his neighbors, but it would be rash of him to conclude that there was no further quality, to him unnatural and inexplicable, which was a real factor in his neighbors' perceptions and judgments. So it may be the case that there are value-blind individuals who are able to reduce ethics to terms of desire and purpose because they are unable to see the true unique value quality.

The dualism of nature and value which Moore's position involves is opposed to any thorough-going monism as well as to certain forms of pluralism. This may be either a recommendation or a condemnation of the hypothesis. We shall not here attempt to decide which (if any) of these philosophical doctrines is correct. But there is one argument casually introduced by Moore which is of peculiar importance in this controversy and which has special bearing upon our immediate problem. Upon the apparently truistic argument that complex entities must be composed of simple entities[35] rests the plausibility of the view that *good* is such an ultimate simple. There is no logical necessity for this assumption. It may be the case that complex entities are merely groups of other complex entities, and that no entity (except, perhaps, such as are purely formal) is ultimately simple, though any entity may be simple for a given purpose or point of view or in a given system.[36] Entities might then be considered like proper fractions, every such fraction consisting, in a sense, of the sum of its halves, each of which is still complex and subject to further analysis, which can never be brought to an end in any simple entity. If such a view is accepted, the claims of ultimate indefinability for the value predicate cannot be credited.

To conclude, we have seen that it is impossible to prove or disprove on *a priori* grounds the view that *A is intrinsically good* is not identical with any natural proposition.

[35] *Cf.* Wittgenstein, *Tractatus Logico-Philosophicus* (1922) §§ 2.02 *et seq.*, 3.25.

[36] Thus the *sphere* is a simple in the Huntingtonian system of euclidean geometry, a complex to be analyzed in other systems, hydrogen a simple for chemistry, a complex for physics, the economic man a simple for classical economics, a complex for sociology.

We can base our choice between this theory and its alternative only upon the empirical confirmation or refutation of the attempted natural definitions of goodness, which we shall consider in the third section of this outline. Furthermore, we have seen that such a test will not settle our problem beyond the possibility of "reasonable doubt."

.30 Either *A is intrinsically good* is identical with some natural propositional function (.31) or it is a propositional function which is not identical with any such propositional function (.32).

This is the application of the alternative just discussed to the assumption of relativism (.3) as the previous treatment was to the assumption of absolutism (.2). By a natural propositional function is meant a propositional function all of whose values are natural propositions, in the sense already explained.

The question is then whether, if the relativistic hypothesis is true, the particular relative propositions which form the subject matter of ethics are definable wholly in terms of the positive sciences or not.

.31 *A is intrinsically good* is identical with some natural propositional function.

This position, which we have agreed to call naturalistic relativism (or relativistic naturalism), has been maintained, perhaps not quite consistently, by the Greek Sophists, and in modern times by Santayana. It is, in its most plausible form, the view that ultimate ethical standards are things chosen, rather than truths discovered. Beyond such choice, on this hypothesis, there is no ethical appeal.

And since this choice is notoriously variable among different individuals, our ethics is based upon relativism. If *A is intrinsically good* means some such thing as *I approve of A*, then it is neither true nor false *in vacuo*, but becomes true in some cases and false in others as the *I* is given a definite reference.

The truth of this hypothesis presupposes an affirmative answer to the following question, "Is it possible that a given event may be truly judged to be good and to be not-good?" There is clearly no logical difficulty in an affirmative answer to this question (or in a negative answer) so that we must look to actual ethical experience to decide the problem. This task can only proceed through the testing of various more definite forms of definition of the ethical predicate, in the light of our ethical experience. Our method of solving this problem must follow the course outlined in the former half of this second section (*cf.* .21 and .22).

As the problem of relativism has been discussed in the first section (.3) and the problem of naturalism in the former part of the present section (.21 and .22), it will be unnecessary to go any further, for the present, into the arguments for and against the hypothesis of naturalistic relativism.

.32 *A is intrinsically good* is a propositional function which is not identical with any natural propositional function. This theory would hold that while the ascription of intrinsic goodness to a given event is a variable, the variable in question is not composed of natural terms. That is to say, although in different references or connotations the value judgment means different things, what is common to these judgments is not something which can be expressed in terms of psychology or any other positive science. There are no conceivable arguments for such a position, since the arguments for relativism are all based upon the ground that *good* is definable in natural terms, while the arguments for the indefinability of *good* are all based upon the belief that goodness is a constant quality which natural terms are unable to approximate. What sort of indefinable constant element could produce relative value judgments through dependence upon a variable is something of a mystery. We may conclude that this fourth alternative theory of the nature of the value predicate is, on the whole, an improbable one. Such a conclusion is of course, like every similar conclusion based upon the failure of affirmative argument, subject to error. If, for instance, we should find that relativism must be true and that no known interpretation of the value predicate in natural terms is adequate, we should be tempted to reconsider our conclusion in the present case. If, however, upon the assumption of relativism we can formulate a satisfactory definition of the value predicate in natural terms, the present theory may be rejected without question.

C. The Definition of Goodness

Inasmuch as the hypotheses of non-naturalistic absolutism (.22) and non-naturalistic relativism (.32) assert the impossibility of analytically defining intrinsic goodness in natural terms, we shall consider in the present section the possible definitions compatible with naturalistic absolutism (.21) and naturalistic relativism (.31). This inquiry is, of course, insignificant under the rejected theory of nihilism (.1).

.210 *A is intrinsically good* is a proposition identical with *A contains a surplus of pleasure* (.211), or with *A is real* (.212), or with *A is the object of a rational will* (.213), or with *A is the object of positive interest* (.214), or with some other natural proposition (.215).

On the assumption of naturalistic absolutism we are called upon to decide whether any of the above-mentioned possibilities can satisfy the needed analysis of the proposition *A is intrinsically good.* The question whether any of these natural propositions is identical with the ethical judgment must be carefully distinguished from the question of whether these propositions afford accurate criteria for the applicability of that judgment. It may, for instance, be the case that everything which contains a surplus of pleasure is intrinsically good and that everything which is intrinsically good contains a surplus of pleasure. And yet, if this proposition can be significantly debated, it must be the case that the two predicates *is intrinsically good* and *contains a surplus of pleasure* really mean different things, as *color* and *wave-length* mean different things. Otherwise the question whether the two predicates apply to the same things (*i.e.* define the same class) would not be meaningful, since there would be not two predicates but one, which was merely stated in different terms. Thus the proposition, "*A is intrinsically good* is identical with a given natural proposition" can be shown to be false either by a demonstration that the two propositions do not have the same truth value in particular cases or by a demonstration that, whether or not they always have the same truth value, their meanings are distinct.

.211 *A is intrinsically good* is a proposition identical with *A contains a surplus of pleasure.*

As we have already pointed out, this definition is distinct from the assertion that the class of intrinsically good things is also the class of things that are on the whole pleasurable. The latter assertion we shall consider in the next section. The present definition has, however, frequently been asserted by hedonists, and its implications have been well pointed out by G. E. Moore.[37] It requires us to maintain that the question "Do intrinsically good things contain a surplus of pleasure?" is meaningless, being the challenge of a mere tautology, namely, "Intrinsically good things are intrinsically good." Only the language in which the concept is expressed has been changed, since the two predicates are held to be identical.

It appears to us that this position cannot be maintained, when once this implication is recognized. The question of whether good things are pleasurable is a real question, as nearly all hedonists and all anti-hedonists have agreed. Its answer is not a mere tautology or a self-contradiction. *A is intrinsically good,* then, is not identical in *meaning* with *A contains a surplus of pleasure.*

.212 *A is intrinsically good* is a proposition identical with *A is real.*

This proposition has apparently been the underlying

[37] Moore, *Principia Ethica,* pp. 17-21, *et passim.*

assumption of a good deal of metaphysical ethics, which attempts to discover what is good by inquiring into the ultimate nature of reality.[38] We need not trace the various ethical systems which have been based upon this proposition, with the aid of varying theories as to the nature of reality. For it is obvious that the real is not always good and that, at least when *real* is identified with *actual*, the good is not always real. This is a belief which we shall further consider under the next section (.2202). Its truth, and the truth of the more modest assumption that *real* and *good* do not mean the same thing (*i.e.* that it is not nonsensical to ask whether real things are good), are sufficiently obvious to permit an outright rejection of the theory shown to be incompatible with these propositions.[39]

.213 *A is intrinsically good* is a proposition identical with *A is the object of a rational will.*

Under the class of ethical theories defined by this assumption are grouped doctrines which found goodness upon the will of a Supreme Rational Being, or upon a transcendental will and reason, or upon the inferred will of an ideally rational man. The theory is, of course, not inconsistent with either of the two foregoing theories, and has commonly been combined with one or the other of them. Of all the attempted definitions of goodness on the basis of absolutism it appears to us to be the most adequate. The question of what is ultimately good does not present itself as far distant from the question of what we would will or approve if we were omniscient. (Omnis-

[38] See Chapter One, § 5 and Chapter Two, § 2 (H), *supra.*

[39] *Cf.* Moore, *Principia Ethica,* ch. 2.

cience, of course, must be restricted to positive domains if we are to avoid a vicious circle in our definition.)

But it appears quite possible that two beings supremely rational (in this positive sense) should will different and incompatible things. As far as we can judge, equally rational individuals do have different ethical standards, and an increase in rationality does not appear to be constantly correlated with an approximation to uniformity in ultimate ideals. We find, in fact, that up to a certain point increased intelligence generally provokes variability in ethical judgment. This would tend to show that, since the rational will may have no single coherent body of ethical valuations, it cannot be used as a basis for the absolutistic definition of intrinsic goodness. Of course, this argument, being based upon very inadequate observation, is not conclusive. But it does seem as if our judgments of value would retain their significance even if the rational will did not direct itself towards a constant ideal. Thus, the question, "Is the intrinsically good identical with the object of the rational will?" is significant, and the two defining predicates which are compared by the suggested common applicability must be distinct.

So our conclusion is again, although less confidently proposed than in previous instances, that goodness in an absolute sense cannot be analyzed into the complex of natural factors suggested above.

.214 *A is intrinsically good* is identical with *A is the object of positive interest.*

The difficulties encountered by the previous attempt to define goodness in terms of a perfectly rational will are avoided by the present proposal, which claims that the meaning of the value predicate may be analyzed into a preponderance of positive interests towards the object of the judgment. Interest, in this sense, must refer to a psychological entity, such as that defined by Professor Perry,[40] without further ethical implications. It is unnecessary to attempt a critical examination of the *balancing* by which the resultant direction of the sum of interests towards a particular end is determined. We attempt a closely analogous inquiry in our treatment of hedonism (.2201), and it seems probable that some meaning can be found for the present complex. Our objections to the suggested analysis of goodness are not based upon the difficulty, impossibility, or insignificance of a "resultant" and all-inclusive interest towards anything. Nor do we base such an objection upon the ground that some intrinsically good things are not the object of such an interest and that some things which are the object of such an interest are not intrinsically good. This we should be prepared to maintain, if necessary, by pointing to the disdain which is commonly attached to the noblest ideals and to the disappointment and revulsion which are attached to the attainment of certain widely sought ends. Such arguments, however, would prove little, for our application of the word *noble* and our disapproval of disappointment and revulsion would be properly open to attack. The most conclusive objection which can be brought against the present theory is simply that the two identified propositions do not really mean the same thing, however often they may possess a common truth value in their application to par-

[40] Perry, *General Theory of Value* (1926), ch. 7.

ticular objects. We do not believe that what is intrinsically good is identical with what is, on the whole, the object of positive interest. And while we should be prepared to admit, upon evidence, that this belief was erroneous, we should not be prepared to admit that it was self-contradictory, that we had been in fact simply asserting that what is intrinsically good is not identical with what is intrinsically good. That the question "Is the intrinsically good the object of positive interest?" is the challenging of a tautology (or a question of philology), that any answer to it must be either tautological or self-contradictory, that no ethical dispute or discourse is possible upon this question, all this appears to be highly improbable, and the position which leads to these implications must be abandoned.

.215 *A is intrinsically good* is identical with some other natural proposition.

Although it is difficult to attain much certainty in the criticism of a position as essentially vague as the present, ethics, like every other science, must take into account possibilities of this sort and utilize in their analysis the best instruments at its disposal.

We have seen that the possibility of an analytical definition of goodness in an absolutistic system depends upon the existence of some natural predicate the applicability of which to the class of intrinsically good things cannot be significantly questioned. That is to say, if goodness means simply possession of a certain natural property, it will not be significant to ask whether that which is intrinsically good possesses this property, or to answer this question, or to adduce any ethical arguments in support of an affirmative answer. We have further seen that in all the suggested definitions of goodness these implications lead to more or less obvious absurdity. It is our final conclusion that any other analytical definition of goodness in an absolute system will be subject to refutation in a similar manner, and thus that the proposition under present consideration is false.

We thus conclude that Moore is correct in his insistence that every natural entity can be significantly valued, *i.e.* that the value judgment passed upon a natural entity is never self-contradictory or tautological. But a natural entity could not significantly be valued in terms of itself. It follows that either (1) goodness, the standard of valuation, is not itself a natural entity, or (2) there is more than one standard of goodness, so that each standard is itself capable of significant evaluation in terms of another standard.

It is by overlooking the latter possibility that Moore has reached the conclusion that all ethical naturalism is fallacious. Our own conclusion is that the only possible form of naturalism in ethics is relativistic naturalism, and this conclusion we recognize to be not a logical necessity or an immediate intuition but rather a precarious inference from the inadequacy of all the forms of naturalistic absolutism thus far considered and the apparent applicability of a general principle found in the analysis of these cases to all further forms of naturalistic absolutism.

.310 *A is intrinsically good* is a propositional function identical either with *x desires A* (.311), or with *A contains a pleasure surplus experienced by x* (.312), or with *x approves of A* (.313), or with some other natural propositional function (.314).

.311 *A is intrinsically good* is identical with *x desires A*.
According to this theory, when any person (and we might without straining our theory admit artificial persons, such as society, within the range of the variable x) passes a judgment of goodness upon an entity, the meaning of this judgment is simply that the person in question desires the entity. This is a doctrine which Bertrand Russell seems to accept in his essay, *What I Believe.* It is perhaps the most obvious interpretation of relativistic naturalism, but it cannot be maintained if the term *desire* is taken in its normal connotation.

Desire implies a lack of the thing desired. But it is quite clear that we find value in things we do not lack. If our valuations of ourselves, of our possessions, of past events, and of present enjoyments, is not to be ruled out of the domain of ethics, we must reject this identification of the value judgment with the assertion of a desire.

.312 *A is intrinsically good* is identical with *A contains a pleasure surplus experienced by x.* The substance of this doctrine is that when any one asserts that a given entity is intrinsically good, the meaning of his assertion is that the entity is, in his experience, pleasurable. In order to demonstrate the truth of this doctrine, it is necessary to show that we ascribe goodness only to entities which afford us pleasure, and that this possession of pleasure is the very essence of our judgment and not merely a universal concomitant of it. It does not appear that either of these contentions is sound. We are all ready enough to admit that experiences which are not pleasant to us may nevertheless be good when occurring in the life of another, and most people believe that experiences which are not pleasant to any one may be intrinsically good. It may of course be true that all such beliefs are erroneous, but there is clearly no internal inconsistency in such a belief. We cannot then maintain the doctrine that what is *meant* by the ascription of intrinsic goodness is the containing of a surplus of pleasure for a given person.

.313 *A is intrinsically good* is identical with *x approves of A.*

It will readily be admitted that when we believe something to be intrinsically valuable we have a certain feeling or attitude towards it which may be called approval or positive interest. It is the argument of the doctrine here considered that the existence of this attitude is all that our intrinsic value judgments significantly assert. Thus the fundamental relativism of values maintained by our theory will lie in the fact that different individuals may and do approve of different things.

Approval, in this sense of the term, must be an attitude rather than a judgment, for a vicious circle fallacy, as we have already suggested, would arise were we to define goodness in terms of a personal judgment that such-and-such a thing is good. As an attitude, approval is definable in natural terms. But the further psychological analysis of this attitude need not here concern us. There is reason to believe that the attitude of approval is itself as clearly discernible as any of the psychological elements into which it might be resolved.

The doctrine in question avoids certain objections which have been raised against the two previously considered formulations of naturalistic relativism. It admits the equal applicability of value judgments to the things we enjoy as compared with the things we lack and desire. It does not equate value with the capacity of enjoyment, and thus admits the significance of all assertions of approval regardless of the logical reasons or psychological grounds upon which such approval rests.

Two further objections to the theory remain to be considered. In the first place, it will be alleged, no doubt, that this theory is inconsistent with the obvious fact that we make mistakes in judgments of value. In the second place, it may be maintained that even if we always have the attitude of approval towards the things we believe good, we actually mean to assert something other than the existence of this personal attitude when we pass a value judgment.

The doctrine that the value judgment is an assertion of personal approval is not inconsistent with the existence of erroneous judgments. Errors of utilitarian valuation are, of course, irrelevant to our present treatment, and are as easily accounted for on the basis of the present doctrine as on any other theory. But it may be admitted that we make errors in intrinsic valuations without prejudice to our present theory. There is no doubt that it is possible to lie about one's state of mind, even though (or because) it is frequently impossible for any one else to disprove the assertion. Our value judgment, like every judgment, refers to something, and this reference may be inaccurate. If so much be admitted, one cannot deny the possibility of honest as well as dishonest error in the belief that a certain entity is approved. We are not omniscient in our introspections. Consequently it may be the case that we suppose an attitude of approval to exist where none in fact exists, or *vice versa.* And even more frequently we must be mistaken as to the nature of the entity towards which this approval is directed. We may often announce the existence of an approving attitude with some assurance, but when we try to break the environment into pieces and say, with any definiteness, "It is this that I value," we are subject to every weakness of the human judgment. Thus, even though the reference of our moral beliefs is not objective in the sense of being commonly observable, it is objective in the sense that it has an object. The possibility of error in moral valuations is accounted for, and the essence of moral education is found in the Socratic imperative, "Know thyself."[41]

The second objection to this theory of value, namely that we mean to assert more than a personal attitude when we assert a value judgment, presents greater difficulties. They are not, however, conclusive, for we may and frequently do believe that our judgments have a more absolute reference than they can possibly have. We may believe, for instance, that a judgment of motion has an objective and absolute reference, when, as a matter of fact, the only significant reference it can have is to an arbitrary though

[41] And *cf.* Wittgenstein, *Tractatus Logico-Philosophicus* (1922) § 5.63: "I am my world. (The microcosm.)"

generally accepted set of space-time co-ordinates. So, if there is actually no absolute standard by which our value judgments can theoretically be tested, the only meaning that can be attached to them is a relative one. Whether or not there can be this absolute reference of our value judgments is a question we have been unable to answer. Our only conclusion for the present can be that if relativism be a true doctrine in ethics, the identification of valuation with approval raises no further special difficulties and appears, on the whole, to be sound.

.314 *A is intrinsically good* is identical with some propositional function other than any of the preceding.

Few valid arguments can be raised for or against a proposition as vague as this. Alternatives of this sort are a logical necessity in the exhaustive treatment of scientific theories which are not analytically contradictory. The possibility in question would be easily ignored in any historical treatment of conflicting theories, and it is in fact one of the greatest advantages of logical method that it fails to hide the possibility of alternative theories which have not been adequately formulated. We are thus reminded of the tentative and probable (or improbable) character of the conclusions we have reached.

But while we have not been able to disprove the present proposition through any rigorous proof of one of its alternatives, the definition of goodness in terms of approval or positive interest seems to accord very generally with the moral data to which a theory of relativistic naturalism points. To this extent the present doctrine, which equally assumes the truth of relativistic naturalism, must be regarded as improbable.

D. The Criteria of Goodness

In the preceding section we were concerned with the definition of intrinsic goodness under the ethical doctrine of naturalism, absolutistic (.21) and relativistic (.31). We found that, while absolutistic naturalism was incapable of support, the relativistic version of naturalism assumed a plausible form in the doctrine that judgments of intrinsic goodness are assertions of personal approval. Under this doctrine the determination of additional criteria of value may be left to positive psychological and anthropological science, which is capable of discovering without further ethical assumptions what those objects are to which the approving attitude is assumed by various individuals. We shall therefore restrict our inquiry under the present section to those criteria of goodness which are compatible with the assumption of non-naturalism,[42] which we have seen to be a plausible theory only in its absolutistic form (.22). The prefix .220 in the following outline thus indicates the assumption of absolutism (.2) and of non-naturalism (.22) and the immateriality of the third of our basic ethical questions ("What is the definition of intrinsic goodness?").

.2200 *A is intrinsically good* is equivalent (in truth value) to *A contains a surplus of pleasure* (.2201), or it

[42] Strictly speaking, none of the following theories is inconsistent with the doctrine of naturalism, but we have seen that naturalism is empirically untenable in its absolutistic form, and all the hypotheses considered below do assume absolutism.

is equivalent to *A is real* (.2202), or it is equivalent to *The universal rule under which A falls is self-consistent* (.2203), or it is equivalent to some other proposition (.2204), or it is equivalent to no other proposition (.2205).

.2201 *A is intrinsically good* is equivalent to *A contains a surplus of pleasure.*

According to this doctrine, which we may call ethical hedonism,[43] the only things which are intrinsically good are things (experiences) which contain a pleasure surplus, and all such things are intrinsically good. This doctrine is a definition of the good, since it asserts that a certain predicate defines the class of good things. It does not, as we have already explained, define *good.*

The defining proposition, *A contains a surplus of pleasure,* is to be understood as meaning simply that A is on the whole pleasurable or pleasant, although some of its parts may contain pleasure and others pain, when taken separately. It will be sufficiently clear, in our further discussion, if we refer to such entities as pleasurable or pleasant.

Since it is impossible to define pleasure in simpler terms and since everybody has an immediate or intuitive acquaintance with pleasure, it is useless to attempt any analytical definition of the concept. However, although pleasure is immediately known, the *word* "pleasure" has been used in various senses, and it is therefore necessary to explain in which of these senses the present doctrine

[43] We shall not here attempt to determine the extent to which traditional formulations of hedonism have coincided with this doctrine. We believe that this is at least a common basis upon which nearly all exponents of ethical hedonism have agreed.

uses the word. This can best be done by a process of exclusion. In the first place, the word is not restricted to the so-called "lower" pleasures, but includes all sorts of pleasure, such as the pleasures of aesthetic contemplation, self-discipline, altruism, and metaphysical argument. In the second place, *pleasure* does not mean the absence of desire or the absence of pain, as the absence of pleasure during sound sleep should show. In the third place, *pleasure* is not identical with the fulfillment of desire. We have all experienced unpremeditated, accidentally achieved pleasures, and on the other hand, things we seek frequently prove to be non-pleasurable.

Pain is to be understood as a negative correlative to *pleasure*, similar to it in including the "higher" pains as well as the lower. That is to say, it is a quality of entities which are less pleasant than an entity which contains neither positive pleasure nor pain (or which contain less *hedonic value* than such an entity—using this expression to refer to painfulness and pleasurefulness and considering the former as possessed of negative hedonic value).

This, perhaps, is all rather confusing. But one can only point to a simple idea, giving rough hints to secure that identification which analytical definitions provide for complex entities. The limitations of the word *pleasure* in this respect are severe. This word has, in our puritanical language, come to have a number of disagreeable connotations (as have such words as *lust*, *sensual*, *sensuous*, *decent*, *moral*, etc.). We have, in order to meet the current of thought that has flowed about the notion now so poorly described by the word *pleasure*, thought it best to retain and, if possible, to rehabilitate the term. Were we freed from the currents and criticisms of the past and careless of the philological transformations of the future we should prefer to use such words as *joy*, *gladness*, *suffering*, *agony*, *happiness* and *unhappiness* to describe the object of our discussion. It does not seem to us that hedonists have been rightly criticized for using the word *happiness* to designate the state of mind in which pleasure predominates. This is the common meaning of the term, which we continually invoke when we speak of happy childhood, happy New Year, etc., and it is rather the critics of hedonism who are to be rebuked for using this common word to denote a state of self-expression, self-realization, virtue, or whatever else is being proposed as man's highest good. Of course, *happiness* is a fine word, almost indispensable, in fact, for a successful ethical theory. One may sympathize with, even if he does not share, the concern which anti-hedonists have shown lest the word fall exclusive property, as the legacy of common speech would seem to direct, to the theory of hedonism.

Certain important inferences may be drawn from the fundamental hedonistic premise, and their elaboration will be useful in our examination of the consequences of this premise. In the first place, it is implied that *A is good* is equivalent to *A with its consequences contains a surplus of pleasure.*[44] In the second place, we can infer, on the basis of the hedonistic proposition and certain additional factual premises,[45] that *A is intrinsically bad* is equivalent to *A*

[44] *Cf.* pp. 131-132, *supra.*

[45] These factual assumptions may be found by substituting *contains a pleasure-surplus* for *is good* (ϕ) in the *definientes* of section 2, *supra,* and substituting *contains a pain-surplus* for *is bad,* etc., in the *definienda.*

contains a surplus of pain, that *A is intrinsically better than B* is equivalent to *A contains more pleasure-surplus or less pain-surplus than B*, and so on through the remaining concepts of ethics.

Hedonism, as its more able exponents have recognized, cannot be proved. The only evidence for its truth can be the obviousness of the value judgments to which it leads, although evidence for its disproof can be produced not only by comparison of its implications with immediate moral observation, but as well by a logical analysis which shows the theory to be self-contradictory or meaningless. In this respect it is similar to every other ethical theory. A number of people have thought, after reflecting upon their value judgments, that whenever anything is intrinsically good it is also pleasurable, and *vice versa*. That all people would arrive at a similar conclusion if the errors in their judgment and reasoning could be eliminated is a matter which cannot be conclusively demonstrated. Yet it is only with respect to the truth or falsity of this proposition that the doctrine of hedonism, as here defined, can properly be criticized.

Hedonism appears to be a doctrine consistent with the writer's value judgments. Although this fact does not prove the truth of the theory, it is a sufficient ground for belief, if all the objections to hedonism can be shown to be irrelevant or invalid. This, then, must be our task, and the objections we shall attempt to dispose of are: (1) that hedonism is inadequate, (2) that it is impractical, (3) that

---

The propositions of psychology thus derived appear to be obviously true, and they logically imply that, if the hedonistic premise is true, the other ethical propositions suggested above must be true.

it is wicked, (4) that it is meaningless, (5) that it is self-contradictory, and (6) that it is false.

(*1*) *The inadequacy of hedonism.* It is frequently argued that hedonism is a "mere abstraction," which does not give us any knowledge of the courses of conduct that are good.[46] This objection is quite pointless. Of course, hedonism is not a code of minute directions which can make a stupid and obedient man good. It is, however, a fundamental basis upon which the desirability of any action can be determined without bringing in any further purely ethical considerations. Whether a particular case of lying will result in more pain than pleasure is a problem which demands no knowledge of ethics and which can better be solved by the psychologist, the anthropologist, or the culprit's father than by the ethical philosopher. The philosopher has performed a task of extreme importance if he shows that the value of an action depends upon factors as simple and definite as pleasure and pain.

(*2*) *The impracticality of hedonism.* Opponents of hedonism have made a good deal of the so-called "hedonistic paradox," that we cannot attain pleasure by seeking it, that pleasure to be got must be forgot.[47] We may reply to this objection first that it is untrue, secondly that if it were true hedonism would not on that account be impractical, and thirdly that the whole question of the practicality of hedonism is quite irrelevant to the issue of its truth. In the first place, this notion that we never attain pleasure when we consciously try to do so has, despite its venerable

46 Bradley, *Ethical Studies* (2d ed., 1927), ch. 3 (Pleasure for Pleasure's Sake), pp. 100-110.

47 Bradley, *op. cit.*, pp. 85-86 *et passim*; Paulsen, *System of Ethics* (ed. and transl. by Thilly, 1899), p. 254.

pedigree, no basis in fact. To accept the challenge of this argument on its lowest terms, people who go out "for a good time" frequently have a good time. But when it is realized that the hedonic end is universal rather than individual, the "paradox" is even more obviously absurd. We do try to make other people happy, and we do succeed. In the second place, even if it were true that we must forget about pleasure in order to produce it, this is no more a denial of the ultimate and supreme value of pleasure than is the fact that in order to be well we must not think too much about health a refutation of the value of health. Hedonism is an answer to the question of what is good, not the question of what we ought to aim at. The latter question is answered by the hedonist like any other moral question. "So aim that as a result of your aim the greatest happiness will be produced. If you are morally strabismatic, as everyone is to a certain exent, then, by all means, don't aim at what you are to hit. Aim at perfect beauty, perfect love, or perfect truth, and whether or not these things are actually valuable, the target that you hit, happiness, will be of value."

Finally, if any of these arguments had a grain of sense and showed hedonism to be an impractical doctrine, they would be completely irrelevant in an examination of the truth of hedonism. It would be no more absurd to argue that, because irrational numbers give us a great deal of trouble in arithmetic and lead to many mistakes, there must be some way of representing them as rational fractions. And yet great philosophers have pinned their faith to this argument. The only proper inference that can be drawn from this argument is that in matters of morality, where scientific disinterestedness is an unattainable ideal, men fall prey to the stupidest fallacies.

The argument that hedonism is impractical is also directed against the so-called hedonic calculus of pleasures and pains. It is alleged, first, that such a calculus is too definite to be applicable, since "one man's meat is another man's poison,"[48] and, secondly, that it is not definite enough, since it can be stretched to justify any action.[49] The first allegation is clearly groundless, for what we compare by the hedonic calculus are not quantities of meat or poison, but pleasures and pains. The hedonist does not need to poison his neighbor with the meat that he himself enjoys. He may, however, attempt to give him equal enjoyment by presenting him with pastry. The same considerations hold when we consider the matter temporally. Certainly, what made me happy fifteen years ago need not make me happy today, but hedonism makes no such ridiculous assumption, and the attacks of anti-hedonists in this respect[50] are completely beside the point.

As for the second charge, it is no doubt true that different hedonists will disagree as to the value of a particular action, but certainly this is not a difficulty peculiar to hedonism. As long as people have different ideas about the natural results of events, they may agree on the most minute ethical code without agreeing in all their deductions from it. No doubt the generality of the hedonic calculus permits a degree of half-hypocritical self-deception in our moral choices, but the possibilities of the very minute church casuistry in this direction have sufficed to make

48 Albee, *History of English Utilitarianism* (1902) p. 274.

49 Bradley, *Ethical Studies,* pp. 101 *et seq.*

50 Dewey, *Human Nature and Conduct* (1922) pp. 202 *et seq.*

the whole subject of casuistry unpopular. Hedonism, then, is not by any means exceptional in being susceptible to divergent practical interpretation and application, and even if it were it would not on that account cease to be true.

(3) *The wickedness of hedonism.* Many opponents of hedonism have attempted to refute it by showing how wicked it is, but after the previous considerations it is unnecessary to consider such arguments in detail. It is enough to state these objections to show their absurdity and irrelevance. Hedonism with its calculus of pleasures and pains makes one a law to himself, since anybody can interpret the system with as much authority as any one else.[51] It leads to egoism, since the only pleasure we really know is our own.[52] It is irreligious. It is a pig's philosophy.

If the relevance of any such arguments to the truth of hedonism could be shown, it would be a comparatively easy matter to refute them. But it is more important to elucidate the common error upon which all these criticisms rest: the elementary failure to distinguish between truth and value. The belief that no distinction need be made between the truth and the goodness of doctrines is always false and seldom good. It is justified by philosophers on the ground that it is always good to believe what is true, and by pragmatists on the ground that it is always true to believe what is good.[53] The former faith is a hasty generalization, contradicted by the deepest experience, but

[51] Bradley, *Ethical Studies*, p. 109.

[52] Bradley, *op. cit.*, p. 94. But *cf.* note (added in second edition).

[53] We intend no disparagement of pragmatism by this easy antithesis. But philosophy, in its original signification, as the love of wisdom, is essentially opposed to pragmatism, which values wisdom or truth only in so far as it affects practice.

withal a faith which is not philosophically criticized, because only those who share it become philosophers. The latter belief is either the product of a similar intellectual optimism or a resolve to use the word *truth* in a new sense. When the distinction between truth and goodness is appreciated, the arguments on the charge of immorality which are directed against unorthodox ethical *theories* are seen to be not only circular (since the falsity of the theory is usually assumed to demonstrate its wickedness), but perfectly irrelevant to the question of whether the theory is true.

(4) *The self-contradictory character of hedonism.* Hedonism is declared by many critics to be a self-contradictory hypothesis. "A state of continuous pleasure," it is argued, "would not be pleasurable." This is of course ridiculous. A state which was not pleasurable could not be one of continuous pleasure. But the implication that perfect happiness is incapable of attainment, since every known pleasure can conceivably be increased, must be taken into account.

Hedonism does not offer us a goal which can be completely reached. It does not presume to establish a "highest" good. But it does serve as a guide for the ethical comparison or valuation of any entities. The argument that, since every quantity of pleasure is at an infinite distance from perfect pleasure, there can be no quantitative difference between finite pleasures and no possibility of moral choice or comparison,[54] is based upon a false notion of infinity and would, if true, show that no finite number

[54] Bradley, *Ethical Studies*, pp. 97-98; Green, *Prolegomena to Ethics* (1883) § 359.

can be greater or smaller than any other. The degree of value of an entity is no more dependent upon its distance from an infinite ideal than is the magnitude of a number dependent upon its distance from a greatest number.

Thus the only significant objection to hedonism, on this count, is that it sets forth an ideal which can never be completely attained.[55] We may admit the truth of this criticism without agreeing that it constitutes a valid objection to the hedonistic theory. Ideals are of two sorts, those which are unattainable and therefore indestructible, and those which are attainable and self-destroying. One may "go west" all his life, without being nearer to the end of his journey than when he started. Yet he has made progress; and his ideal has not failed him. Of this type is the ideal of happiness. There is another sort of ideal, represented by the categorical imperative, "Go north." Such an ideal is capable of complete realization, but at the journey's end one finds himself stranded at the Pole without a working compass. So the reaching of any ultimate goal must destroy the significance of morality. In Heaven there is no compassion because there is no suffering, there is no courage because there is no danger, there is no virtue because there is no temptation.

The dilemma is a real one, fraught with all the tragedy of man's existence, and whether or not hedonism chooses wisely in pursuing an unattainable and never-failing ideal, a direction rather than an end, it has at least made a logically defensible choice.

(5) *The meaninglessness of hedonism.* The hedonistic

[55] Bradley, *op. cit., passim. Cf.* Bentham, "The Influence of Time and Place in Matters of Legislation," ch. 5, § 2, 1 *Works* 171, 193-194.

claim that every event or set of events which can be described as intrinsically good can also be described as containing a pleasure-surplus rests upon the assumption that in all such events different pleasures and pains are comparable or commensurable. For if there were, in an event or in the artificial sets of events upon which our more complex ethical judgments rest,[56] incommensurable elements of pleasure or pain, we could not ascribe to the totality a *pleasure-surplus*. But we know, the critic of hedonism contends, that pleasures and pains are not subject to quantitative comparison. The concept of a *pleasure-surplus* is therefore as meaningless as the concept of a *round square* or a *green thought*—or, at least, if it has a meaning, that meaning must be restricted to limited domains of commensurable experiences and thus cannot be co-extensive with the domain of ethics.

The hedonist does not answer this argument when he retorts that the problem of the commensurability of values presents far graver difficulties in every other ethical theory, that freedom, personality, reality, self-expressiveness, and interest are not more easily weighed and measured than pleasure, that only the Cimmerian unintelligibility of most other ethical theories has made commensurability seem a peculiar difficulty of hedonism. The challenge remains to be answered. The pervasiveness of the ethical problems it raises should only make us the more scrupulous in its examination.

Let us note, in the first place, that as a presentation of a psychological difficulty in our ethical calculations, the objection is true, important, and irrelevant to the truth

[56] See § 3, *supra*.

of hedonism. It is the business of ethics to explain rather than to deny the difficulty of coming to correct ethical judgments. We are here concerned only with the claim that quantitative comparison of pleasures and pains involves not merely a psychological difficulty but a necessary antinomy in the logical structure of hedonism. Perhaps if this contention can be refuted, the actual psychological uncertainty and difficulty of our hedonic comparisons will not so readily be exaggerated as is the fashion today.

Before considering the validity of this objection we may prepare the way by disposing of two common formulations of the problem which have raised just doubts as to the possibility of its solution. There is, in the first place, the view that our hedonistic calculations must strike a balance between pleasures and pains, discovering how much pleasure neutralizes or balances a given amount of pain.[57] To this the objection is raised that pleasures and pains are different things, and do not, in any strict sense, balance or neutralize each other. No doubt the language to which this exception is taken is metaphorical and inexact, but we cannot believe that the fact described is non-existent. All we do when we "balance" pleasures against pains is to consider an event or a group of events as a whole and pass upon this whole a positive judgment of pleasurableness, or compare it, in respect to the contained pleasure, with some other whole. The assumption underlying this procedure is *that the quantitative comparison of any two events or sets of events with respect to the contained pleasantness is al-*

[57] Laird, *Study in Moral Theory,* pp. 107-108.

ways theoretically possible. It is this assumption alone which can properly be criticized in this connection.

In the second place, the nature of the quantitative comparison which hedonism requires has been somewhat obscured by the habit of referring such quantities to the dimensions of intensity, duration, and extent (*i.e.* number of persons affected, clearly commensurable with duration). When Bentham put forward these dimensions of pleasure (along with certain others of purely instrumental significance), he was concerned only to point out the characteristics (or "factors") which demand consideration when we compare and evaluate quantities of pleasure.[58] He had no illusions as to the possibility of multiplying intensity by duration. But his critics have, almost with one accord, fallen squarely into the error which they lay to hedonism. They have assumed that areas are quantitatively determined by a multiplication of length and breadth, and that pleasure-quantities can be determined only in a similar fashion, by multiplying intensity and duration or extent. But since this is manifestly impossible, hedonism must be meaningless.[59]

This is of course absurd. It is no more possible to multiply length and breadth than it is to multiply intensity and duration of pleasure, or apples and oranges. Multiplication is an operation which applies only to numbers. Areas, lines, and all other quantities are neither numbers nor in any way dependent for their significance upon numerical treatment. Modern developments in the philosophy of mathematics have made it clear that no *a priori* reason,

[58] "Table of the Springs of Action," 1 *Works* 195, 206.

[59] Laird, *op. cit.*, pp. 108 *et seq.*

no formal mathematical proof can be given for the proposition that physical spaces of the same length and breadth are equal in area. The truth of this proposition is simply a matter for immediate spatial observation (or mathematical inference from such observation), as is the truth of the proposition that areas vary in proportion to the product of certain numbers applied to two different dimensions. The fact that we can apply numbers, by the use of yardsticks, to lines and areas is of great practical importance, but it cannot serve to validate the propositions in question, since the use of such numbers depends upon immediate observation that a yardstick in two different places or pointing in two different directions is of the same length, and that areas bounded by lines equal in this sense, are themselves equal. The immediate observation that pleasures are quantitatively equal when such dimensions as intensity and duration are equal, and that they vary in certain ways when these dimensions vary, is strictly on a par with the primitive basis upon which the comparison of areas is based.

Thus, again, the only principle which hedonism needs to maintain is that pleasures are quantities which can be, by direct observation and by inference from such observation, compared and significantly asserted to be equal or unequal. That assumption we must now proceed to examine.

The allegation that different pleasures are not susceptible to quantitative comparison rests upon two fundamental and popular assumptions in regard to the nature of quantity whose falsity has been conclusively demonstrated.[60] It is commonly assumed, in the first place, that all quantities are theoretically, at least, divisible. It is then argued that, since every given pleasure is an indivisible unit, there can be no quantitative comparison of pleasures. In the second place, it is assumed that quantitative comparison is dependent upon measurement. Since it is impossible to superpose one pleasure upon another, and since there is no system of measurement by which the number of units in two pleasures can be ascertained and numerically compared, it is thought that pleasures cannot be quantitatively compared.

Both assumptions are false, and although a rigorous demonstration of this point would take us far afield and could serve only to reword the arguments brought forward by Russell, it is necessary that we show the nature of this error and its application to our present problem.

The assumption that quantities must be divisible is based on the view that quantitative comparison is simply a numerical comparison of the number of parts in the compared quantities. That this is false is proved by the possibility of applying quantitative comparison to quantities which are relations (*e.g.* distance) and which cannot conceivably be divisible, and to quantities which consist of an infinite number of parts (*e.g.* spaces, temporal durations) which, although necessarily equal in the number of such parts, may be significantly compared. So we may significantly compare the value or the pleasantness of two events without assuming that the quantities of pleasure or value are divisible. All that is necessary is that it should be significant to say that one event is better or more pleasant

[60] Russell, *Principles of Mathematics,* Part 3.

than another. That such judgments are significant is a proposition which can be validated only by its immediate obviousness.

The assumption that quantitative comparison is dependent upon measurement is ambiguous, and inconsistent with the theory of hedonism only in the sense in which it is false. If by *measurement* is meant the calculation of the number of parts in a quantity, then measurement is inapplicable not only to pleasures but also to space, temporal durations, and indeed to all quantities except "quantities of divisibility."[61] In this sense, measurement is not presupposed by quantitative comparison. A second, more complicated meaning may be given to *measurement*, on the basis of which pleasures are measurable in the same way as spatial quantities. To quote from Russell's *Principles of Mathematics*: "Let it be agreed that, when the distances a_0a_1, a_1a_2, . . . $a_{n-1}a_n$ are all equal and in the same sense, then a_0a_n is said to be *n* times each of the distances a_0a_1, etc., *i.e.* is to be measured by a number *n* times as great. This has generally been regarded as not a convention, but an obvious truth; owing, however, to the fact that distances are indivisible, no distance is really a sum of other distances, and numerical measurement must be in part conventional."[62] It must be noted that the equality upon which this sort of measurement rests is something for whose existence we can have no other evidence than immediate obviousness. Superposition will not help us, since that process applies not to distances but to physical objects, and depends upon the assumption that the object

61 Russell, *Principles of Mathematics*, pp. 182-183.
62 *Ibid.*, pp. 180-181.

moved does not change its size, which is the very point at which we have to rely upon immediate observation.[63] Nor can the existence of measuring rods help us in the least, since here too there is a process of superposition which depends upon the assumed constancy of the length of the measuring rod and of the objects to which it is applied. Yardsticks are indeed of practical value, and it is not our purpose to deny that a much greater degree of accuracy and agreement can be attained through their use than is possible when we come to measure pleasures. But this conclusion is only natural in view of the far greater complexity of the subject matter with which we deal. It does not affect the validity of measurement as applied, in the sense defined above, to different pleasures. We regard two distinct and independent pleasures taken together as a single pleasure, in the same way as we regard two distinct and independent distances, for purposes of measurement, as a single distance (relational addition), and in this sense we may say that one pleasure is twice as great as another, when the second is equal to a quantity of pleasure which, combined with its equal, produces a quantity equal to the first.

The complexity of the process is real, but no greater than the complexity of spatial or temporal measurement which long familiarity makes us overlook. When it is realized that pleasures may be measured in exactly the same sense as lines or intervals of time, the theoretical importance of numerical measurement is seen to be almost negligible. To quote again from Russell, "Those mathe-

[63] Our reliance upon immediate observation is even more obvious in the comparison of temporal durations, where superposition is inapplicable.

maticians who are accustomed to an exclusive emphasis upon numbers, will think that not much can be said with definiteness concerning magnitudes incapable of measurement. This, however, is by no means the case. The immediate judgments of equality, upon which (as we saw) all measurements depend, are still possible where measurement fails, as are also the immediate judgments of greater and less. Doubt only arises where the difference is small; and all that measurement does, in this respect, is to make the margin of doubt still smaller—an achievement which is purely psychological, and of no philosophical importance. Quantities not susceptible of numerical measurement can thus be arranged in a scale of greater and smaller magnitudes, and this is the only strictly quantitative achievement of even numerical measurement. We can know that one magnitude is greater than another, and that a third is intermediate between them; also, since the differences of magnitudes are always magnitudes, there is always (theoretically, at least) an answer to the question whether the difference[64] of one pair of magnitudes is greater than, less than, or the same as the difference of another pair of the same kind. And such propositions, though to the mathematician they may appear approximate, are just as precise and definite as the propositions of Arithmetic. Without numerical measurement, therefore, the quantitative relations of magnitudes have all the definiteness of which they are capable—nothing is added, from the theoretical standpoint, by the assignment of correlated numbers."[65]

[64] Or, Russell might have added, the *sum*.

[65] Russell, *Principles of Mathematics*, pp. 182-183.

When the mathematical errors that have been described are laid aside, the application of quantitative comparison to pleasures is seen to be perfectly valid. That we find significance in the judgment that such and such a day was the happiest in our lives, that a given pie will give more pleasure to six boys than to one, that one man is more wretched than another, or that one gift will make our friend happier than another gift, is the only basis which the theory of hedonism requires to attain meaning. That this basis is given by experience can hardly be denied.

But it may still be maintained, perhaps, that pleasures are subjective in a sense in which physical data are not, and that therefore the comparison of quantities of pleasure cannot go beyond a single individual's experience. It does not appear to us that this contention has any plausibility beyond that with which long philosophical discussion and criticism may have endowed it. Our observation of space or time is just as subjective as our observation of pleasure. Both are intuitions which science can only clarify and codify. "So far as reality is concerned all our sense-perceptions are in the same boat, and must be treated on the same principle."[66] Physics, as a natural science, is based upon sense-data which are influenced at least by such variable factors as the observer's perspective or space-time location. The space-time world of one's immediate experience is just as subjective as the world of thought or feeling. In either case, there is a set of immediate data, and a hypothetical reduction of these immediate data to a common or "objective" system, with a final translation of these "objective" entities into the immediate observations

[66] Whitehead, *The Concept of Nature,* p. 44.

of other individuals. The inference that certain people will observe an eclipse, which I make on the basis of observations within my private space-time perspective and by means of certain laws which have been only inductively established (to the extent that they are not formal and tautological) is the core of physics. Without such inferences, physics could not be empirically verified by more than one person, and there would be an infinite number of irreducible physical systems. Without the observations upon which these inferences are built, physics could not be an empirical or natural science even in this narrow sense. Thus the laws of dynamics, for instance, which ascribe velocities and accelerations to bodies and measure these velocities and accelerations in terms of a time which is itself measured by moving bodies (the earth, clocks, etc.) on the assumption that their movement follows the laws of dynamics, would be a circular system of empty tautologies if we did not give content to the entities dealt with by a "subjective" intuition or observation of time and space.

To this procedure of physics and natural science in general, a complete parallel is found in our hedonic comparisons (and as well in our ethical comparisons). We have certain experiences of pleasure and pain. We observe, with more or less care, the conditions under which they arise. We infer, on the basis of certain laws (again, only inductively established, and therefore uncertain), that under these conditions other people (or even ourselves, at other times) will have similar experiences. As in physics, we pass from one private world into a common world and beyond that again into another private world. At the end of this long journey we make the judgment that Henry is very happy when vacation time comes and that James will be less happy when the dentist drills his tooth. That these judgments are significant cannot plausibly be denied. That they are sometimes false and frequently true is also indubitable. It is on the basis of assumptions exactly similar to those which any natural science makes, that men bring moral order into their lives and escape the solipsism of the moment from which one embarks only at his peril but within which neither meaning nor thought exists.

(6) *The falsity of hedonism.* Granted that hedonism is a meaningful doctrine, the question of its truth or falsity is the only issue of real importance in our present study. The first three arguments taken up in this section have been considered only in order that their irrelevance to this issue might be made clear. There is, however, a psychological importance in those objections. For when the absurdity of the arguments upon which the case against hedonism is commonly based becomes clear, we may come to believe that the chief objections to the doctrine rest upon misapprehensions and that these irrelevant and inconclusive objections would not have been raised if there were actually obvious errors in the hedonistic hypothesis.

Even on this issue numerous irrelevant objections have been raised, which we shall briefly dispose of before proceeding to the real point in question, which is whether or not the conclusions of the hedonistic hypothesis lead to manifestly false value judgments. In the first place, antihedonists have almost always attacked psychological hedonism,—the doctrine that men *do* actually seek *their own* greatest pleasure.[67] This doctrine is quite irrelevant to the hedonistic doctrine that men *ought* to act in a way productive of the greatest pleasure *for all concerned.* Equally irrelevant is the objection that right action is not always pleasant.[68] The hedonist maintains only that the right action with its results contains more pleasure than any possible alternative,—it being irrelevant to the value of the action whether this pleasure is experienced by the agent or by others. A further objection, of opposite import, is that hedonism values future goods above present goods,[69] but while this is justified by mis-statements of the dependence of value upon the results of actions, it is quite unjustified when we measure the pleasure involved in the act with its results.

Finally anti-hedonists have shown that all proofs of the doctrine are inconclusive,[70] and this is certainly true, although the inference that the doctrine is therefore false is certainly invalid. The chief defenders of hedonism have seen that, like any other fundamental hypothesis, it is not capable of proof, but must be judged solely on the basis of the judgments to which it leads.

After this monotonous but necessary prelude, we can at last come to the real point of the issue. Are the value judgments in which hedonism results untrue? Here we are faced with a real difficulty. The only basis on which we can humanly judge of the truth of these or any other

67 Dewey, *Human Nature and Conduct,* pp. 199-200; Paulsen, *System of Ethics,* pp. 253, 258; Green, *Prolegomena to Ethics,* §§ 340-346. But see § 351.

68 A. E. Taylor, *Problem of Conduct,* p. 327.

69 Dewey, *op. cit.,* pp. 204-207, 265.

70 G. E. Moore, *Principia Ethica,* pp. 66-74; Bradley, *Ethical Studies,* pp. 112-116.

ethical conclusions is a set of personal judgments which are themselves subject to error. Indeed if our personal judgments were not subject to error, an ethical theory could not be of the slightest value. But this difficulty is not one peculiar to ethics. It is germane to all science which is not purely formal. We cannot verify the law of gravitation except by noting the agreement of its conclusions with our immediate physical judgments,—and these judgments, although based upon direct observation, are frequently erroneous.

Of course, people do agree in their physical observations more than in their moral observations, but the extent of this difference is greatly exaggerated, on both sides of the comparison. The belief that men, upon entering a laboratory, are temporarily endowed with infallibility is a popular myth, which has superseded, in certain communities, an equally widespread belief in the infallibility of popes and kings. No great scientist is blind to the degree of honest error involved in physical observation. People—and scientists are people—see to a certain extent what they want or expect to see, and scientists, like moralists, have interests and expectations. On the other hand, moral observation is by no means as chaotic as popularized anthropology has caused many moderns to believe. Most so-called moral differences are simply differences of belief as to natural causality. A man who believes that talking to his mother-in-law will result in the rotting of his corn will evaluate the act differently from one who entertains no such notion,—but this is not a difference in purely ethical observation. As far as the ascription of purely ethical judgments is concerned, the men are simply valuing two different complexes, and neither disagreement nor agreement is possible.[71]

In order to secure the possibility of agreement or disagreement, we must take care that the objects presented for observation are actually the same for each observer. This is best accomplished by offering objects for purely intrinsic valuation, ("If the world were to end tomorrow" is a proper protasis for speculation on intrinsic goods), but even then remnants of our instrumental judgments are apt to linger in the clearest moral faculties. However, to the extent that we have secured identity in the objects viewed, a great similarity of moral judgment will appear. It is to this fundamental agreement that any absolutistic ethical theory must, practically, appeal in the testing of its doctrines.

It is our contention, first, that most of the conclusions of hedonism accord with a wide body of moral observation (in so far as such observation is directed to intrinsic values), and, secondly, that none of its conclusions is manifestly false. If both of these propositions can be maintained, we may inductively confirm the hedonistic doctrine in as valid a manner as can be applied to any other scientific law.

The first of these contentions is naturally not susceptible of any conclusive demonstration. We believe that when the precautions of moral observation suggested above and further elaborated in the remainder of this section are observed, this proposition will be found to be true. The second contention is more easily examined within the confines of an essay. Its demand is that we take up the typical

[71] *Cf.* Laird, *Study in Moral Theory*, pp. 104 *et seq.*

"hard cases" which anti-hedonists have presented, and show that their proper solution is not inconsistent with the hedonistic theory.

These cases fall into three types, corresponding to three ways in which hedonism is susceptible of refutation. In the first place, something may be shown us which is intrinsically valuable although it does not contain pleasure. In the second place, something may be given which is pleasurable but not intrinsically valuable. In the third place, it may be shown that of two entities the less pleasurable is the more valuable, that value and pleasantness do not vary in direct proportion.

G. E. Moore has offered us a typical case of an entity devoid of pleasure yet supposed to be intrinsically valuable:

> Let us imagine one world exceedingly beautiful. Imagine it as beautiful as you can; put into it whatever on this earth you most desire—mountains, rivers, the sea; trees, and sunsets, stars and moon. Imagine these all combined in the most exquisite proportions, so that no one thing jars against another, but each contributes to increase the beauty of the whole. And then imagine the ugliest world you can possibly conceive. Imagine it simply one heap of filth, containing everything that is most disgusting to us, for whatever reason, and the whole, as far as may be without one redeeming feature. . . . The only thing we are not entitled to imagine is that any human being has or ever, by any possibility, *can* live in either, can ever see and enjoy the beauty of the one or hate the foul-

ness of the other. Well, even so, supposing them quite apart from any possible contemplation by human beings; still, is it irrational to hold that it is better that the beautiful world should exist than the one which is ugly?[72]

To this we can only reply that there appears to us to be no difference of intrinsic value between the two worlds, and that, if anybody is careful to discount his natural feeling that after all somebody might see the worlds, as well as the difference in the pleasantness of imagining the different worlds, he will probably agree with us. But, as we have already suggested, in cases like this, where utilitarian values are apt to project themselves into our consciousness masked as intrinsic values, it is extremely difficult to place much confidence in our conclusions. This is especially pertinent to the claim of the anti-hedonist that virtue or wisdom is intrinsically good even if it is not pleasant. It is almost impossible to make introspectively the highly artificial and unusual separation between the intrinsic goodness of these qualities and their instrumental value in promoting happy life. But when we succeed in making that abstraction, it seems that honesty and dishonesty, love and hate, wisdom and ignorance, do not differ in intrinsic value. Would it be a good thing to make everybody more wise or more beautiful or more honest than he is now, if nobody, either of the present or of the future generations, were made any the happier by the change? We cannot think so, and we believe that most people who are able to see exactly the situation that has been described would agree.

[72] G. E. Moore, *Principia Ethica*, pp. 83-84.

The second set of objections to the hedonistic doctrine is that some pleasant things are not intrinsically good. Again there is a good deal of danger of confusing the issues by presenting examples in which we are distracted by instrumental values. Anti-hedonists, from Plato to Moore, have regularly pointed to the pleasures of sexual perversion as the clearest example of intrinsically bad pleasures. Let us accept this challenge, assuming for the sake of argument that these perversions are really as pleasant as our traditional moralists have portrayed them. Let us see whether the hedonist's claim that these pleasures are intrinsically good is really as repugnant to common sense as has been claimed.

It is easy to recognize that what is intrinsically good may be, from a utilitarian point of view, very bad indeed,—but it is very difficult to think consistently in these terms. Somehow intrinsic value appears to be more important than instrumental value. So we find it difficult to think that an act which, in our opinion, must have evil consequences can be intrinsically good. This is a psychological, not a logical, difficulty. It offers one explanation why people object to the hedonistic proposition in question, but it does not show that proposition to be false.

A second ground of objection which is equally invalid from the point of view of logic lies in a natural failure to perceive exactly what it is that we are judging. In the case in question we are supposed to be judging an act or a set of acts which involve the pleasure of the agent. That being the case, it is a misleading abstraction to view the act apart from its pleasure. Yet this is what one who finds the act intensely repugnant is almost bound to do. It is as impossible to imagine a disgusting act as pleasant, merely because we are informed that somebody else finds pleasure in it, as it would be to imagine a symphony as beautiful merely because some lunatic or critic finds aesthetic enjoyment in it. The person with a strong horror of the acts in question is no more in a position to see their pleasantness than was the scholastic teacher of Galileo's story in a position to see the sun-spots that Aristotle had not written about. And if he cannot see the real object of his judgment, what weight can be given to that judgment?

A third source of logical confusion which may account for the anti-hedonist's denial of value to certain pleasurable experiences arises from a failure to distinguish between the question of whether an act is good and the question of whether the act ought to be praised.[72a] Socially the moralist has commonly served the function of inducing people, through the organization of verbal rewards and punishments, to do unpleasant things that are socially useful. Moralists have thus been led to withhold praise from naturally pleasant acts or experiences, whether useless or useful. This denial of approval may be socially justifiable —since the commodity of praise retains its value only on a scarcity basis—but such approval is not for that reason false.

Here, then, are three misapprehensions upon which objection to the hedonist's disposal of these difficult cases seems usually to rest. If they can really be surmounted, there is no reason to believe that the hedonistic judgment will be repugnant to general moral opinion. There may be some with minds flexible enough to see what they are judg-

[72a] *Cf.* Chapter Two, section 2 (C), *supra.*

ing and clear enough to rid it of all its instrumental values, who yet regard the acts in question as intrinsically bad or as perfectly indifferent in intrinsic value. If the hedonist has any such opponents, then *cadit quaestio.* One of the disputants must be wrong, but which there is no way of telling. (We have, of course, assumed the principle of absolutism throughout this discussion.) But at least the hedonist's position in this controversy is not manifestly absurd, as his critics have claimed.

Another line of argument to prove the existence of pleasurable experiences devoid of value takes the following form. Pleasure and the consciousness of pleasure are different things, if the word *consciousness* has any meaning at all. Now if there are any pleasures of which nobody is conscious, it is clear that they would not be intrinsically good. Therefore the hedonistic hypothesis must be false.[73]

The specious force of this argument is due to a pun on the phrase "consciousness of pleasure." If this means the knowledge that we are happy, then this knowledge is certainly not a necessary element in intrinsically valuable experiences. The knowledge that we are happy may add to our happiness, but, on the other hand, it may lead to the disintegration of that happiness. But if "consciousness of pleasure" is taken to mean pleasurable consciousness, then, since pleasure is realized only in consciousness, it is nonsense to talk of unconscious pleasures. The happy individual must be conscious of something. Accordingly, this argument that "pleasures of which nobody is conscious" are valueless is invalid, whether we understand by this phrase "pleasures in whose enjoyment one is not conscious

[73] Plato, *Philebus;* Moore, *Principia Ethica,* pp. 87-89.

that he is happy," or "pleasures in which one is not conscious at all." Only by mixing up the two meanings of the phrase does the argument acquire its specious force.

The contention, then, that entities which contain pleasure are not always intrinsically valuable receives no adequate support, and we may conclude that the implications of the hedonistic doctrine in this respect are not repugnant to common moral observation when that observation is freed from certain elementary misapprehensions.

The final set of objections to the hedonistic hypothesis attempts to show that the intrinsic value of entities does not vary in direct proportion to the pleasure they contain. The hedonistic proposition which is attacked is that, of any two entities, the one which is more pleasurable is intrinsically the more valuable. Again, the claim is put forward that this proposition proves to be absurd and incompatible with general ethical observation in certain crucial cases.

With one accord, moralists have called upon the pig (or the oyster) to demolish the hedonistic argument.[74] Can anyone honestly doubt that an ordinary human life, virtuous and full of unsatisfied desires, is really more valuable than the life of the well-fed pig whose every want is satisfied? As this challenge is typical of the anti-hedonistic contentions on this point, it will be well to examine it with some care. If we can discover that it owes its psychological appeal entirely to a number of logically invalid inferences, we shall be able to gauge its real force.

In the first place, this argument involves the common confusion between pleasure or happiness and the satis-

[74] Plato, *Philebus;* Carlyle, "*Jesuitism*" in *Latter Day Pamphlets* (1850), pp. 28-31; Ritchie, *Natural Rights;* Paulsen, *System of Ethics;* Bradley, *Ethical Studies;* Moore, *Principia Ethica.*

faction or absence of desires. It is assumed that because a pig has no unsatisfied desires it must be happy, and that a man who has many such desires must be unhappy, or at least less happy. Both of these assumptions are simply absurd. Pleasure is not the absence of unsatisfied desire. If it were, books and islands and irrational numbers would be much happier than any waking man. Dull and stupid people very frequently achieve a placid contentment which is quite devoid of joy, and there is no reason for believing that pigs, when they are well-fed, are happy in any degree appreciably similar to the happiness that we know when our emotional and intellectual development is in its fullest flower. On the other hand there is nothing incompatible between the existence of happiness and the co-existence of many unsatisfied desires. It is not a matter of common experience that those whose life is a perpetual search for some unattainable ideal are really less happy than those who have no unsatisfied needs or yearnings. Accordingly, the alternative between the satisfied pig and the unsatisfied Socrates is quite irrelevant to the issue before us.

Now anti-hedonists have generally assumed that the experimental pig is not only satisfied but supremely and ecstatically happy, and that his fellow subject and counterpoise is not only less satisfied but less happy. Since the case is only a hypothetical one, they have a right to describe its conditions. But these conditions may be such as systematically to mislead our judgment, and if that is the fact no weight can be attached to such judgment unless its dangers are clearly recognized and circumvented. We have seen, in the first place, that a stress upon satisfied and unsatisfied desires (rather than pleasure) tends to confuse the problem that is to be solved. Even if the pig's happiness is expressly postulated, the fact that this assumption is made upon an invalid ground and is intrinsically absurd tempts us to pass our judgment not upon the states of pleasure, which are unreasonably inferred from the difference in unsatisfied wants, but rather upon the difference in these wants. And such a judgment in favor of Socrates is not inconsistent with the doctrine of hedonism.

But when we have clarified the problem and put the choice squarely between the intrinsic value of an ecstatic pig's life and that of a less happy man's life, a second difficulty presents itself. Most people do not really believe that pigs live ecstatic lives. The intensest pleasures we know all depend upon a highly complex nervous system, which pigs do not possess. Our reaction to the choice presented us is therefore about the same as our reaction to the question, "Do omniscient stones know more than less wise philosophers?" Our unwillingness to answer the latter question in the affirmative is not based upon a conviction that philosophers who were less wise than such stones would know more, but rather upon a perception that the question put involves a false assumption. So, if the moralists who have put questions like this have themselves confused a question of fact with a purely hypothetical question, endeavoring to demonstrate that pigs really are very happy, is it any wonder that the less acute general opinion to which they appeal has commonly made a similar mistake in apprehending the problem and passed its judgment upon the pigs of the real world rather than those of the moralists' porcine elysium?

It seems that if we are able to overcome the natural confusions to which this problem leads,—the confusions just outlined, as well as those already alluded to in our previous discussion,—no inherent absurdity will be found in this most extreme of hedonistic judgments. Endow a pig with the most intense joys you know, the pleasures you derive from love or tennis or aesthetic enjoyment or intellectual artistry or anything else that is equally joy-giving, and no difficulty will be found in the judgment that this pig's life is more valuable intrinsically than the life of a less happy human.

This last example is typical of the other cases in which philosophers have seized upon hedonistic value judgments as inherently absurd.[75] It will be found that all these cases involve one or more of the distracting elements we have noted. Either the case is one where the act condemned by hedonism is instrumentally more valuable than its alternative, leading to a mistaken judgment through the common confusion of intrinsic and instrumental values, or it is of a nature to blind one's vision of the pleasantness involved in the "lower" alternative, or it involves a confusion between pleasure and the absence of unsatisfied desire, or it proposes an absurd hypothetical case which is not taken seriously by the jury, who proceed to offer a verdict upon the real issue of fact rather than upon the judge's interpretation of that issue.

If these confusions are recognized and overcome,—or, better still, if we restrict our test cases to situations which do not suggest these misapprehensions, then the value judgments of hedonism are seen to be in very general accord with common moral observation (of intrinsic values). At

[75] *Cf.* G. E. Moore, *Ethics* (1912), pp. 236-238.

no point do they become absurd, although there is frequently a good deal of room for intellectually respectable disagreement. This is only natural. People do honestly disagree, even when all confusions of thought have been overcome, as to what is intrinsically valuable, just as people do honestly disagree, to a lesser extent, in objective but indemonstrable judgments of color. Towards this agreement and disagreement two attitudes are possible. We may hold that the question is not one of truth or falsity, that judgments of value (and perhaps, also, all other immediate judgments, those of color, space, time, etc.) are ultimately relative to individuals, and that human beings are sufficiently similar to make a very extensive agreement quite natural.

Or else we may hold that when people disagree on a question of intrinsic value one or both must be wrong. If this be the case, *i.e.*, if our absolutistic hypothesis be true, then we can decide whether particular value judgments are true in the same manner by which we determine whether judgments in matters of physical observation are true. Suppose that people disagree as to the color of a particular object (*i.e.*, as to the similarity of this color to a certain standard color). How will they decide which view is correct? Undoubtedly they will first discover whether a preponderant majority of people agree in one judgment. Then they will examine the vision of the dissenters to discover possible physiological abnormalities. They may examine the spectacles of the dissenters. And if by these means the difference is not seen to rest upon a pure misapprehension of what it is that the dispute is about or upon some hindrance to the vision of this object, there is only one more step that can be taken. The wave-length of the light from the object is measured, and compared with the wave-length of objects upon whose color the disputants have agreed. And the inference is made that the disputed object is of the same color as that standard which has the same wave-length. This inference, be it noted, is not logically conclusive, although nobody, in the case of the colors, would actually challenge it. From the fact that all light found after analysis to be (within a certain margin of error) of a particular wave-length has been observed to be orange, we cannot deduce that a new example of that wave-length will be orange. There is no *a priori* justification for a correlation between color and one of the many elements which appear in every color-situation, namely wave-length of light rays. The inference is validated only by our inductive assumption that color and wave-length, found to be correlated in a number of instances, will exhibit that correlation in all other instances.

The moral of this parable is too obvious to require elaboration. In our examination of hedonism, after taking all our laboratory precautions we are still faced with ultimate disagreement in certain cases. Then we can only call upon a correlation observed in a great many other instances to hold between pleasure and value, and offer the inductive (and therefore only probable) inference that here, too, the judgment which agrees with this correlation is the true one.

We have not proved the hedonistic hypothesis either by refuting the attempts to disprove it or by showing the basic agreement of its conclusions with logically refined moral observation. Such a proof, of this or of any other ethical theory, or indeed of any theory of any applied science whatever, can only be a trap for tired minds. But examining the hedonistic hypothesis in a scientific manner we have found it to be (on the assumption of absolutism and non-naturalism) clear, abstractly susceptible of refutation, and generally confirmed.[76] This is enough to make it an acceptable scientific hypothesis, exerting a greater claim upon our belief than any rival theory. It is obvious that no "fighting faith" is given by this calculation of probabilities and alternatives. That can easily be attained, when occasion demands, by a review of the absurd arguments which the critics of hedonism have accepted.

.2202 *A is intrinsically good* is equivalent to *A is real.* Of all the alternatives to the hedonistic theory sketched in the previous section, this is certainly the simplest and perhaps the most widespread. The special forms of this theory well nigh exhaust the list of traditional ethical systems.

In its most obvious form the theory is simply the sanctification of everything that exists and the denunciation of the non-existent. "Whatever is is right." Since this theory is in obvious conflict with the data of ethical experience it is necessary only to point out the logical fallacy upon which all the arguments in its defence rest in order to justify our rejection of it.

Inductively it is found that many things which appear at first sight to be bad really have good results and are on

[76] The reader will find many points briefly touched upon in the foregoing analysis developed more adequately in: J. S. Mill, *Utilitarianism* (1863); Sidgwick, *Methods of Ethics* (1874); G. E. Moore, *Ethics* (1912); R. M. Blake, "Why Not Hedonism? A Protest," (1927), 37 *Internat. Jour. of Ethics* 1.

the whole, from a utilitarian point of view, good. Thus death and sickness accentuate the joys of life and health, suffering brings purification in its train, hunger increases the zest of food. It is then inferred that all things which appear to us to be bad are really good. The argument is logically defective, since it is equally true that many things which appear at first sight to be good prove, on more mature consideration, to have bad results. Life and health increase the suffering attendant upon death and sickness, etc. If the arguments of theodicy had any validity they would show merely that our first judgments in matters of ethics are always completely erroneous. That certain actual objects and events are bad is as obvious a fact as this world can exhibit, and no argument based upon the nature of other events can show this recognition of evils to be erroneous.

The various metaphysical, theological, and scientific formulations which have been given to this theory do not substantially affect its substance. Metaphysicians have argued that, since the real world is composed of forms or essences, the most formal form or the most essential essence must be the highest good, that since the real world is a complete harmony, the good is that which is harmonious, and so almost every metaphysical system has produced its ethics.[77] Similarly theologians have argued that since everything obeys the will of God, obedience to God's will is the criterion of goodness. Scientists, too, have often thought that because everything obeys the law of evolution or the law of adaptation to environment, obedience to such laws must be the ultimate test of ethical value.

[77] See quotation from Russell, pp. 23-24, *supra.*

Underlying all these arguments runs an inductive inference that is snapped as soon as we find a single real thing to be bad. That some real things are bad is an ultimate fact upon which the significance of ethics rests, and beyond which reason cannot legitimately carry us.

.2203 *A is intrinsically good* is equivalent to *The universal rule under which A falls is self-consistent.* Although we believe that this is the essence of the Kantian moral system, we shall not be concerned to justify this belief. Our present task is merely to ascertain whether or not the theory in question is true.

This doctrine is used to demonstrate many excellent ethical rules. We must not steal, because if every one stole there would be no property and thus no possibility of theft. We must not lie, because if every one lied there would be no plausibility in lies and therefore no possibility of effective lying. We must not torture dogs, because on the same general principle a big giant might torture us before we got the chance. Upon the efficacy of this mode of argument in moral education we pass no criticism. Its logical validity, however, and its meaning are open to serious question.

The most obvious meaning of the doctrine under consideration is: (1) that there is a single universal rule under which any given act falls, and (2) that when and only when this universal principle is self-consistent, is the act in question intrinsically good.

On this analysis the logical fallacy underlying the doctrine is immediately manifest. The second statement in question must be meaningless, since the first is false. That is to say, no particular event determines a definite rule under which it falls.[77a] This is elementary logic, but it is often forgotten in discussions of morality. Its application to the present problem is not difficult to comprehend. A given instance of lying may be brought under the category of lying, but with equal logical validity and often with more human significance, it may be brought under the narrower categories of "telling a lie for reasons of modesty," "telling a lie to save a friend's life," etc., or under the wider categories of "conversing," "acting," etc. Some of these categories may be capable of universal sanction, others not. By a judicious selection of universal principles, one can demonstrate, on the basis of this theory that anything is good or that anything is bad. This, in fact, seems to be the outstanding attraction of the present doctrine. One might show, for instance, that writing philosophy is bad, since if everybody wrote philosophy all the time, everybody would very soon die of hunger and cease to write philosophy. On the other hand, the killing of Socrates need awake no moral qualms when its righteousness is tested by the self-consistency of the logical universal, "Every teacher of philosophy who lives in Athens at the present day and goes by the name of Socrates is to be executed."

These brief considerations suffice to show that the doctrine in question, if taken to affirm a unique determination of universal categories or principles by indiyidual cases, must be false. If, on the other hand, it is recognized that any act falls under an indefinite number of classes and is described by an indefinite number of universals, the only sensible meaning that can be attributed to our theory is

[77a] See Chapter One, § 6, *supra*, for an analysis of the legal product of this fallacy, *viz.*, the doctrine that a particular case may uniquely determine a legal rule or principle.

that the universalization on which our criterion of value depends refers to *every* applicable universal or to *at least one* universal (not uniquely denoted). It is clear that neither of these principles can offer a significant criterion of value. As for the former alternative, it is difficult, perhaps impossible, to imagine a single act whose adoption by every one would not result in a practical inconsistency (and throughout this discussion we are speaking of practical inconsistencies). As for the latter alternative, it is clear that if any act is possible at all, one can formulate some class of which it is the only member, and thus lay down a universal rule applicable to it and free from inconsistency. Both the wholesale pessimism of the former interpretation and the boundless optimism of the latter are denials rather than explanations of ethics.

.2204 *A is intrinsically good* is equivalent to some other proposition (than any of the three preceding).

Again we are faced in our alternatives with a vague and broad possibility in regard to which little of any importance can be said. We might go on to abstract from this domain further ethical theories of a more specific character and proceed to their consideration. But in the end we should still face this inevitable alternative, and we have no hopes that our own further delimitation of this field would be profitable. The three theories of the good already treated in this section are more or less typical of any understandable alternatives.[78] Moreover, in our examina-

[78] The endeavor to deal with ethics in ethical rather than philologic terms forces us to omit a discussion of verbal doctrines which we do not understand. Such, for instance, are those popular theories which seek to define the good in terms of "power," "self-expression," "personality,"

tion of hedonism we have reached the conclusion that hedonism is probably true, if any absolute system of ethics is true, which implies, of course, that any absolutistic theory inconsistent with hedonism is false. Whether there are theories which, although stated in different terms (*e.g.* in terms of interests), are equivalent to the theory of hedonism, in the sense of agreeing with the hedonistic valuation of every entity, is a problem which it is unnecessary to treat. For our purpose throughout this ethical discussion has been simply to discover some standard by which the good, and hence that part of the good which we call the good life, can be measured. The solution of this problem does not demand that we discover the *only* adequate doctrine. For these reasons we submit the conclusion that the proposition of the present section is either false or, if true, not incompatible with the doctrine of hedonism. This conclusion must have at least the probability of our previous conclusion in regard to the truth of hedonism.

.2205 *A is intrinsically good* is not equivalent to any other proposition.

This is a final ethical possibility which denies the existence of any criterion of goodness. It implies that the class of good things has no defining predicate other than goodness. Although there is no reason why any one should believe this proposition, its abstract possibility must be allowed. Certain superficial grounds for its plausibility may, however, be refuted.

The proposition in question is not simply that there is

"maturity," or "self-renunciation," to say nothing of the many inmates of metaphysical harems which never appear in public unveiled and whose anatomy it would be indecent to discuss.

no natural quality identical with goodness. That has been an assumption underlying all the present treatment of non-naturalistic ethics. The further contention is made, in this doctrine, that there is no natural quality or relation peculiar to good things (in the sense, for instance, that a common wave-length is peculiar to yellow things), and none of the arguments in favor of the former claim can properly be applied to the latter.

There is a second misinterpretation of the present theory which may give that theory some plausibility. We may easily confuse the proposition that no simple or unanalyzable predicate can identify the class of good things with the proposition that no predicate of any sort can define that class. The two propositions, however, are wholly distinct. To say that wisdom and beauty and love constitute the good is to propose just as definite a criterion of goodness as can be attained by a doctrine which equates the good with a single one of these entities. That there are, in fact, any ultimately simple entities, is a proposition which may easily be disputed. The necessity of a more complex determination of the good than any thus far suggested cannot support the validity of the present doctrine. Even a complete enumeration of all good things would offer us a means of defining the good in natural terms. "Being 1 or 2 or 3" is a perfectly adequate definition of "positive integer less than 4," and it is difficult to understand why "the good" should not be definable at least in some similarly complicated manner.

Finally, since the present doctrine is both absolutistic and incompatible with hedonism, its greatest probability must lie within the measure of the probability that hedonism is false, and some other absolute system true. For these reasons, we believe that the present doctrine, that goodness is an absolute quality, not definable in natural terms, for the existence of which no positive or natural criterion can possibly be found, must be rejected.

4. CONCLUSION

To summarize the conclusions of the present chapter, we have come upon two theories of ethics which, so far as the vision of the present writer extends, appear equally valid as explanations of the world of value. On the one hand, there is the theory that intrinsic goodness is relative, definable, and identical with a relation to an approving individual. On the other hand, there is the theory that intrinsic goodness is absolute, indefinable, and equivalent in application to positive pleasantness. Between these incompatible alternatives we have discovered no rational basis of choice, nor have we been able to show with any conclusiveness that other ethical alternatives are untenable. It is in the shadow of these doubts that our legal philosophy must make its very beginning. The conclusion is not a pleasant one. But the stories philosophy tells do not all have happy endings.

We can reconcile ourselves to failure by the reflection that "uncertainty is the lot of every branch of thought and knowledge when verging on the ultimate."[79] We can rest in this uncertainty and be glad that what we have attained is at least *docta ignorantia.* Or, less patient with the universe, we can fly forth on the pinions of faith,—but know-

[79] Cardozo, *Paradoxes of Legal Science* (1928), p. 135.

ing not whether ours are the wings of Daedalus or the wings of Icarus. Finally we can hold to the light of reason, faint though it be where we most need it, and find uncertain but not useless steps to moral knowledge.

It is a conclusion to which we have been forced in our survey of possible ethical systems that the standard of the good life has been most adequately formulated by the theory of hedonism, if any absolute formulation of this standard is possible. Beyond this remains only the alternative of ethical relativism, in which there is still room, of course, for a hedonistic ethics, but only as for a personal standard coordinate, *sub specie aeternitatis,* with all the other standards which have been accepted by men.[80] To those whose moral feelings run in the pattern of hedonism, this qualification and this doubt may appear unimportant.[81] It is only from a transcendental viewpoint that we distinguish between a world where an eternal realm of values subsists beyond the sure sight of man and one in which there is a fundamental moral anarchy, a clash of ultimate and ephemeral standards beyond which appeal is as impossible in reason as it is in life. When the world is dead we shall not wake to see that values too have vanished. That super-worldly vision is tragically and perhaps fortunately denied to man, and its issue is uncertain. "We

80 Of course, if the theory of ethical relativism be true, each of the legal ideals and each of the ethical ideals that we have rejected retains a personal validity. Neither the standards enforced by actual law nor the total "resultant" of individual ideals can claim an ethical, logical, or rational priority over the various ideals of judges, political philosophers, or criminals.

81 Thus Bentham, who regularly uses the language of absolutism, seems at times to admit that all ethics is relativistic. He writes, in the *Anarchical Fallacies:* "I say, it ought not to be established; that is, I do not approve of its being established; the emotion excited in my mind by the idea of its establishment, is not that of satisfaction, but the contrary." 2 *Works,* 495.

still shall fight . . . and we may leave to the unknown the supposed final valuation of that which in any event has value to us."[82]

Whatever the ultimate nature of the moral world may be, the political task of hedonism is plain,—in thought, the translation of the books of the law into the universal language of human joys and sufferings,—in practice, the struggle for the attainment of ideals thus discovered. To the criticism that this labor is baffling and tedious, the hedonist will answer, with Spinoza, that all things excellent are as difficult as they are rare. To the objection that the undertaking is a fruitless one, he will reply by pointing to the works of Bentham, in which are set forth and to which we largely owe every important legal reform of the nineteenth century.[83] And if it is alleged that the values he seeks to attain are ephemeral and evanescent, rationally devoid of objective significance, he will reply that it is human happiness he loves, and that if this love can have no ulterior justification it can need none, that if the kingdom of heaven within us be a dream it is, like life itself, a dream from which we can never wake.

Here, then, whether in truth or error or dream, our ethics culminates and the task of positive legal science begins.

[82] Holmes, "Natural Law," in *Collected Legal Papers* (1920), p. 310, 316.

[83] To note only the most striking and concrete: the simplification and cheapening of legal procedure (it is to Bentham that we owe even the word *codification*); the liberalizing of the law of evidence; the extension of compensatory damages (*e.g.* to death actions); legal recognition of the rights of animals; the inheritance tax; the international (another word invented by Bentham) limitation of armaments; the abolition of serfdom and slavery; the humanization of punishment; the liberalization of the law of divorce; public health legislation; the nationalization of education; the development of social statistics.

CHAPTER FOUR

LAW IN LIFE

1. THE FUNCTION OF POSITIVE SCIENCE IN LEGAL CRITICISM

WITH legal criticism, as with every other sort of measurement, it is not enough to own an accurate yardstick. One must also see precisely what it is that he is measuring. There is need here for further instruments of the surveyor,—barometer and sextant, theodolite and camera, telescope and microscope. The realm of law in which we seek to take measurement has its unbridged streams and pathless forests, swamps and ravines and unconquerable mountains. In tidier lands where a Platonic deity geometrizes and all things are squares, the ethical philosopher may lay his yardstick alongside the objects of his concern and announce his results with assurance and finality. Here in the domain of law he finds that determining the shape of the areas he is to measure presents difficulties no less forbidding than those he has encountered in his search for a standard of measurement immune to the distorting influences of temperature and atmospheric pressure.

The problems of legal criticism do not appear to us at first blush in the human context which gives them ethical significance. Before us is the cryptic symbol,—the decision of a court, the statute of a legislature, the act of a policeman. How are we to unravel its intricate human significance?

It is idle to hope that the interminable controversies of ethics may be forgotten in formulating a program for the positive, scientific study of law. For those who disagree upon the fundamental values of life will disagree as to what consequences of law are worth investigating. One who finds the source of all value in the color yellow will have little patience with a legal science that does not determine how various legal decisions affect the yellowness of houses, people, and trees. One who finds absolute ethical values in an esoteric and irresponsible "legal reason" or "justice" that vibrates in judicial decisions and statutes—though the heavens fall—will deem positive study of "law in life" wholly useless. And the rejection of all ethical absolutes will not help legal science to forget the war of ethical schools, since relativism gives to every individual the assurance of irresponsibility in the affirmation of his own personal ideals. Agreement as to the proper scope of positive legal science is, under relativism, as accidental as agreement upon the locus of intrinsic goods.

The ethical conclusions to which we have attained in our analysis of possible ethical systems must therefore be the starting point for our delineation of the scope of positive science in legal criticism. For a legal criticism which finds in happiness the substance of all valid moral judgment, it is the task of positive science to link the ceremonial show of the legal process with the joys and sufferings of sentient beings. This task will have a limited relevance to legal criticism which follows other ideals. Even those who think that pleasure and pain are devoid of ethical significance may find that the search for these elusive entities follows paths which must be traversed in moral criticism of other varieties. And of course those who, rejecting all ethical absolutism, find that their own feelings of moral approval are responsive to joy and suffering in the situations that they judge, will demand of positive science the same focus that the absolutistic hedonist demands. The rejection of absolutism, does not, as we have seen,[1] eliminate the possibility of ethical error. The relativist must be perfect not only in his introspection but as well in his understanding of the object he is judging, before he may say, "In my heart I approve of this law. Therefore it is, from my viewpoint, good." Thus, while we cannot, on *a priori* grounds, refute the relativist who claims that he approves a given decision whose consequences he cannot trace, we may well ask whether the approval he feels is directed to the fragment of the world's experience that is actually implicated in the legal symbol before him or to a mythical context which is the creation of his fancy. If every ethical absolute is an illusion and man has no moral knowledge beyond that which his heart's desire creates, one may still ask of positive science that it reveal the wider nature of legal facts as a prerequisite to the passing of even a personal valuation upon them. And if, as we have argued, most individuals do have moral reactions to the joy and suffering they see about them, the attempt to reduce legal elements to complexes of pleasure and pain will be conducive to clarity of legal-ethical controversy even if it is not a task which the nature of things imposes upon legal scholarship.

[1] See Chapter Three, § 3 (C), *supra*.

To enumerate the effects of laws upon man's happiness is not the purpose of the present chapter. We shall be concerned only with the more modest search for the lines of causation which connect law with such effects, lines which by shifting from one culture to another give to identical legal elements contexts of varied significance in different times and places. We seek not for the messages of the law but for the code with which its cryptograms may be deciphered into the understandable ethical language of pleasure and pain. Can we find here, in the realm of positive science, as we have thought to find in the realm of pure ethics, beneath a chaos of irrelevancies, some factors of constant or universal significance for the valuation of law?

The answer to this question depends, perhaps, upon the level of our search. These factors of constant significance in the positive analysis of legal elements we can hardly discover in the portrayal of a given body of law as it functions in a particular society. The modesty or laziness which shrinks from a concrete portrayal of the effects of law in furthering or hindering the good life for the society in which we live finds sober support in the recognition that historical accidents have largely determined the mode in which our society responds to its lawmakers. And yet, it is certain that we shall not find these elements of law on the level of the *a priori.* For the law itself is an accident. There have been and there may be again societies without courts, and no peculiar characteristic of the legal order can be ascribed to an eternal need of the human spirit.

A third level of inquiry remains, the level of empirical uniformity on which we have searched for ethical standards. It is not rash to expect that in the rich diversity which legal experience records we may come upon some factors present in every legal order, linking the language of law with the life of the people. To define and enumerate these factors is a task that is perhaps neither presumptuous nor quite useless.

To divide the inquiry which these considerations delineate in a manner least destructive of the organic interrelations of our subject matter is not an easy task. With some diffidence we propose three divisions in our analysis of the complete positive nature of legal elements. We shall first of all consider the meaning of a given legal element in its relation to the rest of the legal order: What is the systematic interaction between the act of one agency of the law and the acts of all other legal agencies? The answer to this question will be framed in terms of official conduct. The problem of law observance will next occupy our attention: Given the total complex of official behavior implicated in any element of the legal order, what direct responses or adjustments will men make in their conduct? Here our analysis of law must be carried beyond realms of official action and we must consider how an awareness of law influences one's conduct in those fields where law commands and prohibits. A third problem we are required to face: What is the significance in human life of such conduct as is directly controlled by the law? To this question our response must be formulated in terms of those experiences which ethics reveals as possessed of intrinsic value.

The three subjects of inquiry are concentric rather than mutually exclusive. The second inquiry includes the first, the third, the second. The systematic behavior of legal officials is obviously a type of human conduct influenced by legal elements, and pleasure and pain may certainly be found in the immediate impacts of legal forces upon individuals as well as in regions of life less directly influenced by the law. What gives point to this trifurcation of our problem is the obvious fact that there are other realms of life than the public conduct of legal officials in which the force of law is felt, and that the human significance of law extends beyond the domain of our behavior-adjustments to legal rules.

2. THE SYSTEMATIC SIGNIFICANCE OF LEGAL FACTS

Simplest of the positive tasks which face one as he attempts to bring ethical insights to bear upon the doings of jural bodies is the task of estimating the jural significance of the jural act. And yet the most serious errors in the accomplishment of this task arise from an approach to the problem dictated by an exaggerated conception of its simplicity.

The appearance of simplicity arises from the fact that jural facts, unlike the facts of physics or biology, generally purport to be self-explanatory. The statute carries on its face its intended effects; the decision of a court, if important, is generally accompanied by a rationale in the form of an opinion; forms which point to an explanatory legal context surround most acts of subordinate legal officials. To take these affirmations of system,—judicial opinions, statutory language, oaths of officials, constitutions, procedural forms,—at their face value is to create the possibility of an autonomous science of jurisprudence.

The function of the jurist, upon this assumption, as of the pure mathematician, is to ferret out the gaps and inconsistencies in the given system, and to suggest new arrangements of axioms and theorems, new definitions, and new formulations of doctrine. The contributions of an Ames, a Williston, a Wigmore, to jurisprudence are one in kind with the demonstration of Veblen that all of euclidean geometry can be stated in terms of two indefinables, *point* and *betweenness*, or with the mammoth labors of Whitehead and Russell in demonstrating that all the propositions of pure mathematics are merely complicated forms of a few simple tautologies of formal logic.

When the systematic jurist has done his task he has done an important work. If he has done it with a mathematical impartiality towards the inconsistent rules he discovers, recognizing in them not a ground for rejecting an "incorrect" rule but only the mark of diversity in systems among which *a priori* choice is impossible, there will be none to dispute the scientific value of his contribution.

It is in these terms and upon these assumptions that learning in the law has traditionally been framed. The practical usefulness of the traditional jurisprudence is an indication that, even if the systematic claims of jural acts cannot be taken at their face value, these claims are neither stale nor worthless. The corrections that the traditional assumptions require will be for many purposes over-subtle and unmanageable in the rapid movements of the marketplace. The limitations of judicial introspection are not matters with which the average lawyer wishes to concern himself, and a jurisprudence which attacks the proclaimed rationality of legal decisions will not commend itself to the bar. But no science can rest upon the lowest level of accuracy that is practically acceptable. And so there has arisen in this country and in this century the call for an analysis of anciently ignored discrepancies between "law in books" and "law in action," between what courts are saying and what courts are doing, between the words of statutes and the conduct of courts "bound" by them, between the instructions to the jury and the laws of jury behavior, between the orthodoxly formulated functions of administrative and executive officials and the actual conduct of these officials, in short between law as principles "laid down" or "recognized" by courts and law as principles of judicial behavior.[2]

"Realistic jurisprudence" has sprung in great measure from the recognition that principles enunciated by courts as grounds of decision often represent nothing more objective than a resolution to use sanctified words wherever specified results are dictated by undisclosed determinants.[3]

[2] See Bentley, *The Process of Government* (1908), pp. 294-297, 165-172 *et passim*; Pound, "Law in Books and Law in Action" (1910) 44 *American Law Rev.* 12; Bingham, "What is the Law?" (1912) 11 *Mich. Law Rev.* 1; Bingham, "Legal Philosophy and the Law" (1914) 9 *Ill. Law Rev.* 98; Oliphant, "A Return to Stare Decisis" (1928) 6 *Am. Law School Rev.* 215; Llewellyn, "A Realistic Jurisprudence—The Next Step" (1930) 30 *Columbia Law Rev.* 431; Llewellyn, "Some Realism About Realism: Responding to Dean Pound" (1931) 44 *Harvard Law Rev.* 1222.

[3] See, in addition to the works cited in the preceding footnote: Frank, *Law and the Modern Mind* (1930); Hamilton "Affectation with Public Interest" (1930) 39 *Yale Law Jour.* 1089; Finkelstein, "Judicial Self-Limitation" (1924) 37 *Harvard Law Rev.* 338; Finkelstein, "Further Notes on Judicial Self-Limitation" (1925) 39 *Harvard Law Rev.* 221; Klaus, "Sale, Agency and Price-Maintenance" (1928) 28 *Columbia Law Rev.* 312, 441; R. A. Brown, "Due Process of Law, Police Power, and the Supreme Court" (1927) 40 *Harvard Law Rev.* 943; Handler and Pickett, "Trade-Marks and Trade Names—An Analysis and Synthesis" (1930) 30 *Columbia Law Rev.* 168, 759; Isaacs, "How Lawyers Think" (1923) 23 *Columbia Law Rev.* 555.

In analyzing the elasticity of traditional legal rules, in pointing to the amount of free play in the joints of the corpus juris, in uncovering the weaknesses of judicial "rationalization," the advocates of realistic jurisprudence have often seemed to argue against the existence of any systematic relations within law. An unrealistic view of single cases as divorced from the uniformities which lend them significance has seemed to pervade much recent writing. Perhaps a preoccupation with the "hard cases" of law which are sent to appellate courts for review and which alone fill the bulk of our reports, case-books, and treatises, has seriously distorted the views of some contemporary "realists." Whether these natural errors of a protestant movement have actually been committed is not an important question. It is, however, important to realize that there is no essential incompatibility between the view that particular legal decisions are significant only in the context of potential decisions systematically related, and the view that law finds its content in decisions of courts. No less in the actual practices than in the explanatory dicta of courts are uniformities and systematic relations to be found. A profound scepticism towards the adequacy of judicial introspection demands a reformulation of principles of judicial conduct, and in this work of reformulation a systematic analysis of the economic and social background, the moral presuppositions, and the psychological habits of thought of judges and other legal officials must play a governing role.[4] Jurisprudence, in ceasing to

[4] For pioneer efforts towards such analysis see T. Schroeder, "The Psychologic Study of Judicial Opinions" (1918) 6 *Calif. Law Rev.* 89; H. D. Lasswell, "Self Analysis and Judicial Thinking" (1930) 40 *Internat. Jour. of Ethics* 354; C. G. Haines, "General Observations on the Effects

be an autonomous science, simply extends the domain in which it seeks systematic knowledge of legal decisions.

It is therefore with no intention of minimizing the importance of recent advances in juristic thought that we put forward the systematic implications of a jural act as the first object for the concern of legal criticism. Fortunately it is an object to which vast practical interests direct unceasing study. The individual who has won a law suit is interested not in the blank fact that a decision has gone in his favor but in a hundred derivative questions to which that fact gives point. What are the possibilities of retrial or review? What will happen if a juryman tells the judge that the verdict was reached by aleatory methods? What facts would an upper court reconsider on appeal? Upon what property may the sheriff lawfully levy for the amount of judgment and what will happen if he levies upon other property? Can the defendant be prevented from fraudulently disposing of his property before execution of the judgment? What remedies are available against the defendant if the judgment is unsatisfied? How long will the judgment remain in force? How may it be renewed? What effect will be given to the judgment by the courts of another state? What questions between the parties will a court refuse to consider in the future, on the ground that they were or might have been raised by the concluded case?

of Personal, Political and Economic Influences in the Decisions of Judges" (1922) 17 *Ill. Law Rev.* 96; T. R. Powell, "The Judiciality of Minimum-Wage Legislation" (1924) 37 *Harvard Law Rev.* 545; R. A. Brown, "Police Power—Legislation for Health and Personal Safety" (1929) 42 *Harvard Law Rev.* 866; W. Hamilton, "The Ancient Doctrine Caveat Emptor" (1931) 40 *Yale Law Jour.* 1133; W. Nelles, "A Strike and Its Legal Consequences—An Examination of the Receivership Precedent for the Labor Injunction" (1931) 40 *Yale Law Jour.* 507.

How may the defendant inflict new harms with legal impunity? Each of these questions might receive a historical answer in terms of one or a dozen new lawsuits. But the problem of significance would re-emerge after each decision. It is beyond the realm of the actual that the lawyer must find the answers to these questions of his client. And beyond the realm of the actual is only blank mystery unless there are systematic connections between decisions. Whether these connections are framed in the pseudo-ethical terms of orthodox doctrine or are framed in language washed, at the suggestion of Mr. Justice Holmes, in cynical acid,[5] and flavored with psychoanalysis, behaviorism, and Marxian theory, it is only in the context which these connections create that a judicial decision has meaning.

Too obvious to be labored is the relevance of parallel considerations in the analysis of other jural facts. The object of a realistic legal criticism will be not the divine vision which follows the words "Be it enacted:" but the probable reaction between the words of the legislature and the professional prejudices and distorting apparatus of the bench, between the ideas that emerge from this often bloody encounter and the social pressures that play upon enforcing officials. Words are frail packages for legislative hopes. The voyage to the realm of law-observance is long and dangerous. Seldom do meanings arrive at their destination intact. Whether or not we approve of storms and pirates, let us be aware of them when we appraise the cargo.

Can we find any formula to collocate the relevant considerations in the task of tracing the reaction between any

[5] "The Path of Law" *Collected Legal Papers* (1920), p. 167, 174.

element of law and the rest of the legal order? Any such formula must take account of at least five factors: (1) The personal moral reactions of individuals to whom the administration of law is entrusted towards the substance of the particular legal element; (2) The professional sense of loyalty to the purpose of the original legal element; (3) The accuracy of the modes by which that purpose is transmitted and apprehended; (4) The professional thought-ways which bring different legal elements to mutual relevancy; and (5) The distribution of power within the realm of law administration.

(1) To the extent that the law addresses itself to an unpredictable future, it must be incomplete. To the extent that unpredicted conflicts demand settlement, authority must be given to the discretion of the law administrator. It is a truism that this authority will be utilized in accordance with the desires of the law administrator, and since no man ever sinks his whole personality into a single role, it is inevitable that such desires as may be called "personal" will in some measure dictate the direction of discretion.[6]

The personal desires and ideals of those in whom law administration is vested can never be wholly negligible in the calculation of the systematic repercussions of a jural act within the jural order. The importance of this factor will, however, naturally be reduced to a minimum where the class of individuals who directly control the legal process is comparatively homogeneous in outlook. Similarly, in particular fields of law where emotional drives

[6] See Bentley, *The Process of Government* (1908), ch. 16; Brooks Adams, "Law under Inequality: Monopoly" in *Centralization and the Law* (1906) Lecture 2; and works cited in footnote 4, *supra*.

are reduced to a minimum, personal idiosyncrasies and biases may be of rather inconsiderable importance.

(2) The play of personal beliefs as to the desirability of a given rule or ruling receives its primary check in the feeling of the officer of the law that his office entails a duty of loyalty to the legal order as such, whatever its content. This loyalty is institutionally strengthened by the oath and badge of office, by the realization that one's legal discretion is limited by his dependence upon other branches of law administration, and above all by the professional spirit which compels allegiance to one's co-workers and to the traditions of one's craft. The trial judge loses professional prestige when he is too frequently overruled in an appellate tribunal. The appellate judge, aware of the tenuous and sporadic nature of his control over lower courts, is inclined to approach a case on appeal with some bias in favor of a judgment of affirmance. A similar tendency towards co-operation plays its part in the relation between court and legislature, legislature and administrative board, court and executive official. So, too, the continuity of a single office naturally induces an attitude of respect towards the use that one's predecessors have made of the authority which one inherits. Whether or not this loyalty be sanctified with such phrases as *stare decisis* and *res adjudicata*, it makes some appearance in every legal system and every legal office. To this professional conservatism many evils, no doubt, may be ascribed, but few will deny its importance in the control of personal bias.

(3) If professional loyalty constitutes an effective check upon the exercise of legal discretion, such loyalty is in turn substantially limited by difficulties in apprehend-

ing what it is that demands professional allegiance. Without authoritative published accounts of the legislative history of a statute, a court frequently finds the orthodox inquiry into the "intent of the legislature" a vain ghost chase. The Common Law of England led a precarious existence in this country, until the middle of the eighteenth century brought a wholesale importation of English law reports, Blackstone's Commentaries, and English-trained lawyers.[7] How much does history owe to the fact that the Corpus Juris Civilis was physically preserved through the Dark Ages while none of the systematic statements of Greek law has ever been recovered? How much does contemporary constitutional law in this country owe to the scantiness of our records of the social legislation which marked the early history of our states and which now offers, only to historians, historic precedent for numerous unconstitutional statutes? How much law lies hidden today in current "memorandum decisions"?

Our problem assumes its simplest form in these terms, but it demands an account of less tangible facts. The shifting sense of words[8] and the shifting lines of conceptual classification have more than once led conservative courts to radical innovation. The incompleteness of most formu-

7 Reinsch, "The English Common Law in the Early American Colonies" I *Select Essays in Anglo-American Legal History* (1907) 367; Goebel, "King's Law and Local Custom in Seventeenth Century New England" (1931) 31 *Columbia Law Rev.* 416.

8 Most curious is the recent history of Lord Coke's mistranslation of the provision of Magna Carta protecting the "liberties and franchises" of freemen, that is to say, the monopolistic privileges of certain landowners to hold courts, as referring to freedom in general. The mistranslation, accepted in apparent good faith by the United States Supreme Court, has been a significant weapon in the judicial annihilation of unwelcome statutes. See Commons, *The Legal Foundations of Capitalism* (1924), pp. 47 *et seq.*

lated legal rules has often rendered near-sighted allegiance to the past pregnant with new heresy, as changes in penalties, in procedural apparatus, or in surrounding substantive rules, give new legal significance to the legal element that is preserved. The most difficult task of the judge is often the safeguarding of a decision from a perverse after-life. But the most emphatic and explicit differentiation of cases which other courts might suppose to be very much like the decided case may be "mere dictum" for the next court. The more or less innocent misreading of past cases is probably the chief source of growth in case law.

(4) The compromise between personal motives and official loyalties which is at the heart of jural conduct finds its expression in terms of those varied conceptual devices by which the force of a given jural act is diminished, amplified, or redirected[9] as it moves through a gravitational field of relevant jural activity. One who rejects the phonograph theory of judicial behavior[10] must approach these conceptual devices empirically, as reflections of certain psychological attitudes rather than as revelations of pre-existent truth.

What a case "stands for," *i.e.*, what rule, or set of potential decisions, it establishes, we have seen to be a problem not in logic but in judicial psychology.[11] The idea of common law as "case law," the doctrine of *stare decisis*, and the "case method" of teaching law reveal with peculiar clarity the important role which judicial habits of classifi-

[9] See Llewellyn, *The Bramble Bush* (1930), pp. 56-66.

[10] See M. R. Cohen, "The Process of Judicial Legislation" (1914) 48 *Am. Law Rev.* 161.

[11] See Chapter One, § 6, *supra.*

cation play in the determination of the legal order. Every legal decision is the decision of a particular case, and by no purely logical process can a universal rule or an application to another case be derived from a particular decision or from any number of particular decisions. Rules of law, like all other rules inductively arrived at, are based upon the assumption that such and such a case is typical of a certain class of cases.[12] But what class a case will be seen to typify is decided by the habitual categories of thought of judges. Different cases are commonly brought under a single rule by regarding the current categories of thought as the "true" or "natural" ones,—a metaphysical error which is not peculiar to judges and lawyers. But the categories of judicial thought, no less than those of common sense or religion, shift with all the winds of doctrine. Things anciently separated by firm sheepskin compartments come to be seen together as "torts," and with the unified concept comes a cross-fertilization of theory. An attack on the "lump concept" *title* supports a division of problems in the law of sales that have been traditionally united, in theory if not always in actual decision.[13] The invention of the word *boycott* or of the attractive phrase *right of privacy* gives vast doctrinal importance to once trivial decisions. The work of Hohfeld in throwing the searchlight of logical analysis upon traditional ambiguities in the words *right, privilege, power,* etc.[14] bids fair to bring into the judicial analysis of precedent a greater discrimination than is yet common.

12 See Bishop Whately's admirable treatment of the logical nature of induction in his *Elements of Logic*, Book 4, ch. 1.

13 See Llewellyn, *Cases and Materials on the Law of Sales* (1929).

14 Hohfeld, *Fundamental Legal Conceptions* (1923).

But each of these illustrations of the variant empirical character of judicial thought presupposes the more general but equally accidental judicial belief in a fundamental separation of powers between legislature and judiciary. Can any one doubt that the popularization of the doctrine that judges make law will modify the judicial attitude towards past decisions and bring with it a keener awareness of legislative problems?

The habits of thought of the legislator are no less dependent upon the shifting sands of political theory. They are commonly less sharply differentiated from popular thought-ways than are those of the judge, because of a greater contact with and dependence upon the general public and because of a less specialized training. But the nature of the legislator's task brings into his thinking peculiarities which are of particular importance in legal criticism directed to the judicial interpretation of statutes or the exercise of the judicial veto. Most impressive is the bovine calm with which American legislatures ignore judicial assaults upon their offspring, an attitude traceable, no doubt, to the fact that statutes are regularly passed because of the pressure of sporadically organized currents of politically unsophisticated public opinion rather than because of the personal aims of the legislators. The common law principle that statutes are not to be extended by analogy sums up a psychological attitude which has nothing of *a priori* necessity about it, and which seems to be breaking down with a growing use by lawyers of statutes as indicia of some "public policy" relevant to a case.

Differences of professional attitude follow the lines

of division of labor within the jural order. Becoming critical where different classes of judicial officials are drawn from different social groups, they culminate in such struggles as those which the common law courts waged with their rivals in the sixteenth century, or in a guerrilla warfare between legislatures and courts such as *Marbury v. Madison*[15] inaugurated in this country. Such divisions are naturally furthered by the doctrine of the separation of powers, and the limitations upon the power of the state which arise from this fact are peculiarly pertinent to the ethical problem of the proper scope of political activity. In the history of American labor legislation, the record of futile legislative onslaughts on professional and economic prejudices of courts occupies a large chapter. But the working out of conflicting currents of professional thought within the legal order depends in the last analysis upon the distribution of political power among the classes of legal officials.

(5) In any legal order extensive enough to demand specialization of function among officials the significance of any legal act will depend in part upon the locus of the act within the ranks of the legal order. The acts of trial judge, court of last resort, sheriff, and legislature, though directed toward a single purpose, have different capacities for good and evil which a sound legal criticism cannot afford to ignore.

The official and unofficial checks exercised by one branch of law administration upon another, which furnish so large a part of the substance of political science, are an essential part of the meaning of jural acts. The ethical

15 Marbury v. Madison, 5 U. S. (1 Cranch) 137 (1803).

significance of Supreme Court decisions on the constitutionality of statutes would be radically altered if a Jacksonian attitude towards the enforcement of such decisions should be adopted by the executive arm of the federal government. Sovereignty, as the power to utter the last legal word, is a complex concept, and the locus of sovereignty varies, in every political structure, with the question presented for legal solution. Considered in its broadest aspect, final legal power always rests in the group capable of amending the most fundamental laws of the state. But if we focus our vision upon less fundamental issues of government, we find the final power to conclude disputes distributed among all the agencies of law enforcement. The local justice of the peace, in an unappealable case, speaks with the same legal finality as the legislature or the highest appellate court. The criticism of any jural act thus demands a calculation of the controls to which that act is subject, and no *a priori* doctrine of sovereignty can be a proper substitute for this calculation. Without an understanding of these controls it is impossible to measure with accuracy the effective limits of action at any point in the legal system or to forecast with any certainty the echoing responses which are forever doubling, destroying, or renewing the voices of the law.

Rough and inadequate as is the foregoing sketch, it is perhaps enough to indicate the nature and importance of the elements which govern the interaction between that in the legal order which we are, at any moment, criticizing and that which we temporarily take for granted. It is enough, at least, to reveal the shallowness of such ethical theory as applies the standards of morality to the conceptual content of a judicial act, and to establish the place of jurisprudence, in the narrowest sense of the term, in legal criticism. Jurisprudence, as the study of the reactions between any part of the dynamic legal order and the rest of that order, is relevant to every valuation of law which is directed to less than the whole law. Its subject matter is not rules of law in propositional vacuum but the field of judicial conduct. It seeks to discover systematic relations of cause and effect within that field and in this task it is continually dependent upon psychology and general anthropology. Such a legal science does not become a normative science by reason of dealing with invocations to morality, any more than anthropology becomes religion by dealing with men's religious attitudes. It assumes its place in the valuation of law as an instrument for the accurate location of a legal element in the context of its systematic jural significance.

3. THE FORCE OF LAW

Given the total complex of legal behavior implicated in any element of the legal order, what adjustments will men make in their conduct? With the recognition of this problem we take leave of jurisprudence as a science dealing with the internal workings of legal machinery and seek the impacts of that machinery on human life. To answer this question in its lowest terms is not to exhaust the positive content of legal criticism, for when we have set forth the social meaning of law in terms of adjusted habits of human behavior, in terms, that is, of commercial practices, the distribution of economic power, the organization of personal relationships, there will still remain the problem of reducing these aspects of human conduct to terms in which our ethics discovers its ultimate values,[16] to terms of individual joy and suffering. This latter problem we must temporarily postpone, restricting our immediate inquiry to the simpler task of tracing the interaction between the jural order and non-jural society.

Scire leges non hoc est verba earum tenere, sed vim et potestatem.[17] In seeking to trace the force and power of law we approach in a realistic manner the age-old problem of the "proper scope of law." The only limitation which general principles of ethics admit in assuming to prescribe what law ought to do is the limitation of what law *can* do.

If we discover that the law cannot make sunsets more beautiful, that it cannot make π equal to 22/7 (although a Kansas legislature once entertained some doubts in this matter), that it cannot put a stop to drunkenness, or that it cannot bring about a just distribution of wealth, we shall be in a position to define more narrowly the class of goods which the law ought to produce. Let us not forget, however, that the narrowness of our final formulation is not a purely ethical matter but a consequence of brute facts which need not be eternal. If it should ever happen, for instance, that smoke legislation and legal control of mechanical weather transformers could ensure the occurrence of beautiful sunsets, their occurrence would be a proper end of law, and arguments that, historically, law

16 The notion that "human experience discloses no ultimates" is carried to its logical conclusion in Professor Underhill Moore's attack, in the name of Behaviorism, upon the possibility of critically evaluating legal institutions. "Rational Basis of Legal Institutions" (1923) 23 *Columbia Law Rev.* 609.

17 *Dig.* 1. 3. 17 (Celsus).

had never been concerned with such things, or that laws of this sort would spoil a harmonious ideological pattern, or that some metaphysically "natural"[18] function of law did not provide for such matters would all be perfectly irrelevant to the question of whether law ought to produce beautiful sunsets.

This is a point upon which most non-lawyers will readily agree, yet its very obviousness demands a word of explanation for the radically different approach of traditional jurisprudence to the question of the proper scope of law. The attitude of the jurist towards the legal presumptions of general ethical theory is the attitude of any craftsman when the ultimate value of his professional aims is questioned.

The blacksmith beats out a beautiful sword of perfect balance and admirable edge. The "natural function" of the sword is to kill people. An ethical philosopher observes as he passes that the sword is a bad thing, that it ought, in fact, to be beaten into a ploughshare.

"Nonsense," is the retort of injured professional pride. "This sword is fitted to its true purpose. Whether it is good or bad is a question for swordsmen, not for moralists. Turning it into a ploughshare would be an unnatural perversion. Besides, the people of the community have asked me to make swords, not ploughshares."

To which the moralist must reply, "Efficiency is not an intrinsic good. Efficiency for a valuable purpose is good,

18 "To begin with, what is 'natural'? Roughly speaking, anything to which the speaker was accustomed in childhood. Lao-Tze objects to roads and carriages and boats, all of which were probably unknown in the village where he was born. Rousseau has got used to these things, and does not regard them as against nature. . . ." B. Russell, *What I Believe* (1925) p. 80.

but efficiency in an unworthy undertaking is a multiplication of evil, and the most expert murderer is the worst. Conformity with a natural function is not a justification for any tool, and until human judgment becomes infallible, and human desires wholly good, conformity with a popular demand will be equally inadequate to establish ethical value."

The attitude of the craftsman and the aesthetic system of critical standards to which it gives rise[19] are common in all walks of life but especially developed and especially obnoxious in conservative and ritualistic institutions like the church and the law. The essence of Pharisaism, the poetic justification of this attitude has been chanted by poets and philosophers from Plato to Bradley and Kipling.[20] There is a convincing simplicity about the apotheosis of efficiency, and the doctrine that life's supreme value lies in doing the assigned job well, no matter what the job is. But the appeal of this philosophy is to our vanity, to the intellectual shallowness which rationalizes its incapacity for evaluating ultimate ideals by denying their existence, and to the personal pride which finds something sacrilegious in the condemnation of sincere but misguided exertions.

The question of the proper scope of law cannot find an answer in terms of history, aesthetics, or metaphysics. Only a realistic tracing of what Dean Pound has called "the limits of effective legal action"[21] can reveal aspects

19 See Chapter Two, § 1 (A) *supra.*

20 Plato, *Republic* *353, 434 (Steph.) *et passim*; Bradley, *Ethical Studies*, ch. 5 (My Station and Its Duties); Kipling, "Tomlinson" in *Verses: 1889-1896*, p. 158.

21 See Pound, "The Limits of Effective Legal Action" (1917) 27 *Internat. Jour. of Ethics* 150. And see M. R. Cohen, *Reason and Nature*, Book 3,

of the good life immune to legal pressures. And this realistic tracing of the force and powers of law is demanded not only in our analysis of the proper scope of law, but in every utilitarian valuation of the law. The human substance of a rule of law is not action commanded but action caused.

Our inquiry into the factors controlling the extent and nature of law observance must begin with a clear conception of what we mean by law. Law, as a body of rules according to which courts decide cases,[22] commands obedience only in a somewhat metaphorical sense. When we speak of "obeying the law" we always think of criminal law, but even criminal law is not, as a rule, framed in precepts addressed to the public. If it contains imperative phrases these are commonly addressed to courts or other judicial officers. And in civil law the lawyer commonly thinks in terms of such propositions as "Where the parties purport to sell specific goods, and the goods without the knowledge of the seller have wholly perished at the time when the agreement is made, the agreement is void."[23] In what sense can we speak of obedience or disobedience to such a proposition?

The difficulty of this question arises only when we attempt to view a particular legal rule in abstraction from its systematic significance.[24] What does it actually mean to

---

ch. 4 § 2; Dabin, *La Philosophie de l'ordre juridique positif* (1929), § 1, ch. 2, par. 2, 3; Bentham, "Principles of Morals and Legislation," ch. 19, 1 *Works* 42.

22 See Chapter One, § 3, *supra.*

23 Uniform Sales Act, § 7 (1).

24 The problem of distinguishing between "complete" and "incomplete" rules of law, and the interrelation between civil and criminal law which a frank facing of that problem reveals, receive illuminating consideration

say that an agreement purporting to transfer certain goods which do not exist is void? It means for one thing (and we here assume a dozen other rules) that the person who was to receive the destroyed goods is no longer obliged to pay for them. If he has already agreed to pay in certain merchandise the merchandise remains his property. To say that the merchandise remains the buyer's property is to say that if the seller or any one else takes it he will be subject to prosecution for larceny, that he will be subject to an action for damages, that he will have no redress at law if the owner injures him while reasonably defending this merchandise.

The most abstract rule of civil law, seen in its legal context, thus reduces to a set of probabilities that under certain conditions certain unpleasant things will happen to certain people either at the hands of a criminal court, or at the hands of a civil court assessing damages (or other penalties), or at the hands of some aggrieved party temporarily endowed with the authority of the law (in much the same way that the judge, sheriff, or hangman is endowed with the authority of the law). To conceive of such probabilities of unpleasantness as commands, and to conceive of avoidance of the situations in which the unpleasantness arises as obedience, is a useful figure of speech. It has the great value of recalling us from the law-treatise's degenerate world of abstractions, in which strange metaphysical entities bearing outlandish names undergo curious metamorphoses to become stranger entities with more out-

---

in Bentham, "Principles of Morals and Legislation," ch. 19 (concluding note), 1 *Works* 151-154. See also M. R. Cohen, "Justice Holmes and the Nature of Law" (1931) 31 *Columbia Law Rev.* 352, 358.

landish names. The sophisticated lawyer in a civilized community can afford to take for granted the simple rules of trespass and larceny which give point to such questions as "Who has title?" "Is there a contract?" "Is there a sale?" When the layman discovers the answer to these latter questions he will commonly act in such a way as to avoid criminal prosecution for larceny, etc. But the legal philosopher seeking a clear conception of the nature of law must see the assortment of threats to which all rules of law reduce. The problem we face is the determination of the efficacy of these threats or commands in inducing avoidance of the acts to which they are attached, that is to say, in inducing law observance.

The solution of this problem demands, in general, a consideration of three distinguishable factors, (1) the knowledge of law, (2) the incentives to law-resistance, and (3) the power of law-resistance.

(1) It is a truism that without knowledge of law conformity to it is an accident. And yet, as Kantorowicz has ironically insisted, knowledge of the law is meager among honorable citizens.[25] The apparent implications of these

25 "This fiction (that every one knows the whole law of a state) contradicts the facts in the grossest manner. The truth is that nobody knows the whole law in its unsurveyable compass, that a few people know a portion of it, that most know nothing at all of it. So true is this that if a private citizen has acquired a thorough knowledge of the law of the state he will usually belong to a class of shady gentlemen. The usurer, the criminal apprentice, the yellow journalist, the fraudulent promoter know the rules which interest them accurately enough; the wholesale merchant, the artist, the officer, the statesman, the husband have only a sporadic acquaintance with even the paragraphs of the sales, copyright, public, international, or family law, without being disturbed in their activities by this ignorance. The traveler in a foreign country makes himself familiar with the language, the history, the art, the customs of the people—not even in a dream does it occur to any one to so much as open its statute books."

two propositions find qualification in several facts which it has become the fashion today to overlook.[26]

The specialization of occupation which is so nearly synonymous with civilization continually presents new situations for legal control and thus gives rise to new rules of law, but with the same force it narrows the sphere in which a given individual need be directly aware of law.

At the same time the specialization of the function of law-enforcement itself relieves the average urban citizen of the occasion to apply a knowledge of law that was indispensable in days of the hue and cry.[27]

Kantorowicz (*sub pseud.* Gnaeus Flavius), *Der Kampf um die Rechtswissenschaft* (1906) 13-14.

26 Despite contemporary panics over the "rain of law" it is still true, as it was in 1866, when Stimson wrote his *American Statute Law*, that "The several states at the present time do rarely change their important substantive law; and the time of the annual or biennial legislatures is mostly taken up with private enactments, charters, revenue laws, and local improvements" (*op. cit.* p. v). Of the 20,473 acts and resolutions passed in our states and territories during 1927 and 1928 (*State Law Index: 1927-1928*), more than half deal with matters of administrative organization or personnel, or with matters of local or temporary importance, such as the fixing of tax rates, the condemnation of parcels of land, etc. All the general laws passed in 51 jurisdictions during two years can be clearly summarized within 300 pages (*ibid.*), *i.e.* in three pages per state per annum. Of these laws the vast majority are directed not to the public as a whole, but to small professional groups (*e.g.* chauffeurs, corporation directors, chiropractors), and there is, of course, a great deal of duplication of statutes among the various jurisdictions. Add to these considerations the fact that much state legislation consists of relaxation or modification of older laws, and the popular myth of legislative overwork ceases to offer a postulate of political philosophy, an argument against the prohibition or the child labor amendment, an unfailing source of editorial copy, and an excuse for lawyers not to read the statute books.

27 The lawyer and the policeman are the inevitable servants of a public which cannot interrupt the exacting labors and pleasures of civilized life to take part in the legal or illegal pursuit of criminals and the general guardianship of community morals. With the growth of specialization we find not only functional divisions in the legal order itself, but a certain institutional organization of the legal interests of the public. Wholly unofficial bodies are supported by the public to give definite form to general

A second fact that must be kept in mind in estimating the breadth and depth of legal ignorance is the set of mechanisms which every developed legal system maintains for the communication of legal knowledge at points of impending conflict. Bills of peace, injunctions, and administrative orders or warnings, are typical instruments for the wasteless conveyance of legal knowledge.

Finally, it must be borne in mind that most law which is not either directed to a small group of individuals or intrinsically interesting to the public becomes known not directly but rather in its disguises. The rules of positive morality by which men guide their conduct are often approximations of positive law, built up out of the dramatic passages in spectacular law suits and the persuasive driblets of legal doctrine that trickle into the lay consciousness in the form of moral-legal maxims. The process is necessarily a slow one. It may take three or four hundred years for laymen to learn that a contract does not have to be in writing. Legal ignorance thus presents a peculiarly acute difficulty in the adaptation of law to short-term social problems.

A little legal knowledge, it seems, judiciously distributed, may go a long way. But with this qualification we return to the proposition with which we began. Not only is conformity to unknown law accidental, but such conformity is no part of the social effects of the law that we are evaluating. An understanding of the mechanisms of legal education, in the broadest sense of that term, thus plays an

beliefs about labor legislation, the prevention of cruelty to animals, prohibition, etc. To these bodies the public more and more transfers the task of understanding the law, as well as the other tasks of practical law reform and law enforcement.

integral part in the estimation of law's social significance. The demand for "justice in the individual case" finds necessary limitations in the educative value of simplicity and uniformity, of dramatic formalism and poetic justice,[28] and of conformity to the content of current positive morality.

(2) Law which does not attach penalties to things that men might otherwise do is of no human significance.[29] Law in action thus appears as a running conflict between desires opposing law and desires behind law. Before examining the weapons used in this conflict we may well afford to take a rapid review of the troops on both sides.

Desires behind law fall, in general, into two orders, (a) those that the law calls forth, and (b) those that call forth the law. Similarly desires opposing law may be divided into (a) those that the law itself stimulates and (b) those against which law is directed.

Ordinarily law, when known, has some gravitational effect upon the network of human desires in the field to which the law is directed. The desire to maintain the respect of the respectable presses personal ideals to conformity with the social ends that law sanctions, even where there is no calculation of the actual enforceability of law. But legislators must take account of the perverse human

[28] The "object all sublime" of Gilbert and Sullivan's Mikado and of Dante is earnestly pursued in many primitive codes. *Cf.* Bentham's list of characteristic punishments in the *Theory of Legislation*, "Principles of the Penal Code."

[29] *Cf.* Holmes, "The Path of the Law," *Collected Legal Papers* (1920) pp. 169-179; Llewellyn, "The Effect of Legal Institutions upon Economics" (1925) 15 *Am. Ec. Rev.* 665, 682. The former of these essays frames the problem of legal analysis in terms of the "bad man," who won't obey unenforced law, the latter in terms of the "marginal individual" who will change his conduct under legal pressure.

joy in doing what is forbidden. Whether or not the desire to kill one's parents was first aroused, as Cicero thought, by laws against patricide, there are certainly many situations in which unpopular laws have stimulated and reinforced the desires against which they were directed. This problem is naturally of particular concern to an unpopular government.

More important than the repercussions of the desires called forth by any law upon the efficacy of that law are the aids and hindrances which the law finds in pre-existing desires. We have already surveyed those desires which are an intrinsic part of the living machinery of law. In some fields of law, *e.g.* workmen's compensation, public utility regulation, and taxation, enforcement does not call for much assistance from unprofessional defenders of law. But there are many fields of law in which legal officials are impotent without the aid of an approving public opinion. Nearly all laws which demand observance by a very large portion of the public are necessarily of this sort. It is of the utmost importance, then, in determining the efficacy of such law to consider the motives which may lead private citizens to aid or obstruct law enforcement. Civil law depends for its operation upon the efficacy of the desire for revenge or compensation on the part of injured individuals, a desire which varies notably with the temper of a people and the availability of the legal machinery. But here, as in other respects, there is no clear distinction between civil and criminal law. In the twilight zone between state operation and private operation of legal machinery, one finds such things as "punitive damages," privately collectible penalties, rewards for the capture or prosecution of criminals, and the power of the citizen to make arrests. The place of these tools in the outfitting of legal rules presents a problem which demands difficult comparisons in the roster of human desires.

More obvious is the need for weighing human incentives when we consider the problem with reference to the potential law resister rather than the potential law enforcer. The problem of arranging and balancing opposing human desires to create effective law is a problem of untold complexity. The tools with which the legislator works are necessarily clumsy. Imprisonment to one man is a social disgrace and economic catastrophe, to another a blessed refuge from bread-lines and wintry winds.[30] The fine which is not graduated to fit the wealth of the offender is a pitifully absurd tool for the control of non-pecuniary offenses. But obviously the clumsiness of these traditional instruments for the control of desires is a function of the inequality existent in a given society. A society which guaranteed the material essentials of the good life to every one, and which rigidly restricted the concentration of wealth, would find the instruments of fine and imprisonment well adapted to most legal needs.

In considering primitive or alien codes of law we are met with many monstrosities which call forth immediate condemnation. But we seldom exercise sufficient discrimination in deciding whether the fault is with the law or with the social opinions which make the law necessary. The retributive theory of punishment appears to most enlightened students to be unsound and barbarous, yet social

[30] O. Henry's story of "The Cop and the Anthem" is re-enacted daily in the lower courts of New York City when thermometers and employment figures drop.

conditions may persuade the most humane of legislators that its incorporation in the law is to some extent desirable. If powerful motives of revenge are not considered in the law they may find expressions of greater weight in human misery than a severity of punishment beyond the limited demands of reformation, protection of society, and example to possible law-breakers. On the other hand, legislation imposing penalties in excess of popular demand, no matter how foolish that demand may be, frequently weakens instead of strengthening the force of law, particularly under a jury system.

All this is not to argue that law must or should restrict itself to a reflection of the will of the public. The public will can be as foolish and as brutal as any individual will. Regularly it is too formless and irrational a thing to serve as a foundation of law.[31] Indeed the reform of the public will is one of the most essential functions of law. But this must be recognized: that the leeway allowed to law beyond the will of the public is strictly limited, and that the highest ethical utilization of the power of law involves the most careful calculation of these limits. "He who attacks prejudice wantonly and without necessity, and he who suffers himself to be led blindfold a slave to it, equally miss the line of reason."[32]

(3) Extensive as is the task of analyzing the human desires upon which and with which the law operates, the significance of these desires in the problem of law enforcement is indeterminate until we have measured the powers

[31] See Bentley, *Process of Government* (1908) ch. 8; Lippmann, *Public Opinion* (1922), *The Phantom Public* (1925).

[32] Bentham, "The Influence of Time and Place in Matters of Legislation," ch. 3, 1 *Works* 171, 180.

which they command. The law is a dynamic equilibrium between conflicting social forces. The calculation of the law's possibilities and effects demands an appraisal of the forces which organized human desires command.[33] This is a problem of practical politics, but the moralist who disdains problems of practical politics must not pass judgment upon political animals.

To frame the question of law's social significance in these terms is not to deny the psychological factors which appear in law observance, but simply to recognize the interaction between thought and conduct. Armies, police forces, and economic institutions, no less than habit of law and order, are organizations of human desire which crumble to dust if the spirit departs.

The powers at the command of law are limited in various ways.[34] For one thing, law as a human institution cannot transcend the limits of human power. The intrinsic nature and ulterior effects of law can lie only in human activity and the results of such activity. The ideals which can be realized through law are therefore limited to the domain in which human action is effective. We need not attempt to bound the realm in which law is forever impotent. It is enough to point to it. The realm of human impotence,

33 Such an appraisal is attempted in two notable contributions to a realistic political science: Bentley, *The Process of Government* (1908), and Bertrand and Dora Russell, *The Prospects of Industrial Civilization* (1923), ch. 10-11.

34 To a certain extent, the problem of the potentialities and limits of law is one of logic, which charts the ultimate limits of rational significance. It is in logical terms that we finally frame the choices which law must make, but what lines of classification are to be selected from the infinite space of logic is not a logical problem. *Cf.* Tourtoulon's suggestive discussion of "pure legal science or the science of possible solutions." *Philosophy in the Development of Law*, ch. 13, § 4.

however, is not entirely constant. Every invention of the physical or biological or social sciences conquers a portion of it. Yet, whatever that domain be, it will always represent the ultimate limits of legal efficiency.

There are narrower limits upon the field of effective legal action than these general human limitations. Law is not only human, and heir to all the infirmities of human flesh, but social, and subject to the further limitations of social activity. Whether or not there is any realm of personal experience which does not have its objectively observable and externally controllable aspects, even the most valiant behaviorist will scarcely deny that what lies within the experience and power of one individual is never wholly within the experience and power of his fellow-men. Thus law must respect the individuality of men, but it need not make a virtue of the necessity. Indeed, the attempts to define this undiscoverable, unpunishable, unrewardable realm of experience are all rather unsatisfactory. With a developed psychology we will no longer laugh at such laws as the English law of treason which prohibited the "compassing and imagining of the death of the sovereign" under penalty of torture and death. There are, as Mr. Justice Holmes has reminded us, many situations in the law today in which a man's life or liberty depends upon the guess of twelve jurymen as to his state of mind on a given occasion. But in so far as we recognize the impossibility of completely understanding or completely describing the individual, we must recognize the impossibility of completely prescribing his experience. And what is empirically of greater importance, we must recognize the cost, for examiner and examinee, for ruler and subject, of applying law's sanctions directly to the less public aspects of man's life.[35]

More definite and stringent restrictions upon the powers of law arise from the peculiar nature of the legal mechanism. The law is a function of the state, and the domain of its effective application varies with the growth or decline of the state's power. In general, the power of the state in primitive communities is very weak, and when it is impossible for us to decide whether there is a state at all it is also impossible for us to decide whether there is any law (distinguishing law from the sanctions of custom and religion which guide human action in all societies, political or non-political). At the earliest stage of political development the physical power behind the law is almost negligible and, as a consequence, the domain of "the politically achievable good" is extremely narrow. The state cannot, and is therefore under no obligation to, control such things as domestic relations and informal agreements. The limited power of the primitive political organization is generally used where it will do the most good, in putting the workings of revenge into channels that do not interfere too violently with public safety, and in establishing a few fixed forms of social and commercial intercourse, to the infraction of which fixed penalties, frequently left to the aggrieved parties to enforce, attach. Such a characterization applies not only to the early law of Rome and to the Icelandic law of the sagas, but as well to international law

35 For a suggestive formulation of the problem of economy in the organization of legal forces, see Llewellyn, "The Effects of Legal Institutions upon Economics" (1925) 15 *Am. Ec. Rev.* 665-666.

in its present infancy.[36] Formalism, the outstanding characteristic of law at this stage, is a necessary principle of economy, through which the law multiplies its actual physical powers by calling into being psychological aids based upon definiteness, narrowness, easy applicability (whence the ethical superiority of trial by lot or ordeal over trial by judge or jury), immediate aesthetic appeal (*e.g.* the *lex talionis*), and security against unpredictable interpretation or outright change.

As the political organization of a community grows in power it comes to include new fields in its domain of legal control. These fields may be annexed from the property of the religious authority, or from the property of common moral opinion, or from the primeval waste, the institutional *res nullius*. Always there is the protest of legal atavists that these innovations exceed the "proper function" of law. No doubt the moral indignation of law-abiding Roman patriarchs when the state entered the field of domestic relations and interfered with the liberty of the father to kill his own children was as bitter as the protest of the United States Supreme Court against child labor legislation. But the arguments of legal absolutism and the prejudice of moral inertia slowly recede before the expanding power of the state and the growing social demand for the utilization of that power.

The law makes most progress where it does not conflict with powerful social forces, so that early law, in order

[36] A further application of this general characterization is illustrated in an article, "Rudimentary Society Among Boys," by J. H. Johnson. Johns Hopkins University Studies in History and Political Science, 1884, vol. 2, no. 11, reprinted in Kocourek and Wigmore, *Evolution of Law,* vol. 3 (*Formative Influences of Legal Development*) (1918).

to secure obedience and perpetuate the reign of law, must be largely a sanctification of the *status quo*. A recognition of this fact is absolutely necessary if we are to avoid, on the one hand, the superficial evaluation of all legal systems by the degree of their conformity with our own, and, on the other hand, the application to present problems of standards that have outlived the historical conditions on which they were based. The progress of law is not, in its most significant aspects, a progress in legal wisdom, but an increase in the realm of jurisdiction dominated by the sovereign power in virtue of its increased physical force. Thus, if the law of early Rome gave sanction to extreme powers of creditors and masters over the bodies of debtors and slaves, we cannot say that the law ought to have been otherwise (*i.e.* ought to have denied those rights) unless we think that the legal forces of the Roman commonwealth could have challenged and subdued the powers of the dominant social class. This seems highly improbable. It was only with the consolidation of Rome's political power that such limitations gradually became possible and actual.[37]

The nature of these problems is totally obscured by the popular emphasis upon intention or intrinsic content rather than result as the determining elements of a moral situation. Commonly a law commanding a good thing or prohibiting an evil is immediately characterized as a good law.[38] But unless we arbitrarily restrict the term *good* to

[37] While the example given above seems to us unexceptionable, it is well to keep in mind Bentham's warning against the too easy assumption that peculiar laws are always justified as well as explained by peculiarities of popular custom. See "The Influence of Time and Place in Matters of Legislation," ch. 2, 1 *Works* 171, 179-180.

[38] See Chapter Two, § 2 (B), *supra*.

apply only to intentions, which is something jurists and moralists never do in their conclusions although they may do so in their premises, this sort of inference is simply illegitimate. For in the type of case under our immediate consideration, a well-intentioned law which attacks dominant interests without a powerful sanction of political force behind it either will be ineffective or, what is usually worse, will provoke rebellion, anarchy, or despotism. The rise of Fascism in Italy is an interesting reminder that this basic ethical requirement of moderate conformity with the will of dominant social groups is never wholly lost.[39]

As a state increases in strength, it can disregard more and more the will of those who, but for the state, would dominate society. A rounded system of "strict law" may develop; and with the further development of political power vast new fields of conduct may be brought into legal purview under the rubric of "equity."[40]

In the modern centralized states of the West the monopoly of internal physical power by the sovereign is probably much greater than ever before in history due very largely to inventions of the last century in industrial machinery (which makes centralization of control pos-

[39] Political democracy, when it is not based upon economic and social equality, is necessarily limited in the effectuation of its doctrinal claims by the power of socially dominant minorities to defy or render ineffective popular legislation. These limitations of actual political power frequently find recognition and rationalization in constitutional restrictions upon the scope of legislation, and it is interesting to observe how, in the United States, growing inequality in the distribution of economic power has gone hand in hand with a growing tendency of courts to draw constitutional restrictions upon popular legislation out of the vague terms of the fifth and fourteenth amendments, the commerce clause, etc. But one must go beyond abstract political theory to discover the empirical bases of this correlation.

[40] For a fuller account of the moral significance of these "stages" see Pound, "Limits of Effective Legal Action" (1917) 27 *International Journal of Ethics* 150.

sible),[41] in means of communication, and in tools of warfare.[42] With the recent growth of political power has gone a tremendous enlargement of the field of possible effective legal control, and a less extensive enlargement of the field of actual control. For, here again, a prejudice against realism in ethical thought, combined with a powerful moral inertia, leads to the limitation of the activities of the state to those realms in which it could have operated effectively a century or so ago. In politics, as elsewhere, conservatism is simply the idealization of yesterday's misfortunes.

The value of laws regulating wages or the liquor trade or parental discipline is a very different matter in a state which has wide powers of enforcement from what it may have been under conditions of past history that would have rendered such legislation vain or politically suicidal. A failure to recognize this basic question of power as pertinent to ethical criticism is at the heart of much loose legal thought today. Theories of political and economic individualism in terms of which our courts have been nullifying progressive social legislation on every front are confessions of past political impotence rather than guides for the future of a growing state.

[41] It is upon this fundamental fact that socialism bases the choice of industries for public ownership or control. A state which cannot coerce millions of farmers may easily assume control of more highly organized industrial realms, *e.g.* factories, power plants, railroads.

[42] Worthy of greater attention than political scientists have given to the matter is the influence of tools of war upon the balance of political powers. Modern democracy can be traced from the development of a cross-bow and musket capable of piercing the expensive armor of the knight. The popular use of firearms grounds democratic revolutions in both American continents, as well as in France. The machine-gun, grenade, and gas-bomb spell the doom of popular uprisings against an army loyal to the existing state. The airplane, until methods of defence against it are discovered, gives to small, energetic groups within or without a nation as yet unrealized powers of combatting a government.

The foregoing sketch of the development of law must not be conceived as a dialectically necessary historical process. It is historically applicable only to states which have enjoyed a continuous expansion of political power, *e.g.*, England since the Conquest and pre-Justinian Rome. The decline of centralized political power in the conquered portions of the Roman Empire, for instance, was followed by notable retrenchment in the domain of legal control, and a similar process seems to have taken place with the breakdown of the communistic empires of the Incas and Aztecs. In the history of most states, one finds only irregular narrowing and widening of the domain of effective legal action as the tides of internal dissension, foreign war, and economic conditions press upon or recede before the boundaries of that domain.

If the temporal variation of political power offers the most useful key to the proper understanding of legal history, its variation with respect to the topography of social institutions is an equally useful key to the understanding of the law of a given epoch. The law is one among many institutions. The direction of its powers is largely determined by a process of competition with organized religion, organized education, the family, professional and mercantile agencies of control, and various other social institutions. The disruption of these agencies throws new tasks upon the law; their development relieves it of old responsibilities.

In this struggle with other organizations of social force, the law recognizes the limitations of its machinery. Operating through courts, it is required by dictates of social economy to concentrate its attention upon facts readily verifiable. Laws against adultery, contraception, and other sexual crimes are notoriously unenforceable. The respect which the law of libel and the law of evidence show for confidential communication is primarily a respect for the limitations of judicial knowledge. The fact that land cannot be concealed gives point to the peculiarly rich development of legal control over real property. The public events of birth, marriage, and death furnish stable fulcrums for legal leverage. The organization of men into permanent groups creates new pressure points for the activity of the law.[43]

Law, again, is a creature of uniformity, and in the human inadequacies of uniform rules are to be found the most pervasive of law's limitations.[44]

Finally, law is threats, substantiated when the occasion demands, by the infliction of suffering. The limitations of fear and violence as recipes for the good life need no elaboration.[45]

[43] Thus the labor union, at the same time that it gives new power, through organization, to the desires of workers, provides a ready instrument for the political control of labor. The right of free speech and the doctrine that equity will not enjoin a libel reflect the practical difficulty of political supervision of expression. But the difficulty of fastening responsibilities ceases with the organization of a trade union, and accordingly injunctions against libel have become frequent in trade union cases, as have injunctions against striking, which were subject to similar practical and doctrinal difficulties in the absence of centralized responsibility. Compulsory arbitration, the effective assessment of damages for injuries occurring in labor disputes, and other forms of political pressure are not legal possibilities until the worker creates pressure points for the state to act upon.

[44] The problem of rule versus discretion has been the subject of many excellent studies in recent years. See, particularly, M. R. Cohen, "Rule versus Discretion" (1914) 11 *Jour. of Phil.* 208; Pound, "The Future of the Criminal Law" (1921) 21 *Columbia Law Rev.* 1; Pound, *Introduction to the Philosophy of Law* (1922) 3; Cardozo, *Paradoxes of Legal Science* (1928) 1-52. For a more one-sided presentation of the difficulties in legal uniformity, see Frank, *Law and the Modern Mind*, (1930).

[45] The tragedy of punishing individuals for the sins of society is no

De minimis non curat lex is, no doubt, often an unworthy anodyne for juristic laziness. Natural reluctance to examine involved social problems and to fashion legal instruments suited to new needs takes eager refuge in an exaggeration of the difficulties of law enforcement. Made-to-order legal philosophies make a virtue of judicial fatigue, bless judicial ignorance, and sanctify the impotence of law. But it remains true that you can't fix a watch with a pick-axe. And though every human good is relevant to the task of shaping political force into the best possible system of law, a living system of law is more than thought transcribed on statute-books. Our legal ideals take meaning only in the human struggles out of which the force of law is fashioned.

4. THE HUMAN MEANING OF LAW

The behavioristic character of law enforcement has inspired a traditional division of life into an internal domain, in which morality is to be the supreme guide, and an external domain which is the proper field of law and beyond which law and legal science have no responsibilities. This division rests upon an unfortunate confusion between the direct subject matter of legal rules and the ultimate human significance of these rules. The limitations of legal machinery narrowly restrict the realm of human life in which law observance can be enforced, but they do not restrict the realm of life in which we must search for the meaning of that law observance. True it is that the

greater than the tragedy of punishing society for the individual's offenses. We are easily tempted to forget how far beyond the individual wrongdoer the effects of legal penalties travel.

jurist, as such, has little to contribute to the study of the ways in which commanded and forbidden modes of conduct ultimately bring into being the experiences in which intrinsic values inhere. But in so far as the jurist presumes to pass critical judgments upon law he necessarily draws upon this study. Legal criticism is thus intimately dependent upon psychology, economics, and general sociology or anthropology.

The contention that all human goods, all parts of the good life, may be affected by the legal order and are therefore relevant to our standards of legal criticism will of course appear far-fetched and fallacious if we consider only the more or less direct effects which law has made upon human activity. In this sense many have echoed the lines of Johnson:

> How small of all that human hearts endure
> The part which laws or kings can cause or cure!

Powerless, indeed, law seems to be in the most important realms of life, in matters of intellect, love, and the ends of human hope and faith. But to consider these elements only as they are immediately and purposefully directed by law is to blind our eyes to the real power and importance of jural activity. Are not our most private feelings and beliefs moulded, in part at least, by our personal contacts, our economic circumstances, our education, our opportunities for recreation and work? And in all these fields of activity does not the law again and again intervene, for better or for worse? In the most intimate of the human affections we can trace the effects of laws concerning marriage, divorce, legitimacy, birth-control, infanticide, decency, and property.[46]

To consider, even in cursory fashion, the real powers of law in a realm where it is frequently said to be without morally important effects or responsibilities, namely the domain of human beliefs, is to become acutely aware of the inadequacy inherent in certain traditional standards of legal criticism. None will deny that man's opinions and intellectual activities form an important realm of ethically justiciable material, and that this phase of life is significantly affected by social determinants, which are in certain realms or aspects of a jural character. But the extent of this control is seldom recognized.

In the first place, organized education is frequently a creature of the state. What is to be taught must then be decided through law, either directly, or indirectly by a delegation of authority to educational officers. One need only note the tremendous differences in the beliefs of, say, Russian and Italian school-children at the present day to appreciate the reality of the state's power in this direction. Of course such differences are most striking in the realms of history, economics, and other sociological disciplines, but not even the teaching of the three R's is unaffected by political activity. Shall it be criminal to teach certain classes (*e.g.* slaves or serfs) to read and write, or shall it be criminal not to do this, or shall there be complete political indifference or more subtle measures of approval or discouragement in the matter? Whether education is to be made universally compulsory, and, if so, for how long,

[46] *Cf.* Tarde, *Penal Philosophy* (1903 [4th ed.], trans. by Howell, 1912) Modern Criminal Science Series, vol. 5, § 87, p. 475.

and under what conditions, is a matter that will affect even beliefs about arithmetic. The question of legal attitudes to private and sectarian schools is assuming considerable importance today. And without leaving the realm of organized education we may note that the state, by endowing research, awarding scholarships, and subsidizing educational institutions or exempting them from certain taxes, may extend its powers of control far beyond the public educational system.

There are other factors in the moulding of belief that are as significant as organized education and equally susceptible to legal influence. The question of the extent of freedom guaranteed or permitted to public expression of opinion has always been of the highest importance in this respect. "Free speech" has been a valuable slogan in man's political struggles, but a slogan of this sort does not solve the real problem of how much freedom is to be allowed to speech. At what point does speech become slander, indecency, instigation to immoral violence, or inducement to breach of contract? The freedom of the press, of course, raises similar legal-ethical problems. Indirectly, opinion is moulded by government disposition and control of broadcasting rights, by laws of copyright and patent, and by tariffs and embargoes on publications, motion pictures, etc. The establishment and control of libraries, museums, and governmental bureaus of information raises further problems of directing public opinion, and legal support or regulation of churches, theaters, and similar institutions involves an influence upon human beliefs that is of great significance.

All these factors are of especial weight in regard to those beliefs that are of a moral nature. A good deal has been made of the influence of moral beliefs upon positive law, but it is no less true that positive law exerts a powerful force upon positive morality.[47] It is largely by reference to existing law that moral beliefs regarding property, contract, status, and the function of government are formulated. Even where belief shades off into feeling, and we deal with man's spontaneous disgust, shame, or reverence, we find that law is not without its influence. By insisting upon certain external standards of conduct, which in turn lead to correlated feelings and sentiments, the law exerts an influence upon our emotional life which has never been accurately acknowledged. Consider the tremendous psychical effects of such legal acts, to take only the recent history of this country, as the Dred Scott decision, the abolition of slavery, the passage of woman's suffrage, the prohibition law, and the declaration of war in 1917. How, in the face of fact so inexorable can we complacently divide life into an inner and an outer realm and prohibit a philosophy of law from entering the former domain in search of its materials? How can we say that man's inner life is, like an Englishman's home, a castle into which the law may not enter? The law does and must enter this domain, whether recognizedly or by stealth, and an adequate legal philosophy cannot ignore the fact or the vast ethical problems to which it gives rise.

Given the modes of external behavior in which men respond to observed law, we have still to find the human sig-

[47] *Cf.* Jhering: "The sense of right has not produced law, but law the sense of right. Law knows but one source, the practical one of purpose."

nificance of such behavior, as it affects the whole life of man.

In this last task of legal criticism, which all the collected volumes of history and science are so far from carrying to a successful termination, we shall not be fatuous enough to offer a simple formula or presumptuous enough to attempt an adequate exposition. All we can offer is a bare and abstract analysis of the problem and a consideration of its relevance and the relevance of its difficulty to juristic criticism and legal philosophy.

Roughly we may group under three heads the factors which determine the human significance of law observance. There is, in the first place, a set of social mechanisms by which our political pressures are transformed and relocated in the social order. We must, in the second place, take note of the significance for legal criticism of man's physical environment as it gives material content to the dealings of men. We have finally to face the machinery of the human soul and to indicate the modes of its response to the impinging social forces which the law has set in motion.

(1) Although the institutions and customs of a society are largely dependent upon law, there is here, as in most phases of sociology, a reciprocal causation. Not only do the sub-legal forces of society help to determine what the effective law will be,—a factor already considered,—but they further determine how this effective law will modify the individual life. Thus they are indispensable elements in the instrumental valuation of law.

What our law of property or contract ought to be depends largely upon the use which people are accustomed to make of particular legal powers. Commercial, religious, and kinship relations lay down the channels through which the stream of legal force will flow. The law guarantees a man certain property rights, but their fruits will be gathered by his first-born child or his maternal uncle, his medicine man or his banker, his customer or his strongest neighbor. Although a cardinal demand for legal economy makes it unwise to distinguish property rights too minutely according to their probable uses, there are certain fundamental distinctions which law at the present day cannot safely ignore. The extent to which a man shall have property rights of testamentary disposition constitutes a problem distinct in many important particulars from the question of disposition during life. This distinction and further distinctions between property devoted to quasi-public (religious, educational, or philanthropic) use and property devoted to private use, or between property for use and property for profit (capital), are exceedingly important, and the habit of ignoring them in abstract discussion of the "right to property" produces much confusion. Not only do such distinctions constitute a valid basis for differentiating various phases of property law, but they provide grounds for distinguishing the law of one social epoch from that of another. To a large extent, the modern social problem of property is based upon a significant trend in the capitalist class from frugal living and constant reinvestment of profits to modes of expenditure less useful to contemporary society and to posterity.[48]

Similarly laws of status must take into clear considera-

[48] See S. and B. Webb, *The Decay of Capitalist Civilization* (1923), pp. 74 *et seq.*, and J. M. Keynes, *The Economic Consequences of the Peace* (1920), pp. 16-17.

tion the social habits determining the treatment of slaves, servants, dependents, and relatives, which determine the benefits and evils that such laws ultimately create. In the law of obligations it is especially important to consider the extent of insurance which is held or can be conveniently held by particular classes, and the less definite mechanisms by which loss is shifted and distributed in all societies.[49] Similar considerations demand attention in criminal law, both in relation to the injury that is punished[50] and in relation to the incidence of penalties. It should be clear that the variability of these social habits and institutions makes it possible and necessary for an absolute standard of ethics to give rise to widely different norms of law in different societies.

(2) It is necessary to recognize that the physical materials upon which social mechanisms work constitute a significant factor in the determination of legal standards. The extension of such materials through scientific discoveries and inventions must generally be correlated with an extension of the legal domain. With the development of radio and aeronautics, for instance, law must cease to restrict itself to the surface of the terrestrial globe. No doubt important political problems will arise when man learns to exploit more efficiently the material and energy resources of sea and air. The problem of human inequality will assume new proportions when medical science discovers safe and practicable methods of transplanting human glands,

49 See Demogue, *Analysis of Fundamental Notions* in *Modern French Legal Philosophy*, pp. 529 *et seq.*

50 See Bentham, *Theory of Legislation*, "Principles of the Penal Code," Part 1.

organs, and tissues from those who are willing to sell to those who are able to buy.

The amount of natural materials available to society in relation to the needs of society is a prime factor in determining the extent to which equality of distribution is desirable. An interesting example of this determination is raised by the law of our western states in regard to the use of water for irrigation. The fact that, in the absence of statutes and upon an identical common law basis, the courts of some states have sanctioned the equal rights of all riparians to the use of water, while the courts of other states have denied any appropriation which interferes with the use of prior claimants,[51] has been frequently alluded to as an example of arbitrary judicial legislation. Although no doubt the instance is one of judicial legislation, its arbitrary nature is not evident. The argument that if all riparians in Illinois ought to have equal rights, all riparians in Nevada ought to have equal rights is typical of legal absolutism, and its superficial plausibility is typical of the eternally plausible appeal to ignorance by which legal absolutism maintains its "evident principles." The significant fact which the argument in question ignores is that equal distribution of water rights in an arid state would afford insufficient quantities of water to practically every claimant, while in a state containing more rivers and rainfall this difficulty will not arise.

Similar considerations, in less striking and more important forms, arise in the general problem of the legal distribution of property. Equality, when it results in a general

51 See Hess, "Arid-Land Water Rights in the United States" (1910) 10 *Columbia Law Rev.* 480.

level of wealth scarcely above the subsistence level, may be less valuable socially than an inequality which secures to a limited class opportunities of cultural and industrial creation. But in a society economically able to assure to all the material basis of a creative life, the social value of Greek slavery or Florentine oppression is irrelevant to the legal problem of allocating property and power.

(3) Jurisprudence, political science, and sociology lead to our final task, the task of psychology, the determination of those channels of man's life through which political and social forces flow to their ethical culmination in joy and suffering. In this task, the powers, desires, beliefs, habits, thoughts, and tastes of man all enter to determine a final answer to the fundamental question upon which the evaluation of any legal element must rest, "What does law do to man?"

Man's *powers* or potentialities are not to be assigned on a simple basis of logic or metaphysics. However persistent is the core of universal human powers and limitations, its determination is a matter of scientific observation and calculation. And in the peripheral realm of variation, the capabilities of men offer intricate problems to which we can give only rough and clumsy answers. It is our purpose only to insist that, whether or not such problems are consciously faced, the answers to them are at the basis of our judgments upon law. To what extent can men be dissuaded from crime by fear of punishment? To what extent can men be happy without private property? Can men preserve the life of the intellect under a mechanized industrial system? These and a thousand similar questions demand our solution. And though we usually appeal to "common sense" for their solution, we cannot hope that common sense is more accurate in these realms than in the intrinsically simpler realms of physics or medicine.

Similarly, we find in the domain of human *desires* material which, whether recognizedly or not, must appear in the substance of legal valuation. We have considered the effect of desires upon the efficiency of law enforcement. Their potency in the transformation of legal forces within the individual life is no less important. All law is based upon certain basic assumptions as to the desire of men to be respected, to get or keep certain things, etc. Progress in legal, as in any other science, must come through the gradual criticism and refinement of these assumptions.[52]

The relevance of human *habits* in determining the effects of law is too obvious to require comment and too intricate to tempt analysis. Suffice it to say that no law can have significance without a firm leverage upon the known uniformities of human behavior, and that the ascertainment of these uniformities is the first, and in many ways the easiest, task of positive juristic science. Much of the social reform of the coming century, for instance, will depend upon a more adequate answer than we have yet discovered to the question, "How far does the profit motive affect the habit of efficient work?"[53]

Modes of thought, popular as well as judicial, play a large part in determining the effects of law. The dependence of law enforcement upon interpretation is obvious and important, but we have alluded to this factor before,

[52] *Cf.* Tourtoulon, *Philosophy in the Development of Law*, ch. 7 (Law and Emotional Life).

[53] *Cf.* Laidler, *Incentives under Capitalism and Socialism* (1933); Bulletin of Industrial Research Group, *The Profit Motive* (1930).

and may now suggest some less patent ways in which belief affects the nature of law. Belief in the law's efficacy is of course partly dependent upon the actual efficiency of the legal order, but it is equally important to remember that this belief moulds the social sense of security and the expectations and conduct of law-breakers with a force that may be far from proportionate to the soundness of the belief. Similarly the belief that what was law yesterday will be law tomorrow powerfully motivates men's responses to legal situations, again to a degree quite incommensurate with the accuracy of the belief.[54] Belief is of course also a causal determinant of many of the factors already considered (desire, habit, etc.).

The *categories* in which we think, no less than the thoughts we recognize are relevant to this analysis. Law, as we have seen, in order to effect economy and social security, must usually be framed in fairly extensive generalities. *De minimis non curat lex.* How these generalities are to be framed must depend largely upon popular habits of thought. If, for instance, no distinction is made in such thought between the killing of a new-born infant by its parents and the killing of one adult by another, both being thought of under the category of "murder," a reason for treating the two cases alike is thereby created (which may, of course, like all the reasons suggested in these examples, be outweighed by more important considerations). For a legal distinction where no material difference is popularly seen gives the appearance of injustice and hinders the enforcement of law. In the circumstances indicated, the kill-

[54] *Cf.* Demogue, *Analysis of Fundamental Notions in Modern French Legal Philosophy*, pp. 368-369.

ing of a child conveys to adults a fear for their own lives. But if, on the other hand, the two sorts of cases are sharply distinguished in popular thought, the effect of a legal distinction between the two cases will be very different, comparable for instance to the distinction which most western people make in moral thinking between the killing of people and the killing of other animals. So, if testamentary disposition be thought of as a property right, its limitation will establish a certain amount of insecurity in regard to other property rights. But if it is generally distinguished from other property rights, as has been the case historically in most societies, this will not happen. The categories of legal and political thought, both professional and popular, are usually vague and ill-suited to the attainment of ethical ends. We attach blame and praise, punishment and reward, to whole classes of activities when it is only a portion of each class that we really want to judge. But distinctions and exceptions become too difficult or too misleading after a certain point, and we use the current classification that most closely bounds the actions we have in mind, relying upon the common sense of juries (or the lawlessness of juries, as their critics prefer to say) and the pardoning power of executives to correct our errors when they become very obvious.

If, as we have tentatively concluded, happiness is the ideal object of law, no problem of legal criticism can be carried to its conclusion without an appreciation of the topography of pleasures and pains. As in every other branch of positive science upon which legal criticism must rely, we deal here with a variable, empirical material that does not assume the simple geometrical forms beloved of moralists. No doubt human beings at all times and places enjoy food, shelter, and dress, but the realm of universal pleasures is less patent when we refine our categories, for what it is that different people regard as proper food or shelter or clothing is highly variable, as is the comparative value which they will attach to the three objects. Obviously, in a country where people like pork or bull-fights or democracy or Mohammedanism, judicial support, tolerance, or suppression of these things should be determined upon considerations inapplicable to countries where these things are detested. An absolute ideal law can be no more specific than the realm of constant or universal human joys and pains.

The topography of pleasures and pains has two functions in legal criticism. In the first place, an appreciation of what it is that makes people happy or unhappy is implicit in the calculation of legal pressures for the moulding of human conduct. All of the studies of legal and social institutions which tell us the force of law depend upon an analysis of human motives which must give respectful attention to the factors of pleasure and pain. There is no source of human pleasure or pain which legal criticism can ignore in calculating the human significance of decisions and statutes. Even the pleasures of simple cruelty demand consideration, for law and customary morality depend in large measure upon men's enjoyment of other men's punishment, which is a major element in the sentiment of justice.[55]

Of equal importance is the role played by the topog-

[55] See Bentham, *Theory of Legislation*, "Principles of the Penal Code," Part 2, ch. 16; Tarde, *Penal Philosophy*, § 5, p. 35, § 91, pp. 505-506.

raphy of pleasures and pains in the final reduction of our analysis of law to terms of intrinsic value. The task of positive science in legal criticism is not complete when it has given us an external picture of man's life as it is moulded by law. Not until we have seen to the spirit within, to its joy and its suffering, can we call upon our standards of pure ethics for final judgment of the law before us.

This reckoning of the human experiences resulting from law in terms of happiness is perhaps the most difficult task which legal science faces, but it is certainly the most fundamental. That it is not wholly beyond the scope of rational solution Bentham's monumental contributions to legal criticism sufficiently demonstrate. A sound legal criticism will correct Bentham's impressionistic surveys of law's effects on human happiness with a more mature psychology and a richer fund of factual social studies than was at Bentham's disposal. But it will not attempt this work of correction until ridicule of the hedonic calculus is undermined by a willingness to examine the actual development of that calculus at Bentham's hands and the actual uses to which it is put in his legal criticism.[56]

[56] See, for example, *Theory of Legislation*, "Principles of the Civil Code," ch. 6 *et seq.*

CHAPTER FIVE

CONCLUSION

WITH these observations we conclude our outline of the positive facts which determine what law is and can be. Desires, powers, tastes, habits, beliefs, even "bloodless"[1] categories appear on our stage, and their activities, though directed by the playwright, go beyond his intentions and foresight. The play, it is, that we must judge, and our review must be written before the play is done.

"But we have written no review," (says the avocatus diaboli). "We have settled the problem of valuing law by announcing that first the nature of value must be discovered and then the 'human significance' of the law surveyed. We have stated the problems of legal criticism,—multiplied them, in fact,—without solving them. And when we have ventured outside the fortress of logical formalism it has been only to engage in purely destructive criticism."

To these charges a plea of confession and avoidance may properly be advanced. In the first place, although we do not seek to evade the label "destructive,"—for while

[1] This predicate appears to be unjustified. Shipwrecked sailors facing certain death from starvation unless they survive a few days kill and eat one man. They are later rescued and brought to trial for murder. Viewing the individual case, there is no great moral guilt. But because the case comes under the current category of murder and because no convenient category of exception or distinction is seen which will not excuse other cases of moral fault, the men are condemned to death. Can we fairly call our categories bloodless after this?

nothing is purely destructive or purely constructive, this essay plainly leans toward the former pole,—we should like to evade certain condemnatory implications attached to that label. It is indeed a curious fact that while undertakers and street cleaners are allowed to pursue their callings undisturbed by the objection that their work is "purely destructive,"—indeed we rather prefer that workers of the former class should not engage in midwifery or those of the latter in provisioning—yet in the realm of the intellect we commonly regard this epithet as a reproach. In this realm, too, there is a need for undertakers and street cleaners,—nor must their justification always be that they are making room for new constructive activity.

More serious is the criticism that we have merely stated the problems of legal criticism, multiplied them perhaps, yet failed to solve them. And while this is to a certain extent true, the formal multiplication of the problems of legal criticism is itself of some value, for most errors of juristic criticism arise from an illicit simplification of the questions that we ought to face. Legal problems are commonly simplified by a reduction to simple issues of ethics or to simple issues of positive fact. But in the former case there are implicit assumptions of positive fact, in the latter implicit assumptions of value, and an adequate legal philosophy must be consciously critical towards assumptions of either realm.

Viewed in the full context of relevant considerations to which our general principle of legal valuation points, the significance of argument is assured and the possibility of solution created. Such solution will depend first upon an answer to the question of what the good life is,—and we have suggested the theory of hedonism as offering the most adequate answer to this question,—if any absolute answer be possible. Secondly, the solution of legal-ethical problems involves questions of positive science whose character we have briefly indicated. To fuse these two aspects and thus to produce material norms of legal activity and standards of legal criticism is a task beyond the scope of the present essay. But in pointing to the very elements which create this difficulty and which make any unchallengeable solution of our concrete problems forever impossible, we are led to reject the numerous theories which claim for substantial legal norms a greater certainty or absoluteness than is involved in relevant ethical and positive considerations. This is itself a material point of some significance.

> It is always something to see where the difficulty lies, although it should be insuperable; and to point out the only means by which the best solution can be given, although that solution should not be so satisfactory as could be wished. It is something to get certain principles, leaving facts in the uncertainty that belongs to them. By showing the real uncertainty of the most conclusive arguments that can be offered on the subject, it will prevent us from giving to less conclusive arguments, more than their due weight: it will enable us to unravel the web of sophistry, and to humble the pride of declamation: it will be of service, in as far as the caution that accompanies a salutary doubt, is preferable to the rashness that may be the result of misconception.[2]

[2] Bentham, "The Influence of Time and Place in Matters of Legislation," ch. 2, 1 *Works* 171, 178.

In answer to the argument prevalent among jurists that "correct" law is certain and constant though ethical norms are variable, we have attempted to demonstrate that even if there is an absolute ethical norm, the standards of ideal law must be widely variant, and highly uncertain.

A recognition of this uncertainty, of the intricate dependence of legal criticism upon the ultimate nature of the good and upon the complicated panorama of changing social conditions, is the first step towards wisdom in legal criticism and goodness in legal reform. It is hard to forsake the multiplicity of absolutes that so easily succor us in our practical valuations. But in the clash of incommensurables we are forced to acknowledge confusion and despair or to look beyond our *media axiomata* to some ultimate principle, beneath which the artificial clarity and the essential incompatibility of our subordinate standards together vanish and leave every problem with the mark of quantity and continuity.

The search for an ethical absolute in legal criticism is not a search dictated by a love of dogmatism. Dogmas our traditional jurisprudence has always had in abundance. Every "self-evident" principle of law or morality to which defenders or critics of our legal order have appealed sets itself up as an ultimate. A spirit of scientific scepticism will press us to reduce to a minimum the ethical postulates of legal criticism. A scientific analysis of the often conflicting claims of traditional legal ideals may not reach the final economy and consistency of a formal absolute, but such an absolute represents at least the direction of a rational legal criticism conscious of its responsibilities and limitations.

The field of ideal law is not a checker-board. It is rather a sea, as vast, as turbulent, as impatient of restraint, as life itself. Rules and decisions and practical standards we set up in our attempt to draw peace and order out of this Heraclitean flux. Actually we can only chart its currents,—to shape them is past human power. By these charts, indeed, we sail, but not by these charts will the sea itself be bound. The success of our sailing will be measured not by conformity to our maps but by conformity to those powers of the deep that govern the realm we have tried to picture.

Far removed is this vision from the cozy and sterile assuredness of the legal Pharisees. But to our greatest judges it has brought at once inspiration and humility, wisdom and the crown of wisdom,—the knowledge of ignorance and uncertainty. In the words of Mr. Justice Cardozo,

> The law like science generally, if it could be followed to its roots, would take us down beneath the veins and ridges to the unplumbed depths of being, the reality behind the veil. The jurist must not despair because his plummets do not reach the goal at which in vain for two thousand years and more the philosophers have been casting theirs. Rather will he learn with some of the philosophers themselves in moderating his ambitions to recast to some extent his notion of philosophy and to think of it as a means for the truer estimate of values and the better ordering of life. He will hope indeed that with study and reflection there may develop in the end some form of calculus less precarious than any that philosopher or

lawyer has yet been able to devise. In the meantime, amid the maze of contingency and regularity, he will content himself as best he can with his little compromises and adjustments, the expedients of the fleeting hour. They will fret him sometimes with a sense of their uncertainty. It should hearten him to keep in mind that uncertainty is the lot of every branch of thought and knowledge when verging on the ultimate.[8]

Such then are the qualifications which must be attached to these natural and significant criticisms of a work like the present essay.

Viewing the problem of legal criticism in these lights, we may avoid the twin pitfalls in the path of comparative jurisprudence,—on the one hand, the evaluation of all law in terms of our own immediate legal ends, on the other hand, the no less complacent fatalism which makes the inevitability of human folly its justification and accepts whatever has been as right. A middle course is charted by the most fundamental truth to which philosophy has arrived: the recognition that unity and diversity, absolutism and relativism, are relevant to each other and distinct, appearing together in every entity and yet characterizing basically opposed aspects of it. The life of legal philosophy is the search for the ethical constant in the ideal of "natural law with changing content." That this constant in natural law is simply its goodness is the recurrent burden of the present essay. What is constant in ideal law is not a body of material commands, but a highly abstract ethical

[8] *Paradoxes of Legal Science* (1928), pp. 134-135.

framework. What is variable is not an ultimate form but a set of social conditions.

From another point of view, this fundamental polarity appears in the relation of existence and value. We have tried to show that the valuation of law involves mutually relevant poles of idealism and positivism, and that no juristic approach that neglects ethics and no philosophical approach that neglects positive science can give us an adequate philosophy of law. The crypto-idealism of Duguit, Savigny, *et al,* is as inadequate as the crypto-positivism of the Kantians, Hegelians, and other formalists in legal philosophy. Each current represents the development of an illicit abstraction made workable only by the unrecognized and therefore uncritical acceptance of complementary factors.

Legal philosophy, when it is sundered from a wider intellectual world, either to be caged in the narrow realm of the existent or to be exiled into an ethereal region of irresponsible desires, cannot live. For in the human world of which philosophy is a part the choice of ideals, which is love, and their understanding must co-exist. That understanding without love is empty, that love without understanding is blind, that the good life is found only in the intimate union of these ideals,—the wedding of reason and faith, as the phrase of another age ran,—these are the most important truths to which men have attained.

INDEX